"In this wild ride of a memoir, Mason covers the barnburning years of a life spent making music, running a business, and learning things the hard way. With power and emotion, Mason covers playing music since age 13, when "the applause was an embrace I had never felt before, sincere and warm in ways that made me shiver," to the dissolution of his band, leaving him broke but not broken, and on to wild romps, moments of pain and beauty, and at long last finding the inner peace he had previously only seen hints of. Frank and funny, Mason shares accounts of the rock & roll life's dark lows and spotlit highs, with welcome insight about bands ("those freewheeling poly-marriages that were sustained by our constant attempts to give birth to our dreams of fame"), music, and life itself." –*BookLife* **Review, *Publishers Weekly***

"*Sex, Trucks and Rock 'n' Roll* is a fascinating memoir by American musician and songwriter Ben Mason. A born performer, Mason, tells of his debauched and selfish life while on tour with his rock band as a young man, a time that nearly saw him serving a serious jail sentence on drug charges. Mason describes his book as the story of his Journey, a journey from a life of excess spent in a blur of sex and drugs, through learning responsibility as 'Big Brother' to the motley crew of misfits that worked for him as movers through to a life of reflection, self-awareness and spiritual awakening.

"I almost swerved this book fearing it might be yet another Born Again Christian epistle that I wouldn't be able to relate to. Mason's spirituality is broad-based and he conveys his beliefs and experiences eloquently.

"This is a very honest book and Mason doesn't hide or try to justify events that put him in a bad light. The last couple of chapters where he describes his home, thoughts and feelings are quite amazing, reminding me very much of James Lee Burke's superb prose on similar subjects, and let's not forget that Burke is one of the world's best known authors.

I get the feeling that Ben Mason's Journey isn't quite over, hopefully if this book is a success the right person will read it and it will be." –**Dave Blendell**, *NetGalley* Review

"A zany romp through the '70s and '80s in the company of some outlandish characters, sort of like the Three Stooges on acid. Simultaneously psychedelic and hilarious; convincing testimony to the fact that you don't have to be an outrageous rock star to live like one." –**Steuart Smith**, guitarist with The Eagles

"A truly remarkable life story, told by the man who lived it. If Ben had not been born a man he surely would've been born a Country Song! A great read!" –**Richard Leigh**, ASCAP songwriter of the century

"Ben Mason has a gift for writing a technicolor world that comes alive. From the screaming guitars and thrumming bass on stage to the ancient hush resting over a green Virginia field, his words are entirely hypnotic. This is one of the best memoirs I've read." –**Beth Harbison**, *New York Times* bestselling author

"*Sex, Trucks and Rock n Roll . . . A Spiritual Journey* covers a lot of territory and I'm glad to be part of it. Watching the author grow from rock star to spiritualist is quite an adventure." –**Jeff Severson**, CBS recording artist and producer

"Regarding *Sex, Trucks and Rock n Roll . . . A Spiritual Journey* I have known Ben since he was sixteen years old and watched him grow as a songwriter and musician (Piano and drums) for many years. It has taken me this long to realize what a marvelous writer he is as a storyteller, purveyor of 'self accounting', with humor and truth. I Love this book!" –**John Wells**, Performing musician, actor and founder of the John Wells Delegation.

"Ben Mason's *Sex, Trucks and Rock n Roll* is a wild ride–poignant, outrageous, raunchy and insightfully spiritual. Ben's journey from glam band gigs to the peace of an ancient river blew away my expectations. Highly recommended!" –**Steve van Dam**, Sire Recording artist, producer and composer of the hit song "Who Got the Hooch"

"With incisive candor and exquisite clarity, Ben Mason's memoir *Sex, Trucks and Rock n Roll . . . A Spiritual Journey* reveals that the quality of a well-lived life can be found in the details. Nothing is left out: the first performances, the easy sex, the hard loves, and the even harder losses . . . until, finally, the restless rock n roll soul finds refuge in the heart. This is a beautifully written narrative, intimate and wise, that exhorts us to look beyond the stage lights—to listen above the keyboard's din—and to realize all that is essential in a singular, human life." –**Leanne Tankel,** Author, *Broken Hallelujah - Notes from a Marriage* and music critic, *Americana Highways,* and writing instructor at Northern Virginia Community College

"*Sex, Trucks and Rock n Roll . . . A Spiritual Journey* is an enormously powerful story of a life full of amazing adventures–all told with great perception, humor and imagery that will linger in your mind long afterwards. You won't be the same after reading this one." –**Ronald T. McMillan,** author of *The Touch,* a D.C. Detective series.

"I've had the honor of reading an excerpt from Ben's memoir, *Sex, Trucks and Rock n Roll . . . A Spiritual Journey.* I'm intrigued! His words seamlessly create realms of tactile emotional experience. Looking forward to this publication."–**Kiaya Abernathy,** Rappahannockradio.com

"Ben writes with passion about his journey in music from the dream of being a musician, to the reality of a rock and roll band, and on to the hard reality about what that life really is and the need to earn a living. It's a winding road that so many musicians have traveled, each in their own way. Ben's colorful account is entertaining, insightful, rowdy, and introspective." –**Paul Reisler,** Composer, songwriter, band leader–Trapezoid, Paul Reisler & A Thousand Questions, and Three Good Reasons.

"*Sex, Trucks and Rock n Roll . . . A Spiritual Journey* captivated me at once. I'm elated to hear these narratives of a man who is strong and yet willing to look at himself and his part in the hardships that came his way. This is a memoir to show the reader that they too can move through darkness toward the Light." –**Ms. JJ Gormley,** Certified Yoga Therapist and Teacher and Director, Surya Chandra Healing Yoga School

"*Sex, Trucks and Rock n Roll . . . A Spiritual Journey* is a very interesting read that inspires through the author's evolution and journey over 25 years. As a fellow entrepreneur and a person who appreciates Rock And Roll I suggest interested readers check it out!" –**Michael O'Harro**, veteran DC club owner

"Mr. Mason is the embodiment of the storied 'complicated man'. The author tells a kaleidoscopic story that doesn't simplify the many facets of a life of curiosity, doubt, and reconciliation. For those of us who refuse the path more traveled, he has created a validating read. We're not alone, after all." –**Ryan Michael Galloway**, author, performing musician and recording artist

"*Sex, Trucks, and Rock 'n Roll . . . A Spiritual Journey* offers an entertaining, mesmerizing exploration of a musician's life journey. Like great music, the book blends vivid descriptions and personal anecdotes of challenges and aspirations that shaped the author's artistic path.

Ben Mason's life is like a great song that mirrors the zeitgeist of the second half of the twentieth century. This hugely entertaining read also reveals that this musician/businessman never abandons his music. He lovingly speaks of all the highs and lows of the rock band afterlife.

Mason has an original voice in *Sex, Trucks, and Rock 'n Roll . . . A Spiritual Journey*. A deeply personal, wild story and compelling exploration that unlocks an enduring pursuit of self-discovery and transformation. He has the heart of a rock 'n roller and the soul of a poet. Read this book." –Rock-Radio legend and author **Cerphe Colwell**, now heard on MusicPlanetRadio.com

SEX, TRUCKS, AND ROCK 'N' ROLL

SEX, TRUCKS, AND — ROCK 'N' ROLL

A Spiritual Journey

BEN MASON

W. Brand Publishing

NASHVILLE, TENNESSEE

j.brand@wbrandpub.com
W. Brand Publishing
www.wbrandpub.com

Cover design by JuLee Brand / designchik.net
Photography and Restorations by Terry J. Popkin

Sex, Trucks, and Rock 'N Roll / Ben Mason –1st ed.
Available in Hardcover, Paperback, Kindle, and eBook formats.

Hardcover: 978-1-956906-84-4
Paperback: 978-1-956906-85-1
eBook: 978-1-956906-86-8
Library of Congress Number: 2023919329

CONTENTS

This is a memoir that spans fifty years of my life. I have shared my memories to the best of my ability and ask forgiveness for how my mind has recalled certain events. It would be foolish to offer my readers anything but what I believe is actual fact. It would also be foolish for one to assume that memories are always 100% factual.

This is a work of creative nonfiction and many names and details have been changed to protect identities.

Ben Mason

This book is dedicated to my sons
Henry Fox Mason and Arlo John Mason.
You are the best songs I've ever written.

It is also dedicated to the memory of their mother,
Susan Anne Hatley, (07-18-1964 to 06-15-2023)

CHAPTER 1

A DRUMMER'S KARMA (1979)

Raisin' babies,
who's got time?

"Love Was a Lie"

It's four in the morning, and I'm still wired. If I stop moving, I'll flop down in the green room with the band and the girls who've been invited backstage. So I throw jeans on over my spandex, zip a hooded sweatshirt over my bare chest and keep loading the truck.

The guys watch me roll the heavy anvil cases across the dock, cracking jokes, and doing shots of tequila some fans gave us. What's the rush, somebody shouts from a doorway. None of them have a girlfriend like Shana waiting at home. And I really want to surprise her.

It gets oddly cold at night in Panama City, Florida. My fingers are numb from all the drumming and piano playing over the last several hours. And the three encores. But loading the gear melts the stiffness as I shift everything into place. I chug grapefruit juice and keep saying no to the shots I'm offered. It takes me almost two hours, but the truck door finally shrieks down, wailing like one last perfect guitar lick.

I can still feel my steady drum stool in my butt bones, but the band truck's seat is soft and inviting and there's a half a box of pizza riding shotgun. I yank the key and toot a syncopated goodbye. It'll be a long drive north up 95 to Falls Church, Virginia. To Shana. Who I haven't seen in a month. As my sweat dries like a second skin, I wonder what she's wearing, where she is, and what she's doing.

I hope she forgives me. What the hell was I thinking?

Freeway lights turn silver. Greasy pepperoni slices make me think how incredible a reunion dinner with Shana will taste. Will we go somewhere kind of fancy or stay home? My taste buds suggest sumptuous scenes as I sing, scattering my lyrics along the highway. Nothing I can hold onto, just ideas that come from what I've been feeling lately.

I've been on a six-week tour with my glitter rock band, Primadonna, playing six nights a week in Georgia, South Carolina, and Florida. We just finished the last leg in an odyssey of stage gear, motels, snowstorms, and dry shaving in dressing room mirrors. Packed every house, signed a lot of bare breasts; got invited back. But now I'm homeward bound.

As coastal clouds gather, roadhouse phantoms tease. They sneak into my psyche, inviting me to relive some walk-in freezer encounter, some tempting hug that became sex on a box labeled Atlantic Seafood Company. The notion of finding real love on the road is as inconceivable as an oyster with a boner. I always believed someone would simply appear and reveal her truest self to me. Beyond the sex. Beyond the way bodies always first connect, until two hungry hearts are no longer starving for what is really real. But a woman hasn't opened up to me in that way yet. Except for Shana.

Some scenes are indelibly stamped into my mind from this swampy palmetto bug tour: A florid-cheeked sheriff, toothpick dangling, leaning into my cab, asking, "Where you girls headed?" No ticket, just a drawled threat, but we were late for our first set. Nobody seemed to notice. One place we played in Florida kept track of our start times, and as the owner handed me a check, he noted his careful deductions for all the minutes we'd started our sets late. That math cost us ninety-seven bucks.

But not at Loony Lenny's in Georgia. As I recall, they even passed around a tip bucket for us as my bare hands beat my toms, striking rims, splattering blood. The lighter fluid stung as doll heads were lit on fire and flaming drumsticks went flying beyond the lights. My sequined vest and spandex didn't keep me from burning myself but my sister's airbrushed paint job on my drum set remains unblemished. Loved that place.

Somewhere in the middle of our tour, around midnight, in South Carolina, I was scream-singing when a Marine jock climbed on stage, head-butting the mic, belting the classic chorus, inspiring drunken collisions on the dance floor. Just before he leapt back into the fray, the monster jock sneered, "You look like a goddamn woman."

The jock's fairy queen cheerleader put something into my palm. Her folded napkin declared, "I want to be your drum stool." As her Marine tossed down shots at the bar, her head tilted left. I followed. "Lock the door," she commanded. A song about jungle love pounded from the jukebox. The Om tattoo on her muscular caramel skin moved with the thump of the bass drum; we were planted on a toilet seat in the terrarium-colored light of a bathroom. Six minutes later she turned her back to me. "Help me with these," she pleaded. I grabbed, pulled; but her white jeans were so tight they'd rip if I tugged too fast. Or a shoe would fly off if she farted. Either way that would be hard to explain to her hammered Marine. My existential drum stool never said her name. All I got was a blank stare when I said, "Thank you, Ludwig."

Same night, in the 2 a.m. set: our chain-smoking, cross-dressing bass player was crouched next to my hi-hat. He liked to grin at me while I was concentrating on a crowd of waving arms. Women's panties fluttered onto the stage, under the collection on the clothesline above us. The Wet Panty Contest: a creative reminder that what flows from the excitement of what we do can become delicately repulsive.

When the tour was extended a week later, we celebrated. Ironing boards, nightstands, and windowsills were littered with beer bottles and plates of hardening southern barbecue and coleslaw. The morning peeked through hotel curtains as two young women returned from my bathroom. With their fingers entwined they were angelic, even with vomit and a spent needle on the tile between them. They dog paddled toward me; my bed was a life raft. This was their vacation: nodding out on a drummer's sticky brown carpet.

A mole-faced roadie suggested we have some fun. Removing his sleeveless jean jacket, he noted the cigarette burns in their pantyhose and described their possible compliance. I kicked him out. He'd drag his pitiful erection down the hall and warm himself with whatever he kept snorting. I'd cover my guests with blankets. Put pillows under their heads.

I'll swipe towels, shampoo, maybe toilet paper. But I won't steal innocence.

Another night. The A/C was roaring, but I could hear the lead guitarist in the next room performing some showy overplaying with his freakish appendage. His philosophy was that he's got to share it; to let it go to waste would be unfair to fans. Shana would say it stretched like a dachshund under his spandex. It's in every publicity shot; the sixth member of Primadonna. Yes, we got paid to wallow in our excesses.

And until now, any regrets were shadows cast by a glittery

performer who everybody loved. Whatever I did would be forgiven; forgotten. But in the tunnel of road light ahead I see something precious. Something I've taken for granted.

A dozen hours into the drive, my mind is conjuring up bizarre images. Outside the truck, giant hitchhikers appear, straddling the highway; I steer between their legs and sing louder than my cassette deck. I stretch as deeply as I can in the body of my craft, like an astronaut, surrounded by infinity and the FM static of my sonic life preserver. I've begun imagining I'm just a few hours from home. But the radio keeps fading in and out, and as I concentrate on what it's telling me, I have to close my eyes to hear better.

And then. A breath becomes one long sigh as I sink into a silence I've been dying to hear. Peacefully lulled, rocked in the bed of a cradle, I'm certain I'm finally home. I remember feeling tender hands reaching under me, tucking me in. It's all so empty, but full of warmth.

Then the whispering jabbering begins and I hear the ripping sound of something being torn from me, and I realize where I really am. I'm in a void. I fight, forcing my eyes open. I rise. Air horns and high beams wrench me back. My arms spin the steering wheel. I hear my impotent shriek as a tractor trailer and cars slingshot by, so close that I see the prayer frozen in a driver's mouth.

Fecal emesis is when a person vomits feces. I can taste mine as I rush my window down. In my side mirror I see faces in smears of blue light. A moment ago, they'd met me with halting hands. As they disappear, they glare at me—condemnation and concern in eyes that close peacefully.

A gauzy blue glow fills the cab. Did I hit my head? Is it ear damage? Maybe. The bass player in Primadonna is almost deaf, constantly cranking up his amp on my left, while my monitor roars through the bombast of the Ludwig drums around me. Headaches from that make sense, but the blue light that settles around me isn't painful. It's comforting. I feel numb.

CHAPTER 2

LIME GREEN SLIPPERS (1964–2018)

*I take too much sometimes,
but I'm a grateful thief*

"The Brownie of Love"

The metal washer eyes of a German shepherd gleam from a head of torn shingle. In this four-foot-long construction, the beast has my left leg, his claws catching pavement painted black on found river wood, open jaws bloody brown. His dead eyes glare down at me as I pedal in the darkness, making up songs about the zoo, girls at school, and ghosts. My singing may have instigated that attack, now that I think about it.

When I was thirteen, I was up every morning at 4:30. I'd steer right at the end of our gravel driveway and pedal up the three loping hills of Walton Lane. Then I'd coast two miles down Annandale Road to a 7-11, where four bundles of the *Washington Post* would be lined up against a wall. I'd snip the metal wires that bound them, fold them neatly inward, and load them into the baskets of my red Schwinn bike. Half an hour later, I'd buy a warm blueberry Tastykake for sixteen cents at Kerlin's Korner and deliver the newspapers to a dozen businesses and sleepy houses in Annandale, Virginia. I'd head homeward from there, slipping my papers behind doors or into mailboxes for the seventy-four houses on the winding streets of my route. I got really good at nailing my targets, slowing my bike just enough to get the *Washington Post* where it needed to land, folded and dry. I was usually home, finishing a bowl of Cap'n Crunch cereal by 6:30. My brother, sister, and parents would just be waking up. I never wanted to start the morning by telling them about another dog attack. I just accepted that as part of my job.

Recently I constructed a multi sectioned piece illustrating those attacks and hung it in my bathroom over the toilet. I'm looking up at it now, and I see myself on a bike, pedaling hard in the darkness. I can see myself looking off to one side, my saddle baskets laden with papers. I've tattooed in some faint addresses where particularly vicious dogs always lie in wait. It's hard to capture their invisibility, but the grim wooden shapes that indicate fences they always leapt over to pursue me look skeletal. There's an unfastened metal chain and a broken lock to show how uncontrollable they were. I glued a vintage toxic spray can called "Dog Off" into the center of this piece. But that stuff never worked.

I did squirt the dogs with Tabasco and vinegar on the last day I had my route, but by then I had scars on both legs from where they'd caught me. I remember panic and how I'd kick and yell at them as I tossed a newspaper toward their owner's front door. Those animals never seemed to understand that I was not a threat to them in the wee hours of those mornings. But I'd never owned a dog, and I didn't know that the hiss of my spokes, and the whirring of my tires on pavement, incensed them. In this story sculpture, I attached an oversized drywall knife painted with bloody teeth. It grins down at me now, reminding me how satisfied they must have felt, ruining the surface of my peace.

My art has always been urging itself out of me, even when I didn't understand why I needed to release its wonder or its waste. I see it in my scribbles as a five-year-old and I see it in the larger works I create now. I see it in every doodle in every notebook I've held onto throughout my school years. I should probably erect a patchwork collage of those doodles into some larger work, and I will. They are a spastic loose-limbed diary, a body of work that grew and yet remains in pieces on shelves, in closets, and under stacks of whimsical moments captured and awaiting sentence.

Every lifetime is a dream, and every moment is an opportunity to fashion the gift of that dream into a masterpiece of art. Even when the dream makes no sense. Even when beauty becomes nightmarish. Even when loneliness leers at me from a canvas and love is a blue smear brushing just outside a window of my studio.

A year before the dog attacks, I was at my aunt and uncle's house in Maryland for Thanksgiving. Something invited me into their basement, and I sat down at a piano I'd never heard anyone play. I became entranced. I began playing D F# A and E G# B over and over. And over again. Those six notes, unnamed and unknown to me at that time, became my first real siren call into silence I had never filled before. I had no idea why those mystery notes moved me like they did. But they were bright and dark colors, they were shapes and structure, and they were a sound story I knew I wanted to listen to and tell others about.

For Christmas, my father showed me how to hold his drumsticks, and bought me a thirty-five-dollar champagne sparkle snare drum at Chuck Levin's Music Store on 14th street in Washington DC. My father's favorite drummer was Gene Krupa, and we saw him at the Showboat Lounge in Silver Spring. All the way home Daddy kept saying, "Hot mashed potatoes and two pork chops." He said that was the lick that

Krupa always used to keep his drum solos going.

I wanted to be a great drummer too, but I was still fascinated by the mysterious offerings from the upright piano in my parent's living room. Both are percussion instruments. But you can't write songs on the drums.

I began entertaining people when I was thirteen, sitting behind part of a Ludwig black pearl drum set in The Infernos. I had no idea what I was doing. I'd taught myself by listening to 45 records in my room. My mother found me a drum teacher, and a piano teacher, and I practiced for hours, determined to master the language of music. But being in a band in front of crowds gave me bursts of confidence that I never knew existed. The applause was an embrace I had never felt before, sincere and warm in ways that made me shiver. I wasn't thinking it would make me rich and famous, at least not then. But I did believe it was what I was meant to do.

The Infernos band card said, "Red Hot Music with The Quality Sound." We did British Invasion covers, wore matching outfits, and came in fifth out of nine in a battle of the bands. We played at church dances, parties, and sock hops. Our bass player drank cough syrup during our jobs. The old-fashioned kind. Codeine can make a fourteen-year-old boy sound like a down and out blues man. Just before he quit The Infernos he pawned our band speakers, so we tried to pawn his bass guitar. Nobody wanted it so we buried it in the woods behind my parents' house.

I'm one of two members who are still alive out of the seven players who cycled through The Infernos. I was their shy drummer, often playing too much or too loud, and confounded by my curly hair. The Beatles had the look that girls adored, so I began straightening my hair by wearing one of my mother's stockings over my head at night. It worked until gym class, which was luckily the last period in the day. But after a shower, I was that guy with the uncool hair again. I thought being in a band would give me some minor celebrity status at school, but I was invisible to the cool kids who smoked in the boys' room. I bought Lucky Strikes because they looked like an album cover in the cigarette machine. I inhaled once and threw up in the woods where we'd buried that bass guitar. Beer made me throw up too. But I did that on my mother's feet in my own bedroom. She came in as I sat on the edge of my double bed, head spinning. She asked me if I was injured from the fall she'd seen me take in the hallway. Her new slippers were lime green, but she patiently toweled up the response that splattered on them and turned off the lights. She dried my face and said, "You'll feel better in the morning." Always my brightness. Always my darkness. And the only one I thought could protect me from the temptations outside my bedroom door.

CHAPTER 3

"LIKE A BEACH BLANKET" (1979)

*Forgive us both
for who we are*

"A Shepard's Heart"

I shoved my sleeve up and slid my arm along the frozen window, breathing hard. The blue light faded. Now I was awake.

I chugged down some flat soda and chewed on what was left of the pizza. I checked my singing voice, hitting a high note; it rang through the cab like a victory cry.

I knew what I could count on: not Primadonna or record deals or a rental house or chocolate and vanilla python boots, but the best girlfriend I'd ever had. She'd be off tomorrow; we could sleep late. Make tea. Chamomile and honey, and our cat Meezer would be curled up nearby while Shana wrote in her journal, recording how much she valued our relationship; how it opened her chakras. She'd usher a wayward hair out of her eyes; and she'd whisper that nobody should be afraid of the truth.

What made our relationship strong, she'd say, was that we were both radically honest. People are bound to have desires. Temptation was the heart browsing but not necessarily buying. Everything was meant to be. I'd missed those sessions. We'd whisper and squint at each other like our minds were having sex. I'd introduced her to Buddhism, and she'd taught me about Eckankar, the study of soul travel. She said we were old spirits. I said she looked incredible for being so old. I'd try not to focus on her skin catching candlelight, as we talked about spiritual stuff. Like attachment, detachment, and Universal Love. The half-moon shaped mole on her cheek always helped me concentrate. The lessons that came with love could keep us in bed for hours.

But we hadn't talked since a Florida show a month ago. Somewhere south of Richmond I heard her voice, rushing by like whispers from her pillow. She said she was disappointed. But I'd been honest. Radically honest.

It had been a month since I'd seen Shana. Our Florida reunion should have been incredible. Shana had flown in to see me at Jo Jo's in Jacksonville. It was a Saturday night. Spotlights illuminated "Primadonna . . . All Week" on the faux castle wall of an old Safeway store, now transformed by flashing strobes, fog machines, and a mammoth dance floor. Jo Jo's flaunted the conceit that sinners needed a playground. Above its gothic entrance was a car-sized elf in a top hat with a lightning bolt shooting out of its ass. Inside, shirtless bartenders clanged firehouse bells and waitresses in Dalmatian bikinis delivered trays of flaming shooters, as the sounds of some hellish inferno poured from vents in the ceiling. When fights erupted, they were halted by bouncers wearing fireman helmets.

Jo Jo's cultivated a disorderly crowd. They stormed in unholy, inhaling the charged air until surfaces became stickier.

By 9 p.m. a dozen girls who'd come for the fifty-dollar cash prize thong contest were disrobing behind the stage, heehawing and passing around a bottle of tequila. I didn't see Shana anywhere. I had my sticks and I warmed up, rehearsing lyrics, and doing paradiddles on the arm of a beaten couch. When I climbed on stage to tune my drums, I knew she was in the crowd. I sensed her grounded energy in that chaos.

But I never saw her. We did five sets, the thong contest streaked by, and finally, there she was. Backstage, holding two flutes of champagne, smiling sublimely. And maybe it was the cocaine, or the coeds, but in that light, I barely recognized her. She'd changed her hair, was taller than me in heels and looked better than all those topless beauties combined.

We kissed, toasted, and as I rested my hand on her butt, she asked me something. Heavy metal was exploding through speakers above us, and we both kept saying, what? She was wondering about the two fans who I'd slow danced with while I sang "Stairway to Heaven" in front of the stage.

We moved toward the dressing room. "Well, that's just me doing my job," I said, and she nodded. I found her ear under her new hairdo, but it felt like when I'm losing the crowd during a drum solo. I told her that fans were persistent. I caught myself just before saying, "I can't believe they were sisters: Blonde and brunette; bouncing on those single beds like kids. Jumping over a campfire!" I thought she'd appreciate how that innocence touched me. I swore I never invited them back to the motel; "they just followed me." Did I say it like that? Now I can't remember.

I'd thought honesty was sacred. A sacrament that brought us closer. Maybe there's no way to tell a story about two sisters like that without it coming out wrong.

Shana didn't wait while I loaded up my drums and piano. I saw her backing away from the loading dock in her rental car. I figured she'd fly home, to our place in Falls Church, on a red eye out of Jacksonville. And that we'd work it out.

The road is rough on relationships, but love is patient, and love is forgiving. Love should definitely mean more than a one-night stand with two goofy sisters from Minnesota.

It was just after midnight when I pulled the brake in the snow-covered parking lot of the church that sat beside our rental house. The highway was pulsing like feedback in my ears. I'd just driven twenty-three hours straight home.

As I unbuckled, I saw our downstairs bedroom light come on. Drizzling snow aroused me as I walked toward the house and the sound of something familiar. My favorite tune, "San Francisco Girls" by Fever Tree, was slipping out from somewhere inside the house. Bits of lyrics wound through the flakes as I slogged forward.

Our glowing bedroom was a comforting beacon. I dropped my rucksack in the snow and stood on the wooden crate beneath the glass.

The window was frost chiseled, but I could see into our room. The curtains were loosely parted. I steadied myself on the brick of the sill. What was she conjuring? Maybe she was wearing that blood orange lingerie I'd sent from Palm Beach. Maybe we'd take some pictures. She'd be surprised; the official Southern Tour schedule didn't have me returning home to Falls Church for three more days.

I saw hazy, familiar shapes. A candle flickered in a dish, a cat curled in a chair, and strands of Mardi Gras beads hanging from our bedposts framed a large naked man's body. I focused on that image as it had to be some kind of flesh-colored body pillow. Then it rolled over and scratched its balls. A fat giant was on our bed, yawning, lolling there like a beached whale. He jammed my pillow under his head as the bedroom door opened.

Shana entered the room in a red bra, climbed onto his side of the bed and sat on him, confidently. The glass was fogging but I could see his mouth moving idiotically as he grinned up at her.

Fever Tree droned languidly. I looked at her innocent face, that perfect nose, the way her lips parted, her eyes … smiling. That beautiful, mysterious love of my life was smiling at HIM. I was numb. Dead.

He barked out something foreign and I heard that puppy wail she always makes, the one with the "oh God" look on her face.

I kept thinking *smash the window . . . stop this assault,* but then she climaxed, crying "oh Karl oh Karl oh Karl" as he lifted her. I slipped backwards.

I'm sure in their chorus of orgasms they never heard my curse when I landed in the snow. They never heard me start my truck and aim it lightless toward the house. They certainly heard it when its steel rear end crashed into that 1935 brick veneer. I didn't make it all the way through. But I shattered bricks, glass panes, and the hot water radiator line that ran up into our bedroom.

My last name is Mason; I would fix all that brick and mortar myself. But that room would feel cold forever.

I called Shana at work a week later. I didn't ask where she'd moved. All she said was her "friend had been scalded" and we wouldn't be getting married. I agreed, as I could still see her red bra coming off, and some bald guy's sausage fingers reaching around her arching back. And that move where he jumped up and spread her out like a beach blanket.

Every now and then I still caught a scent of her: honey ginger; sweet until it got in my mouth. Then it was as bitter as the shampoo she left in our shower. That was the taste of trust.

What I couldn't spit out was the taste of my own medicine. People said I clicked my teeth together when I was drumming. Losing her trust in us was something I might be chewing on forever. Or until I forgot her . . .

CHAPTER 4

REWRITING MY LIFE'S SONG

(1980)

Leave that life
you think you own

"Come on Home"

There was still a glow about Primadonna. Even in faded T-shirts and cutoffs, we looked like rough and ready rockers arriving to pose for candid publicity shots. There was a radiance to it all, watching familiar cars and motorcycles pulling into my driveway, radios blasting, as if we were going to rehearse one more time.

Mike was in a jovial mood and had his new acoustic guitar with him. I overheard him telling Richard that he had a song idea about somebody's soon-to-be ex-wife. "Not my fault," he kept saying as if there was already a chorus to refute that. The bass player and other lead guitarist, also named Michael, were less expressive.

Everybody knew why we were having this Sunday meeting at my house in Falls Church. Nobody asked where my girlfriend or all the furniture was. The six of us sat on worn Anvil cases and passed around beers as the numbers in my yellow expense book spoke soberly. We had a truck full of gear, five years of performing together, and boxes of T-shirts and publicity posters. But if it hadn't been for girlfriends and parents we wouldn't have been able to turn on the lights.

It had taken us three years, but we'd paid off the gear my mother had cosigned for when she'd made a down payment to the music store that had supplied us. We'd never have had that crisp four-way sound system if it hadn't been for her. If it hadn't been for Richard and his brother Joe, who ran our live mixing board wherever we played, we wouldn't have known what gear to buy. And when that equipment broke down, Joe and Richard always found a way to get it working during breaks between sets. Yet in the five years we'd been slogging it out on the road, we'd never gotten a raise from anywhere we'd performed regularly. They offered us free meals and drinks but gas prices and the costs of blown speakers had gone up. Drumsticks, show clothes, and guitar strings had become more expensive.

Those years were a rollicking ride of weirdness and joy, but mostly immeasurable benefits came from being in Primadonna. We never had a tip jar because they'd always been more physical than financial. And staying overnight at a fan's house always meant free breakfast or even lunch. And many of those women turned out to be incredibly decent people. Single mothers, college girls, lab technicians, nurses, lawyers, and even a state representative. I'd had to give a gatehouse security man a complicated password to be allowed to drive onto her property. "Park behind the old stables," she'd said. "My husband's gone until next Sunday. But don't worry about that. He's been living in the guest house since we separated."

We'd done it all. Signed with RCA/Sunberry/Dunbar, and Interworld Records, gotten the best veteran management we could attract, followed the advice of our producers in New York who had written hit songs, and paid our bills by going on the road. We'd performed at every bar and nationally ranked arena that would have us, up and down the east coast, and even into the Midwest. We lived and slept in the truck, or in fine hotels. We'd cooked fish on hot plates in motel rooms and been served five-course dinners on white linen. And we still laughed at the times we'd passed out on sprung couches in dressing rooms that should have been fumigated.

We'd done showcases for labels that wanted to sign us, filled stages with all the glory we could afford, hired a choreographer, and created a light show with explosions and fog and even threw fake rocks out into crowds on special occasions. But everybody forgets. Unless you have a hit song on the radio, and have the power of payola, an off-the-books system employed by record labels who paid radio stations to keep playing the songs they'd invested recording expenses in, you're just another rock band, making a living by playing wherever you can.

We were unlucky to come along just as the payola scandals of the late '70s were hitting the national news. DJs and mobsters and record label executives were no longer sharing the same sleeping bag. But we still believed. And wrote songs. And rewrote songs and kept digging into the darkness toward the gold we knew was waiting just for us. Until the label and the management deals made our dreams feel like we'd been digging our own graves.

And now, after years of reaching for those flames of gold, we were letting go. An unspoken toast was raised. To dreams, still smoldering on cassettes in a closet.

Maybe someday, we all hoped. For now, we sold our equipment to my brother's band and split the proceeds equally. We were damn lucky to have found a working band that needed literally everything we had, immediately. When the truck and the rehearsal room were empty of all we'd used to make a living, I closed those doors. But in my head I could still hear that throbbing body of work; the parts I'd played and the camaraderie I'd miss. I said goodbye to the screams for encores. And as they faded, I imagined a blank page where I could rewrite my life's song.

CHAPTER 5

THE BIRTH OF BIG BOY MOVERS (1980)

Born to move,
I got wings on my heels

"Single Shoe"

I was almost thirty, renting a 1935 house, driving an eighteen-foot truck to get around. No more putting on mascara and setting doll heads on fire while bouncing on a drum stool. No more stages decorated with women's panties. No more feeling guilty because I can't give some girl my drumsticks.

My first and last straight job was when I was thirteen. I got up every morning at 4:30 to deliver the *Washington Post* on suburban streets in Annandale, Virginia, pedaling a red Schwinn bike with twin saddle bags. Rain or shine. My mother would drive me in our VW Microbus if there was a blizzard. I pedaled those hills for three years, making about sixty bucks a month.

When I quit, I needed to turn in my last collected monies and tell my *Washington Post* manager, Mr. Hamilton, that I'd taken a job as the drummer in a new band.

"Come on," he shouted in response to my knock. "What can I do you for?"

I found him in his bathroom, squatting on the toilet, staring at me over the sports section. He flushed his cigarette and said I'd be sorry I quit him.

I wonder what he'd say now that I was an unemployed twenty-nine-year-old.

It was time to get creative. I had confidence, knowing I'd been successfully selling the services of the band. I would make calls for hours, and I actually enjoyed it. For all my rocker lifestyle, I was organized too—kept notes, and my doodles were artistic, displaying the vibe and emotions of agents and club owners I dealt with. I had the blankets we'd used in the studio to muffle my bass drum, and four parkas that Shana had left in the closet. Most importantly, I had a big truck.

I ran an ad in the *Washington Star*. "White Truck Movers, $25 per hour. You call, we haul." *Washington Star* management called, chastising me for running a "racist ad." I had four minutes before the next ad deadline to give them a new name for the heading. "Big Boy Movers" rolled off my tongue, and my brand was born.

The phone rang immediately. I said we had years of experience moving things. Cash only, at the end of the move. No more silver-toothed club owners writing me a check I had to split six ways. I kept it simple: I offered the truck, the muscle, and the promise that whatever had to be moved, would get moved.

My first customer's name was Brandy. She and her roommate wanted me to move them for seventy-five dollars, cash. I threw everything in the back of the Ford E350 that was finally free of stage lights, speakers, racks, amps, and drum cases. I didn't have a map, but I found my way to Greenbelt, Maryland.

I couldn't park directly in front of the apartment building they lived in, and they were skeptical I could do the move myself. They sat on their patio and drank coffee as I carried out boxes and small furniture. I heaved Brandy's mattress over my shoulder and loaded it and the box springs. I finessed the triple dresser by taking the drawers out, turning it upside down and sliding it down the stairs on the thick parkas. I had never moved lamps and pictures and plants, but I nestled them in-between boxes and at soft angles to keep them from being crushed. When I ran out of padding materials, I borrowed sweaters and jackets from an open box. At the very end, I took off my T-shirt to protect the bowed front of a Governor Winthrop desk, an antique with a fine patina.

It took me two hours to load the girls up. When we got to the drop-off, Brandy called her boyfriend Thad, and he arrived in a convertible with shades on. "You call yourself Big Boy," he crowed. What he didn't realize, in his blustering 6'4" state, was that being short has an advantage. Lifting furniture is all in the fulcrum, and being low to the ground, I could recalibrate more easily when the weight on my arms shifted. Thad had never carried eighty-pound speakers up the stairs of the Old Mill Tavern outside Scranton, Pennsylvania. Thad had never unloaded and loaded a lightless truck for three separate gigs in three separate states on winter nights with stoned band members. Thad had never duck-walked in January sleet, with makeup running into his eyes, carrying mic stands, his right hand wrapped in gauze, fisherman's glue sealing the gash that was always open after six sets, right where a 2B drumstick meets flesh. I felt a wave of what used to rule me, prodding me to prove something to myself, to my ego, and to guys like Thad. But I was a mover now, not a performer in a spotlight.

That day I made seventy-five dollars in four hours. It would have taken two nights at the Crazy Horse for me to earn that much. I got home at 4 p.m. instead of 4 a.m. and nobody shouted "Free Bird" or "Stairway to Heaven" while I was working. Nobody said I was flat on that song by Queen, again.

I told my cat Meezer that Daddy had a new job and fed him the high-dollar canned food I couldn't afford before. I told him that Big Boy Movers wasn't just a rock and roll dream. It was our new reality, built on muscle and gumption. And four parkas out of a closet in a house with a patched-up brick wall.

Three months later, on a sunny Saturday, I held a 4" x 6" piece of paper with a name, a phone number, and a DC address. I'd noted that Susan Werner lived in an apartment, in Georgetown, up twenty steps, and was moving to the Berkshire, where there was a small freight elevator. I'd noted that she had ninety-four boxes, four shelving units, a dining table that I could disassemble, a seven-foot-long bookcase, two chairs, a sewing machine, wooden crates, a stereo, and eight framed pictures. In big letters I'd written, "SHE HAS TO MOVE TODAY."

I'd quoted her $135, but we'd agreed on $100, cash. But then, in her kitchen, I showed her my notes, because she lived up fifty-eight steps and had much more to move than what she'd told me. She admired my careful handwriting and agreed to pay an additional twenty bucks for her miscalculations.

Susan Werner, an athletic grad student, offered me iced tea, and wanted to know how I was going to do this move by myself. I couldn't afford to hire a helper, yet, but I wasn't going to admit that to her. Her mother was there and had the same misgivings, adding that "The walls have just been painted, so, be careful, Mister." I was motivated by Susan

Werner's watchful anxiety as I flew up and down the stairs, loading everything in ninety minutes until even my shoes were drenched with sweat.

My truck cab pulsed with "A New Shade of Blue." It was a Primadonna standard, a set-closer in fact. I wrote that rocker when we were off the road at my house in Falls Church. I still love the dramatic tenor that soars over meaty power chords ("I've got a new shade of blue, remembering nights with you"). As the song built up, I played the hi-hat part on my steering wheel, remembering the thrills that used to empower Primadonna on stage. The new shades of blue that I'd been seeing were as ethereal as music, but so far, I was the only one in the audience when they appeared.

Primadonna could still get signed, I told myself. We'd even gotten together six weeks earlier at a friend's studio to do some recording, certain we might have a hit left in us. It was a song of mine called "Don't Ask Me How My Nights Have Been Without You." We sent the mix up to our connections in New York and they promised to shop it around, but we hadn't heard anything since then. I was thinking that Big Boy Movers was making more and more sense as I wound around Washington Circle, and I was wishing the guys were with me. But none of them wanted to be household movers. Nobody wanted a "straight job."

The Werners took the Parkway. Trucks couldn't go on Rock Creek Parkway. The mother scolded me saying, "You wasted time." I reminded her gently that I wasn't working by the hour. Maybe I should've been.

I commandeered an old chaise lounge at the loading dock of the new apartment, its metal wheels squeaking with purpose. I loaded it up and filled the elevator a dozen times. It was exhilarating work. Not like a waitress flashing me, but the pay made up for that. I was making more on a single move than I ever did for a whole week of playing at any bar on the east coast.

In the half-lit hallway, an elfin senior nosed her walker toward my loaded chaise lounge. Her delicate hand stroked the white metal flowers that graced the top of it. "I'm Mrs. Vivian Mounds," she said with a stern look. "Where are you taking my husband?" She patted the chaise lounge and rolled on into the shadows.

As I packed the elevator with boxes, a WWII peacoat fell out of an open container, marked Salvation Army. There was a stack of letters under it. The top one was clearly addressed to a Colonel Mounds. I wanted to stop the elevator, find the old lady, and return it to her. But I was drenched in sweat, and figured my customer might have an answer.

At the end of the move, Susan Werner asked about the Salvation Army box. She said it wasn't hers. As I was leaving The Berkshire, I saw a large photograph of a handsome couple in the lobby. They had both passed on the same day in hospice. The man was in uniform, she was in a wedding gown. There would be a "Celebration of Life" in the community room later that afternoon. I recognized that stern elfin face. And Vivian Mounds was smiling at me.

When I told my mother about Vivian Mounds, she smiled. "I'm glad you've got that truck," she said. As we hugged good-bye, I thanked her again for buying it. She had sensed what was needed, and burned a path straight toward where I was eventually meant to be.

CHAPTER 6

MY MOTHER'S FIRE (1961-1976)

A silent woman is usually screaming inside

"Learn to Listen"

When we first moved to Annandale in 1961, my mother liked our attractive house, but she didn't like the restraining style of the neighborhood. She said the neighbor ladies all wore cashmere sweaters and turned up their noses when they passed her mowing our front yard in her shorts and polo shirt. They were military officers' wives, coiffed and unemployed, raising children who'd never had a pony that would stick its head in a kitchen window to eat an apple out of a girl's hand, and whose fathers didn't brew Kentucky bourbon in a copper still and let their twelve-year-old daughters try smoking a cigarette. I assumed my mother appreciated the conveniences of our new life. My sister and I could walk to school, joining other kids on our street, as we passed shop windows filled with temptations, both tasty and whimsical.

Later my parents bought a Frank Lloyd Wright-style single-level a few miles away. It backed up to several acres of woods. Not quite as primitive as where we'd lived in Delaware, but the neighbors were friendly and welcomed us as we played hide-and-seek with more roughshod kids than the clean cut military boys who'd lived near the stores where they taught me to shoplift. This house was all red cedar and stone, glass-sided, with a green fiber sky-light and a flat gravel roof. It had a backyard for my mother's gardening and a big mauve overstuffed chair beside the fireplace where my father would read and write in his journal. It gave my parents solitude and my mother a sense of unbridled freedom. She thrived there.

Mama blew through projects like an unquenchable blow torch. When I was twelve, I watched her shoving a gas lawn mower up the hill behind that house, blazing a trail deep into the woods where I'd smoke my first cigarette a few years later. She slapped me hard once when I was eleven, the word *Goddammit* had crossed my lips, but maybe she had her anger from how she'd followed her parents' rules and been denied. Maybe she'd wanted to blame God too.

Her father wouldn't send her to Broadway to pursue her dance career. He made it clear that his daughter should get married and have a family; that performing on stages would never lead her toward a respectable life. He was conservative in his views about how women displayed their bodies, though he did have his night out to see a "show" at the Moulin Rouge when my grandparents took me to Europe in 1963. In his diary he wrote about a "little French beauty, all painted up like a movie actress." My mother was denied even that professional option, and though she occasionally taught dance, she never got to publicly share the skills she'd mastered that validated her dance degree.

So she gave her dreams to me, her bourbon and ginger rocking on the table as she banged it, screaming "Go man, go," over the racket of my drum solos in nightclubs filled with smoke and adoration.

During our early Annandale years, she found me a drum teacher and a piano teacher who taught me the chord method, so I could focus on singing and writing songs. By the time I was fourteen she insisted that my father buy me the rest of a real drum set, and he did. But for some reason, he neglected to buy me a hi-hat. So his metal standing lamp was my way of keeping the eighth notes steady for The Infernos.

My mother wasn't always expressive about her inner emotions; her standard advice was "toughen up." But the budding poet in me was a talent she encouraged, and she loved the first real song I completed at the family piano. It was called "The Zoo Song." I was sixteen then and had taken my girlfriend Karen to the National Zoo. I sang "you let me be like me, and that's what matters most to me." Garfinckle's Department store actually used most of that line and my melody for a jingle that our band barely got eighty-five bucks for.

My mother's fire could be as vibrant as the African polyrhythms I attempted as I drove our neighbor Stan out of his mind. He lived two houses away, and when he'd storm down and tell my mother to shut that kid up, she'd spin around and tell Stan to go to hell. She'd be dancing in her shorts, and my father used to say most of Stan's complaints were because he enjoyed arguing with her, especially on hot summer afternoons when my almost complete drum set would thunder until dinner time.

She let our band, the Infernos, practice in her sewing area/playroom while she watched Maryland basketball on TV and ironed. And as I got better, and joined a band that needed a big sound system to play large venues on the road, she told my father she was writing a check. It was an advance on my inheritance she said. It was her father's stock gains that created the bank account that check was drawn on. We paid her back. At our performances, she was far from being a silent partner, but she'd earned the right to howl at the fire she'd helped create.

My mother's fire was unquenchably hot, her light was always shining to help me find my way. But sometimes I would hear a bourbon bottle clink against a glass, and a cabinet door would slam shut. Her silence would wait for my surrender of what to ask, which was always, "are you OK?"

And the answer my mother always gave me was . . . "I'm fine."

I wish I'd found the words to ask her why she was so elusive. I don't think I ever stopped trying to plumb that depth of shadows in my mother's heart.

CHAPTER 7

FOUR-WAY ORGY (1980-81)

*Life is shaking you,
hold on and breathe*

"Born to Believe"

Pick up any phone. Dial 560-5611. Even if it rings and goes dead, imagine a question about moving services. Like . . . do you guys charge by the hour . . . or are you flat rate? If something breaks, how do you handle that? Are you insured? It was never hard to answer those questions. But I had to really learn to listen between the words to know what I was agreeing to do. That infinite commitment is still there, beyond this realm of technology. And the silence you hear on that dead phone is as deafening as the Big Bang of Big Boy Movers beginnings.

I always answered, "Big Boy Movers," with a slight aural lift on the word Movers. I used an assertive but conversational tone, even if I'd been sound asleep. I was raising a baby, and that wailing phone was how I fed it.

I let words tumble from the caller, allowing them to stumble as they imagined what they wanted from me. It was more than just moving services. It was about how we connected from a distance. We were creating something. I had to learn to listen.

Sometimes, sensitive details would worm themselves out of the conversation as I priced the move. In pick-up or drop-off descriptions, or in the listing of an inventory, the tone would shift, and people would begin telling me about the separation, the marriage, the accident, the divorce, the graduation, the death, the birth, the illness, the new job or job loss, the downsizing, the old house, the landlord, the roommate, the violent ex-boyfriend, the new girlfriend, or the retirement home. Callers would say things to me that only a complete stranger should hear, unable to judge, unable to question, unable to doubt. So I listened.

I wanted to say just the right thing. I'd murmur to replenish the support, but I was a sieve, catching what remained as stories poured from vessels that were often still breaking. I wasn't frustrated; a move was being booked and money was being made. But sometimes the confessions revealed too much detail and I felt anonymous, like a hotline operator. I knew it was unprofessional to pry, but when the conversations turned darkly personal, I would inquire a little more deeply and if the caller asked for help, I would give it to them. I had the numbers of law enforcement officers and private investigators, and I would share those if I felt that the caller was in danger.

I let them talk, imagining Big Boy Movers lifting all that mattered from the flood that I heard rising on the other end of the line. No amount of applause ever made me feel like that. But it was never about me. I've seen grown men and women burrowing into someone's shoulder as a dresser was being carried in or out of someone's life. I've caught the last look at rooms where someone spent countless hours, where they gave so much of themselves to work that they never thought they'd miss.

Moving day is your world dismantled, your material existence handled by ex-cons with names like Creeper, guys you certainly don't want in your house, farting in your kitchen and leering at the pictures which you meant to pack, but forgot, and now some mover with a nose ring is eyeballing your cleavage in your alabaster wedding dress.

Customers would talk to the movers. "Would you like water? What are you looking for in my nightstand? Yes, that's for massage. I'll pack that drawer. Where's the guy I talked to on the phone? He promised me five men, there's only three of you. Who's that in my hammock? Please put that down, that's loaded. Did your shoes leave those black stains on my rug?" All appropriate questions, but not always compassionately answered.

Life doesn't promise us a perfect performance. Sometimes in the stage lights you have a hair lip and a tiny dick. And that's how any Moving Day could be. But at least the moving business didn't offer promises of advancement in exchange for a bad deal. When booking agents lied to Primadonna, we still did the gig that underpaid us or slept in the band truck when promised accommodations weren't available. We imagined a random record executive happening to be in the audience at one of our gigs, hearing us play, and coming backstage to offer us a record deal that was better than what we already had. Like you see in the movies. We imagined a tour where we would open for Cheap Trick, or some other hot band, that would take us to venues where thousands of people would see us and scream for encores. We always dreamt of jetting around the world, touring as an opening act or as the headliner.

We didn't talk about it much, we just kept giggin'. But I believe what drove us was that we knew we were artists who wrote great songs and sang them from the heart—the signatures on our record contracts proved that some labels believed in us too. Having one of our songs chart in the top 40 was a constant glorious dream, but what motivated us was making the music, the energy of performing it, and the audience accolades.

When the band was on fire, I let everything I was worth burn in The Golden Light on stage. Big Boy Movers rose from the band's ashes to show me that business grows a dollar at a time, not a dream at a time. Like melodies that still floated into my head from the ether, I heard essential business questions in my mind. I wasn't on stage, but I found new ways to use that gift. Creativity is a blessing from the Divine.

The questions I had to ask customers to price their moves could be lyrics, but they paid the bills like no song of mine ever had: How MANY steps are at the place you live now? Is there a LONG walk? (If this was a rock song, I'd bring in a steady kick drum on fours right here) Can we get the truck CLOSE to the elevator, or is there a long carry THROUGH the garage? You have a SMALL piano? Is it a BABY GRAND? Are you taking your washer/dryer/freezer or refrigerator? (A power chord would begin now, an E suspended 4th). Will you be PACKED and READY to move (bass guitar would thump in here) with the elevator key RESERVED? Will you transport ALL the pictures, plants, and lamps in YOUR vehicle? (Hi-hat on fours would start now) Does your PARTNER/LOVE INTEREST know you're moving out? Does he/she have any GUNS in the house? (Snare, acoustic guitar, and right-hand piano would charge in here) If so, will you have LAW EN-FORCEMENT present on moving day? (Vocals enter here) Do you have enough SPACE in your storage unit to accept ALL the inventory we're moving that day? Will you agree to PAY us at the end of the move with CASH? Do you understand that we can't accept POST-DATED checks, food stamps, or furniture for payment?

The unpredictable dance of moving day often became a four-way orgy. There was chemistry in every truck. The love and hate for what movers do became an elixir that each crew brewed on the job. My movers were Everyman—rural, urban, tongue-tied, verbose, patient, and reactive, using reptile brain mechanisms to get to that place where the body surrenders and the mind accepts the intolerable. The part-time helpers I hired rarely stayed more than a week. Yet I handed out tools and coached them on what could be complicated issues on a given move.

They huddled and separated to put furniture into place, while senseless objects remained unaware that a human partner was in control, and sometimes losing control, as their padded stiffness was lifted and twisted into position, their wooden legs scraping the wall of a truck, straps and blankets yanked around them, cursed at for being too delicate or unwieldy. "Asshole," a rasping voice would say to them, "get in there." Finally the voices would fade, the door would roll shut, and peaceful silence blanketed everything.

CHAPTER 8

JOHNNY Z (1982)

Life is more than what the living can see

"Rappahannock"

I couldn't believe that Shana called me. I still had a naked picture of her in my wallet—looking over her shoulder at me from under a snow-covered hemlock in Pennsylvania, her pear-shaped ass as perfect as the ivory flakes that laced her hitched-down jeans. But more pitifully, I still harbored hopes that somehow, no man would ever appear in her life who could offer her the same adventurous lust that had led her from her failed marriage into my bed, and all the way into that netherworld we called our spiritual awakening. I held the phone like a delicate seashell in my hand, thinking I'd hear some echo of that past. But after we both said hello at the same time, she began talking, as if what I'd seen through that frozen window of our bedroom had just been a dream. And as she gently spoke, I began to wake up.

She was very matter-of-fact, and there was no bitter castigation as she told me about the new man in her life. He was a higher-level initiate of Eckankar, and in fact, they were going to be getting married on his colonial-era property out in a rural area an hour west of Falls Church. He was a third-generation builder and had introduced her to the concept of renovating older homes into new livable spaces. He had a beard and couldn't have sounded more unlike me. I was good at building ideas into song, but she had found someone who used his hands to create structures that could make a family a decent living. I wanted to say congratulations, but part of me still saw our legs entwined under that parachute in my old bedroom where we first discovered how our bodies and souls could become one.

So I let her talk, her sweet husky voice was patient, and she said she still loved me, but in a different way.

My growing study of Buddhism felt like arms around my shoulders as I sat in my little nook above the front door and listened to Shana's voice. It felt like I was being reminded of a bigger picture.

It took me back to an LSD trip I'd had a few years earlier at my parents' house. The Buddha had appeared so clearly to me then, and his smiling comfort had forever changed how I saw my life from that night forward. I hadn't expected that to happen. I was curious about Eastern philosophy, but finding myself in front of the Buddha on my very first acid trip was an awakening I took very seriously. For several hours during this trip, I was always at the back of an area filled with kneeling supplicants, and always staring directly into the calm, slightly smiling face of the Buddha. Every question in my mind rose like a blossoming flower and was received and returned to me with answers that I knew came directly from the Buddha. I had wondered about my reincarnation; who had I been, who would I become? I stared into the darkness of the bathroom and in the dim light of the mirror, I saw all the beings I had been. Native American, African, Caucasian, Asian; and as the Buddha silently explained this to me, I felt his assurance that all was indeed perfect; that I was meant to be born again, to die and live again, and that my creative pursuits were to honor my creation by the Divine. He comforted me, he made me feel loved by the power of all that is. I wandered through my parents' house, and everywhere I looked I saw his sacred assurance. It was hard to believe that I was walking in what felt like a spiritual wilderness, but I wasn't lost. I was being given the opportunity to experience the continuation of a journey that had begun many lifetimes ago. I was being asked to kneel and I did, with the other supplicants, as the words " trust, faith, and love" settled in my ears. Still, I was apprehensive of where all this might lead me.

On the phone, I wanted to tell Shana how I'd been struggling with my awakening, but I didn't. I wanted to tell her how much I'd missed her, so I told her I'd written a song for her. In that dwindling afternoon light, I felt a perfect silence holding me. I closed my eyes and told her it was good to hear her voice. We didn't make any promises to meet or pore over what had run so quickly past us. She'd called for a reason: she asked me to hire her spiritual guide, Johnny Z, who was looking for work.

I said of course. I'd been doing most of the jobs by myself, but some items were a challenge to move solo. A week earlier, I'd had to pay a stranger twenty bucks to help me lift a freezer into the truck. Summer was coming, the phone was really starting to ring and with a dependable second man on board I could assure callers that Big Boy Movers wouldn't let them down. And I admit, I wanted to stay connected to Shana.

Johnny Z quickly became more than just a helper. He made me appreciate the message on my answering machine that declared "Leave the dirty work to us." Finally, this was us—partners, not another helper misreading directions on a clipboard that my ex-Navy Captain father had given me when I was a paperboy. Helpers were hard to find, and rarely stayed with me for more than a move or two. Johnny seemed committed. I called Shana and thanked her. I kept it brief. I could feel her reading my mind.

Johnny too was an Eckist, and on our third move together, as we set a couch down into the truck, he asked me if I could feel the energy that was coming from the center of the sofa. "So much love here," he nodded, bowing toward the worn cushions. I wasn't sure what he meant, but he was quite clear. He explained how humans emit strong physical sensations through their lower chakras, and as love is made, or as love is shared, just in the sitting, that energy is naturally absorbed by the fibers of what makes fabric. Johnny explained that living material, which once grew as a plant, went through its own process of translation until it became what we see as the sewn material fashioned into objects like couch cushions. "The fabric holds it," he said reverently. Just like a rock holds the light of the sun and turns it into warmth we can feel with our hand.

I saw a winding tear in his eye as we hefted a heavy nightstand up the ramp into the truck. "He never thought he'd see the light go out," Johnny said. The lady we were moving said her late husband had always gone to sleep reading his paperbacks. Johnny said he could feel the warmth of that man's light on the nightstand as we set it down into the shadows of the truck.

Johnny validated my growing sense that the Universe offers us the ability to feel warmth, as life everlasting, and to know light as pure spirit. He and I had long talks and he offered me a mantra to use in my meditations. He lent me some books to read. He knew so much. Some of it was hard to grasp, but I was open, and answers began appearing to me as I meditated. I read all I could about Buddhism, Christianity, as well as Eckankar, and even when I felt myself confounded by what were distant concepts, I heard the silence that I began to accept as peace.

CHAPTER 9

THE FEVER (1982)

*I took a bullet but
I'll be fine*

"Life, Love, Sweet Satisfaction"

At first, I thought, it was regular exhaustion—I just needed a large coffee. Johnny and I pulled into a 7-11 and I settled back into the driver's seat, while Johnny munched on his raw ginseng and tofu. "For the lower chakras," he said, and I readied myself for yet another account of how incredible his new girlfriend was in bed. But my fogginess lingered as Johnny rambled on.

There was a dull ringing in my head.

"Hey man," Johnny said as he turned off the radio. "Did you hear me? You missed the exit man."

We were on our way to a move in Silver Spring, Maryland, so I took the next exit and handed him the paperwork. "Should be ok," I said. I'd moved this customer two months earlier, and it was a relief to have a helper. The customer had helped me lift his piano into the truck, and I wanted to avoid that. But I couldn't remember if the guy had been upset with me, or if the piano had even been moved off the truck with his help. Had a neighbor come over and volunteered? I felt clammy as we pulled up to the house where the move would happen, trying to remember if I'd left on good terms with the customer.

The customer's front door was open; he was securing it

with a strap of some sort and he waved, all grins. I waved
back, but when I reached for the truck door handle, I could
barely push it down; in fact, it felt as if it was locked. My
instinct was to kick the door open, but my left foot, which
I'd just used to push down the parking brake, wasn't cooper-
ating. All of a sudden, the signals from my brain seemed to
not be getting to my body. I was spellbound, as transfixed as
when that blue glow had filled my cab after my near-colli-
sion on 95. My coffee and the doughnut that had fallen into it
remained in the cup holder. I reached for them, and nothing.
"Something's not right," I told Johnny. "See if you can get the
customer to come over here and talk to me."

Johnny's eyes were flinty stones of fear. "What's going on
man?"

I said, "I can't see."

Johnny helped me open the door between the seats that
goes to the back of the truck. I dragged myself onto the pads
in the box of the truck and lay there in the dark. I kept my eyes
shut, but I couldn't move, as if there was some fuel draining
out of me from a seeping wound I couldn't find. Gatherings
of soapy blue light softly settled over my eyes, a signal that
hadn't ever been sent before. Strangely, it felt as comforting
as a baby's blanket.

I had no power to draw a deep breath, but I told Johnny to
give the customer All Star Mover's card; I had one up there
somewhere on the dash. All I could focus on was how my
fledgling moving company was failing, slipping away from
me, in front of one of my first loyal customers. The customer was leaning into the cab, talking, but I couldn't hear his
words. He didn't sound upset. He sounded scared. I heard
the door slam and Johnny starting the truck, and I remember
saying I'm sorry sir, and smelling exhaust and gasoline and

the mustiness of moving pads.

Johnny delivered me to my house in Falls Church and carried me through the back door. He helped me crawl up the stairs to my little bedroom nook. I woke up as he was explaining that a bad strain of flu had been hitting the DC area.

He said, "Rest and water, brother," as he gave me the rest of his ginseng to chew on.

After Johnny left, the weakness spread through my body, and I was sweating like I never had before. I was barely able to strip off my work clothes. But even in this condition I wasn't going to let this bug put Big Boy Movers out of business. I trusted that customers would call, that the answering machine would record numbers, and I'd call them back tomorrow when I felt better. But I didn't wake up for three days.

I lay in that attic bedroom for almost a week, unable to get to the bathroom except by crawling to it. I think the fever spiked on the sixth day and so I lay on the cool tile; my face resting beside the toilet. I wasn't hungry, and I knew I hadn't eaten for several days. I forced myself to drink water, remembering that is what really keeps the body alive.

There were shuffling sounds, mostly at night, like the caresses of a feathery fan, but whenever I opened my eyes, I saw nothing. Just a faded shadow of cool blue, wavering in and out of my little nook like a tide that washed over me serenely. Sometimes it made a sound, a whisper, not my own, telling me to let go, but I wasn't sure what I was hearing. None of it made sense.

I found sanctuary in that foam-floored nook above the front door of my house. The heat and the coolness came and went, charming me with whispers of old voices, and the imperceptible shadows of healing blue hands.

The angles of the nook slanted down at the head and foot

of each end of my foam mattress. This miniature cathedral ceiling was draped with yellow and red dyed Indian sheets, stapled to pine rafters. A three-foot entry door was in the middle, and a white knotted rope pulled it closed from inside. There was a narrow casement window for light and ventilation, and as I cranked it open, I saw my neighbor, Siggy.

Siggy was a chesty-voiced Lucille Ball lookalike and she'd agreed to feed Meezer. She came up to my room with a sandwich on a plate. We had a one-sided conversation as I faded in and out, but she asked if I'd been bitten by a tick. I woke up shivering in a pool of sweat at sunrise. Feeling like a child again, I called my parents.

My father and brother drove me to our family doctor in Annandale. They carried me into his office. After all things typical had been ruled out, my father asked, "Does he have Rocky Mountain Spotted-Fever?"

"No, and he doesn't have Cat Scratch Fever either. He has Fifth's Disease," declared the confident man subbing for our family doctor who was on vacation. "Take him home; if his fever goes up, put him in a bathtub full of ice." An hour later, in a bathtub full of ice at my parents' house, I remembered. While I was gathering clothes off a floor during a move in Reston, Virginia two weeks earlier, I'd pulled a tick off the inside of my left arm.

We were at the Fairfax Hospital Emergency Room twenty minutes later. Then I was in a hospital gown on a gurney. I got a mega shot of tetracycline and was told that if I had come in a day later, I'd be rolling through the back door in a bag.

I was face down on my stomach when a doctor began examining the spots on my body. I heard his flat voice say, "Yes, come on in." There were hushed giggles. A class of student nurses gathered in the small room around me. My naked buttocks were the subject. His lecture was stern as he lifted my gown, saying, "It's unusual to have a patient go this long untreated, so his spots are dramatically defined."

The doctor told the student nurses I was a lucky young man. I wondered if they could see my testicles. Was my penis tucked under or down? I opened one eye and saw white shapes bending over me, so close I could smell their feminine mists. As the doctor rubber gloved an engorged lump on my butt cheek, he said, "This larger one displays how long he's had Rocky Mountain Spotted Fever." I heard the clicking of cameras. I let the doctor have his moment. But I had a burning recollection. No tick bite had made that engorged lump. I'd sat down on a flaming doll head after a drum solo at Shooter's in Delray, Florida.

I'd miss twenty-four days of moves. I'd lose and regain twenty-six pounds and be one of fourteen people in the state of Virginia to be stricken with Rocky Mountain Spotted Fever that year. I'd also be one of two who'd survived it. The hands of the Divine had lifted me, and if they were blue, I'd seen them in that void that almost swallowed me.

The Universe wanted me to live, doing what I never dreamed I'd be doing. Hopefully that Divine intervention would send me some guys who wouldn't quit on me. Because Johnny Z was already leaving.

CHAPTER 10

DAVO, GINO, AND BILLY (1982)

We knew times of innocence

"Annandale"

Johnny Z was moving to Roswell, New Mexico with his new girlfriend, Joanna. But the Eck had imparted some wisdom that he was told to pass along to me. The Eck had told him that the Universe was sending good karma to all of us. Big Boy Movers was going to be to expanding. Johnny said every moment on Earth is perfect, and that every moment gives us exactly what we need. I thanked him for that, but now I needed to scramble to find another helper for Saturday's moves.

I needed helpers. I needed guys who wouldn't overthink what had to be done. Pick up the object, put it in the truck, and not injure themselves or break what we were moving. Guys who wouldn't talk too much about the science of it; it's not that complicated, it just has to get done. And I needed guys who'd stay longer than the twelve days Johnny Z had given me. But I understood, after all, we hadn't done any moves for twenty-four days while I was sick.

So when plumbing salesman Davo McMurphy approached me in a parking lot, I was ready. He had big man confidence and a lead singer's body language. I'd gone into Annandale Plumbing Supply to buy rubber anchors to fasten to the side of the truck box wall. We'd talked about how to keep hand trucks and dollies from going haywire and banging into customers' furniture. He trailed me outside. "Hey man," he said.

He lit a Marlboro and squinted back at the store. He wasn't an unwieldy bulky guy, but there was a bull-like presence about Davo, as if he could break through a fence if necessary, but overall, my impression was that he didn't want to be too uncool to break through anything. But he had a plan and he wasted no time pitching me. "Ben, we're ready. Five bucks an hour. Me, Gino, and Billy, man. We can load, move, and I can drive." He studied his cigarette. As I watched it smoldering against the neon light of the plumbing supply sign, Davo lowered his voice.

"We're living at Bernie's, you know Bernie, right? The party supply guy? Jesus Christ, we're sleeping on hay in a stable, setting up Moon Bounces for birthday parties, wearing little cowboy hats, leading kids around on ponies. Bernie's not paying us because he said we're living free in his barn. We're crapping in trash cans!"

He stopped talking and lifted his chin. Every man has his pride, and it hides inside him as words fail. I sensed he'd waited a long time to trust somebody like me with his frustrations. He looked out at the traffic on Columbia Pike. Before I went out on tour with the band, there were music stores, record shops, and places where American rock and roll cranked into the wee hours. There were diners that served hot dogs and had Elvis songs on the jukebox. There were fights in country bars between guys with names like Cecil, Lemmy, and Tom. Now Annandale had been reborn. The Pentagon families that had sent their kids to Annandale Elementary and Annandale High School (where I graduated) had reshaped their family trees, through marriage and life's lucky happenstances. Vibrant diversity had brought a delightful array of ethnic food to markets and restaurants, and Davo and I both commented on how our hometown was not the Annandale where we had once ridden our bikes. I caught the glimpse of a man who sees how fast things change, and who knows when to take a chance with a stranger.

He sold me. Basset Hound eyes and a Beatle haircut, leaning like a showman in the glare of the store window. Zero moving experience, but I trusted his big bear physique and the promise of a plan. Davo would drive, move furniture; even work the phone. At five bucks an hour. As long as he, Gino, and Billy could live in my basement for free.

Big Boy Movers. It was like I was in a band again. Not a great band name, but I'd be driving, and we'd all arrive at and leave one location, together. It wouldn't be to and from some bar or club, but we'd be in the old band truck. We wouldn't be in glittery outfits wearing makeup, but our clothing would kind of match, and we'd be ready for work. And instead of a vehicle full of heavy musical gear, we'd have lighter types of equipment necessary to do the job we'd been hired to do. We'd make the same kind of crude jokes en route to the venue or rather, now, to the location of the move. And instead of struggling in darkness and streetlight, we'd be loading and unloading in sunshine and daylight.

I was obviously the band leader, but I led with a light touch, letting Gino, Davo, and Billy each find their way. On the moves, the four of us jammed, fitting our talents together to load the truck and to keep what felt like our audience happy. We didn't intend to entertain them, but I did sense that customers appreciated how we moved in harmony through the day, as if the relocation of their belongings was a concert of delicate delivery, a hopefully seamless set of physical work that was at times as graceful as any set of songs I ever performed on any stage with a rock band. As furniture rolled successfully in or out of the truck, it felt like what I'd been missing about being in a band. Guys working together to create something bigger than what just one man could ever do by himself.

This new trio inspired me. Davo had carefree confidence, Gino could beat anyone arm wrestling, and Billy, with his southern Virginia drawl, knew something about everything in the universe. I drove, we moved people, and the four of us drank cold beer at the end of the day, like we'd just finished an invigorating gig. But those rock and roll audiences never tipped us as generously as our Big Boy Movers customers did. And that cold cash began to feel more satisfying than any dressing room quickie ever had.

Now that I was in a different sort of band, I wondered about those women sometimes. What always rose in my mind was an aching question: was I a father? One of my Primadonna bandmates had consoled me, reminding me that I was easy to find. But what if the woman I'd gotten pregnant had given the baby up for adoption? What if the mother of that child had passed away? I kept seeing a little girl, looking up at the trees, waiting for me to lift her onto a branch, or to set her into a swing that I'd gently push. It didn't seem fair; this anxiety was seeded deeply enough in me that over the years it had taken root. And there was no way I could ever know the truth.

CHAPTER 11

YOU'VE GOT TO SEE THIS GIRL

(1982)

*The rainbows and
the butterflies*

"The Other Side of Love"

Three years into the business, the bank account was growing. We had real moving pads, hump straps, and six dollies were bound to the walls of the truck. We looked like roadies, checked out women, and wore our blue-collar bravado like stage clothes on the sidewalks of DC.

I caught a glimpse of myself in an office window as I hoisted a file cabinet into the air. I had arm muscles and was sweating through my T-shirt. Not a glimpse of rhinestones in that spotlight. And no mercurial touring schedule loomed over this new ensemble. Shippers called daily, leaving messages after hearing, "Thanks for calling Big Boy Movers! Don't dread moving day, leave the dirty work to us!" I'd always miss the road life adventures and the thrill of satisfying an audience. But I did not regret the choice I had made.

Pay phones were lifelines for our burgeoning enterprise, and on a lunch break in September, I found one in front of a Burger Chef on Route 7 in Sterling, Virginia. I was booking a move with the receiver to my ear when Davo mouthed the words, "You've got to see this girl."

I followed him inside.

She was eating fried chicken, delicately probing her mouth with her finger between bites. She had sunset-colored hair and when she walked past, her narrow belt became a vein of tourmaline circling tantalizing hips. Her strong jawline said old family prestige, but the economy of her dining choice said working girl on a budget. She was cheerleader cute. And an iconic beauty.

I wasn't sure about the forefinger toothpick, but she carried herself like a model. She angled her tray toward the trash container and with a discreet bump she nudged open the Burger Chef door. She glanced back. I watched her approach the driver's side of a cobalt blue Triumph Spitfire. "Man, you got to follow her," Davo said.

The Spitfire was turning left on Route 7, westbound. Davo was insistent: "If you like her, go get her. She looked back at you, man." I'd just booked a last-minute move in Annandale, but I turned the key and the E truck roared in agreement. Gino and Billy were stretched out in the back. "Hell yeah," Gino said.

I hit every intersection perfectly, keeping the blue Spitfire in view until its taillight blinked left and she blended into traffic on High Avenue. I got the green, as she turned onto a private road. "Go," Davo commanded, "we're movers, we're allowed." Billy's sharp eye caught her getting out of her car, at the rear of a building jutting from a hillside. Its entry had a closed gate and a guard in a steel booth stared us down as we eased past. It was probably a government outpost, anonymous, like all the others. The black dullness she'd disappeared into was just a banal dead end, there was no destiny at play here.

But she was a redhead, driving a blue Triumph. The

vibrant images of how easily she'd been followed to this wasteland made me wonder if she thought a maniac was tailing her from Burger Chef.

A month later I pulled into the Burger Chef on Route 7. There was a cobalt blue Spitfire in the lot, and a redhead was in the driver's seat, hair hiding her face as she adjusted her rear-view mirror. I noticed the piano store in front of her car. Her window was down. It never crossed my mind that my directness could be threatening—a stranger, in torn cutoffs and a tank top, approaching and then coming close enough to make eye contact.

I asked if she was looking to buy a piano. She was wearing a candy pink top and white-framed sunglasses. She tilted her head thoughtfully. I sensed curious caution, but I continued, saying, "I play piano, and I saw you here the other day, so I thought maybe you knew this piano store."

She turned off her ignition. I knelt in the shadow beside her car and introduced myself; she removed her shades. She had pecan brown eyes. A flotilla of gold flecks spread across them and the way they sparkled reminded me of a magazine cover. "I'm Bobbi Jo McCall," she said. I shook her extended hand and she asked if I was a performing musician. I said yes, but that I wasn't trying to make a living from it anymore. I might have mentioned record deals and TV and then I heard myself asking her for her phone number.

The humor of the Universe darkened as a hard rain began falling. Bobbi Jo handed me a piece of a Burger Chef bag and rolled up her window. I sprinted for shelter as Route 7 swallowed her blue Triumph in that October thunderstorm.

At the phone booth I punched in the number, wondering if she'd suddenly realized I was that maniac who'd followed her in his truck. The number she'd given me was out of order.

Got that dial tone that sounds like a robot saying "idiot, forget it, idiot, forget it." But it was a Lovettsville, Virginia number. It was long distance, so I redialed with the 703 area code. It rang but nobody answered.

I got through a day later. Bobbi Jo said she'd come down to Falls Church on Friday night. She sounded comfortable about taking our musical conversation a step further.

Still, I wasn't surprised when she stood me up. Was I too intense? Too far away? Too interested?

But I'd changed the sheets, shaved, put on a skinny tie, and made a dinner of miniature lobster, sprout salad, and French bread. I had pink champagne, which eventually I popped and drank. I did a three-flight apartment move the next day, hungover, telling my helper, Michael Cooper, that women were born without a moral compass. But at eight that evening, as I was sitting naked at my piano, writing a song about lying-eyed cat women, I heard gravel churning in my driveway.

A cobalt blue sports car was pulling up behind the Big Boy Movers truck. I answered my front door in a bathrobe. "Hello stranger," she said. "Sorry I'm late."

• • •

Roberta Josephine McCall was living with her parents in Lovettsville, Virginia. Her mother had never been on an airplane or driven a car, and her father had only been out of the state of Virginia once. Bobbi Jo had been a semi-pro cheerleader and a lingerie model and had sailed for a year through the South Pacific with a female crew, on a yacht owned by Tip Munson of Munson Van Lines. She'd flown to an island near Samoa and had a threesome with the pilot and a wealthy Indian politician. She'd gotten pregnant by one of them and had given the baby up for adoption.

This was imparted over stoned Wheat Thins and cheese as we drank chilled wine. Bobbi Jo was enthusiastic about exotic places she'd go back to if she could afford it. It inspired me to wonder about what I hadn't been able to do.

Like buy some decent furniture. The purple slipcover I'd tossed over the free couch I'd gotten on a move had "character" Bobbi Jo said. But my coffee table was only as attractive as the magazines which were spread across it. A *National Geographic* got us talking about Europe and I told her how much I wanted to return there. I showed her my glass animal collection from Venice, and we agreed that a trip to an auction house would be a fun way to get a great deal on things, like a dining table. Dinner had been festive on two folding tables, but an antique dining table with vintage chairs was something she said she could help me find. Then she asked me about my old piano.

My musical passions hadn't diminished, and after selling all my Primadonna gear I had missed having electric keyboards and a tape deck to do some simple piano/vocal tracks on, as well as a drum machine. But I sat down at my 1935 Knabe spinet piano and played Bobbi Jo a song I'd been writing, and she said, "You should record that." I didn't attempt to explain why those golden dreams were still unresolved, and still unworthy of what it would cost to recreate them. Maybe the money would come in ways I had yet to imagine. Like silent music growing in my heart, everything I'd never had before would fill my house like the enchanting melody I kept hearing in Bobbi Jo's voice.

She responded that my moving business would be lucrative.

CHAPTER 12

IT'S NOT A DATE (1982)

*Your touch is gospel
on my skin*

"The Only One"

We didn't call it a date, we called it going downtown. Plans began forming as we sat on my back deck.

It made sense to me that Bobbi Jo would want to go somewhere exciting, where there'd be a crowd. I knew she'd been a dancer, entertaining guests on South Pacific cruises. I knew she liked rock and roll, and so I began telling her about my younger brother Jimmy's band. They're loud, I warned her, but Friday night they'd be at the Crazy Horse, and we could get in free. She wanted to know if I was going to be playing with my brother that night. I was charmed by her sense of brotherly love, but I gently explained it was his night, and that for once, I wanted to go to a bar and just be part of a crowd. I'm not sure she understood this concept.

As we sat on my back deck, I told her that my brother and I were close, but that we were almost exact opposites. And I made sure she knew I wasn't complaining. In fact, she said that she and her younger sister had come up the same way. "But you both play piano, right?" she said.

My little brother Jimmy took to my parent's piano with a more complete appreciation of its offerings than I ever did. He was seven years old when he began pedaling his bike up Walton Lane where Mrs. Haycock patiently taught him things I could barely grasp. I continued my chord method studies and worked on my songwriting, and though Jimmy didn't sing or write songs or play the drums, he whopped me regularly with his ever-expanding jazz and classical piano licks. I got used to being amazed at his dexterity, and by the time he was eight years old he knew my chord language and could speak it in circles around me.

I always felt like his student. But as I grew into being a band guy, so did he, and he learned from my choices and my mistakes. I began noticing that the young teen players that he had jamming with him were more skilled than half the older guys I was doing gigs with in bands that he always came to see. He was one of my biggest fans and one night after a Primadonna drum solo at some club in Alexandria, he gave me a bear hug and said that if I could do drum solos like that every night, I'd be famous. I had no idea what he meant and as I patted his eighteen-year-old shoulder I was afraid to tell him the truth. I had no idea what I'd just played, and I never knew what I was going to play during any solo, on the drums or the piano. That was the difference between Jimmy and me. I made it up as I went along. But he could hold his music in his hand, and recreate it perfectly every time, like a baker following his personal recipe. I was grabbing my ingredients out of thin air, be they lyrics that arrived as I sat at a piano, or, in the vocal lines I would twist during live performances, with players who often got annoyed by my extemporaneous inspirations. But when I hit the note, when the music rose like spirits from my heartstrings, audiences felt my passion, and its rapture would silence a room until applause rained down upon me and the fire that had been set on stage.

The other side of this lack of consistency was that I could

easily fall from some lofty place I believed I had reached. I had many bruises to my ego as I made dressing room apologies to bandmates who wondered why I couldn't play the same great parts every night. I believe I knew that I was born to follow my own musical path, but I still wasn't ready to celebrate that freedom.

When I left Primadonna, Jim's band continued to rock, following the model we had. They didn't tour but they cherry-picked their local jobs and only played at the best clubs. They were outstanding, and sounded like golden thunder, and I was so proud to see my little brother's fingers flying across the four levels of keyboards that encircled him like an alien craft.

I wanted Bobbi Jo to meet my little bro and when we went downtown, it felt like a homecoming at The Crazy Horse. I wanted her to see what it was like for me to play there, to let her feel the crush of people in the place as the dance floor opened up. To let her hear the bartender calling my name, clanging his bell and grinning at her cleavage as he handed us beers. I wanted to share the moments flying past us as we were enveloped in smoke and rock and roll and I wanted to see her elation as she looked into my eyes, with that pulsing desire I could never touch from behind the drums on stage. I wanted her arms around me as we danced, and I didn't want to be anywhere but in the chaos, as my brother's band roared like a jet on the stage behind the bar. For once I just wanted to feel everything and not think about who was flat or sharp or if my bass drum was too loud. And as we spun under the strobe lights, I caught my little brother's grin. He'd seen Bobbi Jo and as he played some complicated funky riff with one hand, he raised the other and gave me our secret Mason thumbs up which is the middle finger held downward, as if you're being blessed and not cursed.

But I'd spent little time on this side of a stage. My hips froze as I chopped the air like a martial arts fighter. I closed my eyes to connect, but I kept hearing misplayed notes, or lyrics I would have written differently. Meanwhile, men were drawn to Bobbi Jo's moves and swept in close to see if they might catch her eye. She'd smile, batting them away with a shake of her head, but then she would pout and her hips would attract a new swarm of admirers.

On a jammed dance floor, under strobe lights, she kissed me. Her lips were gentler than I'd imagined. Her hair covered my face like peach blossoms spinning in clouds of cigarette smoke. She lifted her hands into the flashing lights and did a little hoedown jig.

We left the Crazy Horse at three in the morning in my black 1976 Corvette Stingray, my first trophy of success. "It's you man," Davo had said. That obsidian phallus was a yacht on the highway, swaying in the current at nine miles per gallon. But it sounded like Neptune's thunder. Bobbi Jo was impressed.

She wanted to see the attic nook I slept in. She crawled in on all fours, her white jeans slipping down, exposing a shiny emerald-green thong. When everything came off, I saw that she was completely shaven. Her easy innocence made it seem like she could be this generous whenever she felt like it.

I told Bobbi Jo I was going out to California to spend Thanksgiving and Christmas with my younger sister, Bitsy. She asked if she could visit. There was a discussion about Big Boy Movers writing off her airfare costs.

Then she promised she'd bring an apple spice cake. Her Stumptown grandma's recipe. I said yes as she was telling me her family had been making apple butter for over two hundred years.

CHAPTER 13

THE BEAR WENT OVER THE MOUNTAIN (1956-1970)

I can see two children, like shadows in the woods

"Still Loving You"

It was a rainy March night, and my sister Bitsy woke me up asking if I "knew where they were." My bedroom was dark, but I could still hear my record player spinning "The Bear Went Over the Mountain." It was an endless fading refrain, and I assumed my little sister was asking me where the bears had gone. But she was crying. "Where are they?" she kept sobbing. "Mama and Daddy. They're gone."

I pushed the highchair from the kitchen toward the living room closet and reached up to find a scarf and a hat for her. I pulled two coats off hangers and helped her step into some rubber galoshes. I had on my new Davy Crockett slippers, and with my stuffed dog Pup Pud under my arm, we left the little barn-red house to find our parents. I was almost five and my sister had just turned three.

The barn red house was at the dead end of Meadow Lane, and in fact, I'm looking at a piece of its 1954 oak flooring on my desk as I type this now. It's small and rough, and in my memory I can see the compactness of that first house my parents bought in Middletown, Kentucky. It was in a new subdivision with sidewalks and I held my sister's hand as we sloshed toward a house that was lit up with green lights. I heard loud voices. People were singing, and yelling for Danny boy, and I wondered if maybe we weren't the only ones who were lost that night. Then a man in a pointy green hat saw us. "Hey you two elves," he shouted. "Where you going?' I believed in elves, and my cousin Rodney and I had seen messages they'd left under my mother's yellow refrigerator. I knew the man was mistaken so I pulled my sister through the wet grass toward the open door so he could see that we were really people.

Smoke bloomed out onto the front stoop as the man in the green hat shouted, "Anybody missing some elves?" My mother was the first to reach us. She knelt and pulled us to her, and everything smelled like mint candy and there was a group of pink faces suddenly all around us. I can't remember what they said, but we got to eat green cake and my father lifted us into his arms. I felt like I was up in a tree staring down on grownups who all decided it was the best time to laugh and lift their hands in the air and swallow whatever was in their drinking glasses.

Our parents weren't mad, and all the way home they kept saying they were sorry they'd scared us. But I didn't know how to describe how lost I felt, waking up in the dark and not knowing where they were. My instinct to protect my sister had happened naturally. But leaving the house and looking for our parents in the rain had been her idea. She's always had that kind of hold over me. Even then.

My sister and I grew like separate flowers in two separate pots in two separate rooms in the house that was my family. We shared the same sunlight, we marveled at the same way we were growing and stretching into a world we knew we couldn't share equally. I would have walked through a blizzard to get her to wherever she wanted to be. But eventually, something kept us from holding hands like we did when we lived on Meadow Lane.

I understand how hard it must have been to be around me. After seven miscarriages, I was my parents' golden boy. My mother once confessed that when she brought my sister home from the hospital, the first thing she did was put her in a crib, and then check on me. I was offered every opportunity first: I got the first bug book and was taken on trips to collect rocks and arrowheads. My parents drove me to Little League games, cotillion classes, boys' choir, piano and drum lessons, and bought me a drum set. They even gave permission for my band to practice loud rock and roll in our playroom on Walton Lane in Annandale. It had exposed cedar rafters and a stone tile floor and a skylight made out of green corrugated fiberglass. My sister might have sung a song with us one time in there. But I never included her in the band rehearsals, I just never thought she was that interested. I also think she was beginning to appreciate a wilder style of music. She never told me our band sounded good. She never said it sounded bad either.

I still have clear recollections of Bitsy and I drawing together as children. The peace in those quiet afternoons was filled with the smell of crayons and freshly sharpened pencils. If we could have drawn out a language to share, it would have been all in colors, and as innocent as when we first watched cows coming up to eat corn that grew along our backyard fence on Meadow Lane in Middletown. Bitsy's brown eyes had looked into mine, and she had said, "I love you brudda Ben." If I could have captured that feeling it would have been with the same colors I saw in that moment. Sunlit yellow, green stalks, and bright brown eyes. She was in a white nightgown, and she was smiling at me like that elf who'd held my hand in a doorway full of Irish green light.

In 1970, my sister ran away to California. She was barely seventeen. I was nineteen. My parents were devastated, but they couldn't stop her. It was like a switch had been thrown in her psyche, and she was ready to free herself of Annandale. She probably barely remembered Middletown, Kentucky, but she was eight years old when my father got a government job in DC. She'd left her tadpole ponds and the endless fields and forests of Hockessin, Delaware, left her friends and the horses they rode together. She'd never found that wonder and kinship in suburban Virginia. But Bitsy also ran away because of me. I was her opposite, a continual reminder to her of everything she wasn't.

But I envied her independence. Her resistance to what had been forced upon her by the changes life had handed our family had made her tough. I caught glimpses of her as a resistance fighter, a rebel who had every right to question how she ended up where she was. I fit in at school. I was clean cut, never got in trouble, and never skipped a class. Teachers and administrators respected me. But I kept a constant vigilant focus which didn't allow me to look for the fun I knew Bitsy was finding as she broke rules I held sacred. She had her own standards, and they were not restricted by parental expectations, school codes, or the ethics of what my little sister referred to for "straight people," referring to a conservative person as opposed to its definition today.

Bitsy started smoking pot and hanging out with hippies and hitchhiked to Woodstock without my parents' full permission. I stayed behind, working that week at a supper club in Falls Church with the John Wells Delegation, making a living playing drums on soft rock songs that my sister called boring. I wish I could have gone to Woodstock. Heroes of mine made history before half a million people and the miracles wrought by those rock gods might have inspired me to quit playing music that often bored me too.

And now I was really looking forward to spending time with her. There'd been over ten years of her coming out to visit our family in Virginia, and times when one of us would say just the right thing to build a six-month silence between us. But phone calls had increased, and we had found a groove again, laughing about a silly radio show with imaginary characters that I'd invented in my head called The Telex show. Total nonsense, but silliness that Bitsy and I thrived on. I'd told her about Bobbi Jo and she'd been receptive, reminding me that since she was a vegetarian, Bobbi Jo and I were not allowed to eat flesh of any sort in her rental cottage. Not even finger nibbling, I'd kidded. I wondered how holiday dinners would work out, but knowing her intolerance for jokes about tofu, I refrained and we moved on to talk about trips to the Anza-Borrego desert, The Salton Sea, and an adventure into Mexico to an isolated place called Agua Caliente. "It's barely on the map," she'd said.

We rented a car when we arrived in California. It felt like we were kids again, heading off into the Delaware wilderness on an adventure. I made no effort to describe Bobbi Jo's worldly experience, but I was anxious about whether my sister would approve of my new companion. I was driving and Bobbi Jo had graciously agreed to ride in the back with Bitsy's boyfriend, Noel. With my sister navigating, we crossed the border at Tijuana and turned east onto a narrow-paved road that had a sign pointing toward "Agua Caliente." Twelve miles away.

Within an hour, the road became a dry creek bed, and we began passing shacks with chickens and donkeys and men sitting on porches with an occasional rifle slung across a hook beside a vividly painted front door.

When the rental car bottomed out, we climbed out and rocked it back onto a more solid surface, reminding ourselves to steer for rock and not sand, as the creek bed twisted along a trail of dusty cactus fence line.

After another hour, we had hit the bottom of the rental car so often that the exhaust pipe now sounded like it was either about to come off, or already had. But one curve later, a flat clearing appeared, and a shallow sparkling creek gently welcomed us to our destination.

Bobbi Jo called out to a man who ambled toward us from a barren shack that was identical to the five other shacks that encircled the clearing. Five pesos, he said. No towels, park over there. We discovered a porcelain bathtub in each dilapidated shack, but as the faucet was turned we were treated to a lush clear jet of steaming water. Agua Caliente. In the privacy of these shacks we enjoyed the finest hot springs I'd ever been in. We ran back and forth from our private enclaves to roll headlong into the chilly creek which was just deep enough to allow us to sink fully in up to our necks.

Bobbi Jo and my sister bonded easily. Bobbi Jo was lightness; my sister, more like darkness that came and went, but the nature of their unique wild streaks was in harmony, and the innocence that had broken both of them out of traditional family molds was tempered by a tough adventurousness that became even more evident as they traded stories. Bobbi Jo had yet to meet my folks, and my sister described leaving Annandale in terms that did not denigrate our family. I was happy to overhear that. It felt as if I was getting her approval of Bobbi Jo, as she was trusting her with such personal Mason history.

As the sun began setting, we realized we were probably four hours from the US, in a car that might not survive the suddenly rising water of the creek we were enjoying.

As we turned for home, I kept my nerves in check by telling my sister all about the break I was taking from the band, though I reiterated that I was still making music. I described how I was building a moving company and how Bobbi Jo and I had met. The wheels of the car would spin helplessly sometimes, but we always seemed to scoot out of whatever muck the creek had caught us in. Then the headlights bounced us up onto a narrow lane which was lined with shacks. Two men blocked the road, their rifles pointed toward our windshield. One said "out" and the other said "trunk." We gave them everything we had in the car. The spare tire, our suitcases of clothing, the little bit of food we'd brought along, and all the money in our wallets. They wanted the seats from the car, but gave up after realizing that it was now too dark to see how they could be removed. The car battery was growing weaker and I managed to convince the men to help me open the hood. When they leaned their rifles against the side of the car, I grabbed them and hurled them into the darkness between the shacks. As they ran for their guns, we threw ourselves into the vehicle and I cranked the key until the engine fired with a gasping cough. We sped down the narrow lane, lightless, with only the sound of solid traction as our guide. I floored the rental car until we finally saw a sign that pointed us toward a numbered road. It was not the one we had originally followed to get to Agua Caliente, but within twenty minutes we were on a highway headed north, seeing signs that read Tijuana and USA.

It took several trips through car washes to clean our rental car, and a backyard mechanical repair by a friend of Noel's to fix the exhaust. But the car was returned and accepted without fuss. I did have to pay for the missing spare tire, but that felt like a pittance. Bitsy and Bobbi Jo had been stalwart soldiers all during that insane encounter, and the toughness that I'd always admired in my sister grew as we shared our experiences about it over the next few months.

And my sister's respect for Bobbi Jo, as beautiful as she was, flowed sincerely, and I sensed her approval of my new girlfriend. I also sensed that she would believe me if I told her what I'd seen rushing toward us at Agua Caliente. Its shape had been as blue as that rising water we had left behind us.

CHAPTER 14

BOYS IN THE BASEMENT (1983)

It's a high pressure morning

"Mambo Genesis"

My sister called our California holiday visit a "long awaited celebration of cosmic connection," as she and her boyfriend Noel lit up some potent pot and we marveled at being surrounded by acres of orange, lime green, and yellow-fruited trees. Waking up every day in a cozy 1905 bungalow was a comfort I hadn't imagined would be as healing. I hadn't thought about Shana for months and my calls home to Big Boy Movers produced no gut-wrenching anxiety. Things were slow. It was winter, but the boys said no pipes had frozen and they were staying warm and keeping busy.

While Bitsy and Noel built their leaded glass window business, Bobbi Jo and I meandered through southern California, and we went from the desert to the mountains to the coast to a hidden palm springs outside a ghost town. All our destinations were less than an hour away, and we began to sexually and emotionally enjoy the dynamic that fueled our harmony. Bobbi Jo had a hunger for new adventures, and I got a buzz watching her naked beauty being dressed for a day or a night out. The freedom and satisfaction inspired me. I sent comical letters and pictures home to my parents, and I knew they felt the same relief that my sister had expressed; my heart was mending with a new person in my life.

But Bobbi Jo's looks became a curious gift, growing

physical proof of what I valued in a woman. The gift included a jealousy check, as men gawked and people made way for her. She could affect a roomful of strangers or passengers on a bus. Motorists slowed and followed us, wondering who she might be. Photographers and agents offered us business cards and discreet invitations. My sister chalked up much of this flirty wheeling and dealing to "typical Hollywood bullshit artists." There was no bit of jealousy or judgment that I ever sensed when my sister would share her experiences with Bobbi Jo. And Bobbi Jo, to her credit, never seemed to take any of these adorations too seriously.

Her hair was too rich to be real, yet it was. Her obliviousness seemed practiced; I saw her tease its abundance, electrifying it to dance on a pillow or across her shoulders. Her face, while glamorous, held childlike wariness. In front of a camera, her naked body, at any angle, was a portrait of sublime lines and unpretentious curves. It was hard not to be constantly aroused by the person I was beginning to fall in love with.

When we got back to Virginia in January, Bobbi Jo was more radiant than ever. Her eyes glinted like brown diamonds as she shook hands and giggled confidently when she met my parents at their house for dinner. My father was his usual conversational self, but I could tell he was distracted by her tan lines, especially after he saw a couple of the Mexico bikini pictures I'd taken of her. My mother pulled me aside as we were leaving and said simply, "I like her. She's a tough cookie."

When Bobbi Jo and I got home, we went upstairs. She hadn't officially moved in, but her pink suitcase seemed very much at home, open on a piano bench in the corner of the room where Primadonna had once rehearsed. The movers had gifted us with a box spring and mattress, and that homecoming gift was a welcome sight. Even the pillows and the new purple moving pad they'd laid across it smelled clean and inviting. We were lying on it naked, when somebody started singing "8675309 I got your number," from the shower one wall away from us.

My rental house in Falls Church was not as I'd left it. Everything upstairs was in place, but in the basement, walls were up, plaster had been applied in rough stucco patterns, and five rooms had been built. Davo had walled off one corner and made it his space, turning my old workbench into a platform bed. Gino and Billy had split the other end of the basement into two rooms, each with a working window and a lockable door. The fourth corner was the utility room, filled with the washer, dryer, and oil furnace. In the middle of all this was the living room. Rugs were down, pictures were hung, couches and recliners were in place, and a TV and a monstrous fish tank rested on an entertainment center. The ashtrays were overflowing, and the coffee table was covered in pizza boxes and beer cans.

There were five new rooms in the basement of Big Boy Movers, but still only one full bathroom in the house.

Billy briefed me when he and Gino pulled in at nine that night. Davo had lost two checks from customers, and scheduled moves that were not ever entered in the book. Twice, a crew had arrived at a Davo job, only to be told that they were arriving on the wrong day. After two weeks of chaos, Billy had taken over the office and was booking the moves. I applauded his decision. Davo would drive and act as operations manager, and Gino would be a mover and copilot. This had been a test of fire, and like a cleansing burn, what had been unable to survive, was forever gone. And as I heard Billy out, I could feel new growth already thriving, toward vibrant health I could not have created without taking a significant risk. Thank God for faith.

I'd seen the boys in action, and I knew they were comfortable figuring out who needed to do what to get a move completed. Davo might have been driving and acting like a crew leader, and he'd probably done well with the customers. But it would have been Billy's careful padding and protection of the furniture as it was fit into the truck that made the pieces of the puzzle fit together. Gino and Davo would have had their logistical opinions, and the muscle to get the truck loaded would have been shared by all three guys. But I had a growing sense that Billy was a more proficient predictor of what could be damaged, and his diligent oversight was key to us getting the moves done successfully.

If I was on the crew, I tried to lead with a light but firm hand, knowing that the only way I'd grow Big Boy Movers was to have people other than me doing the moves. But I still enjoyed doing solo moves. I probably did about one a week. No distractions; nobody asking, why are you doing it like that? And I liked inventing ways to handle whole inventories by myself.

As confident as I was in my solo abilities, I felt drawn to be part of a band of working men. And just like the other groups I'd performed in, all the founding players had arrived at the same time. In fact, they were nested in the house I'd recently emptied of rooms of musical gear, and driving the truck once used to get my bands to stages, where audiences would appreciate all the equipment we'd bring with us to do our work. It would often be more than even one truckload, as vans and cars would transport things like fragile guitars and special effect gimmicks. This same concept held true during moves, as fragile items were often loaded into customers' cars.

Each of these three new members exhibited the same quirkiness that had endeared other characters to me in all the bands I'd played in since I was thirteen. The whittling out of a pecking order had already begun between these three, but for once, I was the undisputed band leader. Still, I had to keep reminding myself that, unlike the rock and roll business, I had scant experience dealing with the nuances of this new business. And none of us had ever played in a band like Big Boy Movers before.

If I would have taken our Life Song record producers' advice five years earlier, I might be on a completely different career track. It would be a solo track, and it would be a career choice involving me, in a spotlight, alone, being groomed as a teen idol, performing songs I'd taken to New York City just months before Primadonna was formed. Cashman and West, the owners/producers/managers of Life Song Records had assured me that "I had the looks. I had the sound . . . and most importantly, I had the songs."

They were songs I'd penned with titles like "Midnight Doctor" ("Every cure is love"), "Gypsy Night" ("oh, love on a gypsy night, I never knew evil could feel so right"), and "Easy Girl" ("She said her name was Easy and she needed a ride, said that mattress in your van, is it the new soft kind?"), and lastly, "Love You All Up" ("I'm gonna love you all up, fill you with everything you've been dreaming of").

My Life Song producers wanted me to return in a month, to record my songs at The Hit Factory, a venerable studio near Central Park. It would all be on their dime. They would even put me up at The Essex House, during the week I would be recording. My sessions with them would allow me to meet, and possibly write with, another unknown solo artist they were working with named Jim Croce.

They bought me lunch, and things looked promising as we shook hands on the 43rd floor in their offices on Broadway. But I took the train home from the Big Apple feeling marginalized. I couldn't see myself in that kind of spotlight. A teen idol? I was a serious songwriter. A teenybopper star? A risky unpaid gamble. Besides, I was a band guy.

And Big Boy Movers felt real. There were no pie in the sky promises keeping me awake at night. There were four of us, and we were creating something as evocative as every bit of the energy a rock and roll band delivers. We would lead our audiences to places inspired by our love of what we do. And get paid one hell of a lot more for the work our band of men would provide.

CHAPTER 15

FREDDY AND THE REALLY GOOD DEAL (1983)

Iron bars and metal bed

"Cathedral Ceilings"

We needed a second truck, so we rented a twenty-four-foot U-Haul for eighty-five dollars a day. The referrals were driving the increase in business, and it was as naturally simple as I hoped it would be, business plan-wise. Offer a service and be clear about what that service would involve. A flat rate would be given based on exactly what was to be moved. Be on time, do the job, be respectful, and stick to the agreements made.

But that was the problem. We often needed two trucks to carry the inventories we were moving. And, if another move came in, then a second separate truck would come in handy for that job.

The U-Haul truck made sense, it was just a few miles away, so Davo drove that and I piloted the E truck, as we'd begun calling the Ford E 350. With two trucks running, I'd saved almost sixty thousand dollars by the end of summer. Profit.

Davo told me about Freddy, a short African American man who had a truck rental business. We could rent an unmarked twenty-four-foot truck from him for twenty bucks a day, Freddy said. And he could even sell it to us. That rental offer was just too good to pass up. It was time to expand our operation, but carefully, rent for a bit, then buy, if that really was possible!

Over the next month, we drove to Largo, Maryland a dozen times to rent Freddy's mystery truck. It was faded orange, had chewed up lettering on it, and used regular gas. All the doors worked, and its long ramp rolled out easily from the rear end. The odometer was stuck at eighty thousand miles, but it drove smoothly, its automatic transmission allowing us to get it up to sixty mph, even fully loaded. The vehicle manual was in the glove box but there was no registration card. Freddy had a form from some truck rental company with his name on it, which he said gave him the legal right to rent it out. The twenty buck price was worth the hour drive to get the truck. I just couldn't understand how Freddy could sell it to us.

There was something slick about Freddy, but his playfulness soothed me. "Hey loan me three hundred and I'll pay you back four hundred," he said over the phone. I was in Annandale, at my parents' house. I saw my reflection in family photos of lawyers, judges, the mayor of Chicago, writers, and executives, all successful and self-reliant. "Sure," I said. I was rewarded a week later when Freddy handed me four one-hundred-dollar bills.

"When you buying my truck?" he asked.

I snorted, "You can't sell it. You don't even have the registration card."

He answered fast, exasperated, "Look here. You buy it, it's yours. You do what you want."

"I need the title," I told him.

In a hoarse whispery voice, he said, "I'll lay it out for you. A big rental company gave me the truck—it was off the books, so there was never a record of it going to me. That's how they paid me. I got another couple of eighteen-footers too. But this one, I need fifteen hundred bucks for it. Hey, don't worry, I'll get you the title."

I couldn't read between the lines of Freddy's wrinkled forehead, but Big Boy Movers needed that twenty-four-footer.

Three days later. "Hey Ben, lend me five hundred? I'll pay you back seven hundred on Friday." Remembering how I'd made money the last time I'd done this, I counted five one-hundred-dollar bills into his hand.

Friday came. I drove into a weedy parking lot in Largo, Maryland with fifteen hundred cash, and Davo in the front seat with me. His big-bodied bravado filled the cab as usual. "Boss," he said, "we're doin' this, stop worrying, ok?" The mystery truck stood alone in the sunshine. A money maker with nobody's name on it. My faith wasn't giving me any directions. This would be my call. A burgundy Dodge van with a peeling Washington Redskins sticker on the rear window pulled up next to me.

Freddy eased out of the van, flicking his cigarette butt onto the ground. "They didn't send it man. They, you know, buried the paperwork. For now."

"Freddy? How can I legally own it?"

He rubbed his forehead. "Look, go put you a new VIN plate on it. Get one off a Ford F-600 at the junkyard." Davo had been telling me this all week; how easy it would be to install a new VIN plate on the door. The one on the mystery truck was half torn off anyway. It was like buying a vehicle with no salvage history. Davo had done this before, or at least he'd heard about how it could be done. Either way, he made it all sound very legitimate. Besides, he said, older trucks get banged up; VIN plates get destroyed all the time.

I counted out fifteen one-hundred-dollar bills into Freddy's hand, and as it closed, I asked about the seven hundred dollar "loan" payback. He said no, that was a separate deal, and he'd have to go to his sister's around the corner. But he'd be right back, with lunch. And he'd check the mail. Maybe that truck title had finally come.

Freddy never came back, not even with the crab cake sandwiches he'd promised. Two hours later Davo and I left Largo, Maryland in two trucks. One belonged to Big Boy Movers. And the other, which we began calling the F truck, still had a pale orange skin on it with faded letters and no legal paperwork to prove who owned it.

My parents instilled a work ethic in me that made them proud. I wondered if the ethics I'd followed to acquire that lost rental truck came from them too. I meditated and prayed in my own silence. I owned my greed for what I knew wasn't a completely above-board transaction. I never fully experienced the relief I'd wanted from that illuminating blue yonder which followed me even on the darkest of days. I had a recurring sense that I would pay for my actions, yet I kept justifying them as necessary shadows my path had led me through, and that my faith had spoken. It had urged me to take the risk, as I had in Mexico.

As I drove to the bank the next day I heard a whispery sound, like static on my radio. At the light it vanished. But it had told me to be aware of the spirit in which I acted. That a man is a god in ruins.

I looked down at my hands on the E truck steering wheel. A reassuring glow encircled my fingers. It was as blue as the afternoon sky above us.

CHAPTER 16

VISIONS OF GREAT (1955)

*We are love, and
love never dies*

"Love Never Dies"

My mother's grandmother, Great, was born in 1861. When she came to visit us at the barn red house in Middletown, Kentucky, she'd dressed in black and was outside on the afternoon that I was told to put on a coat, because it was cold. I didn't want to, but, as Great pushed my sister Bitsy in a baby carriage down our short driveway and onto the sidewalk, I reached into my coat and found some warmth in the pockets. I asked Great if she or Bitsy were cold, and Great came close and lifted her veil so I could see her eyes. There was a flashlight brightness in one of them, but they were both blue and staring as hard into mine as I could stand. I was trying to see what she was looking at me like that for, when she said, "No we're fine, thank you," and with that, she passed by me.

But the feeling I had gotten from her stare kept passing through my mind like the story my father had made up about somebody named "Lampy Lamp" who had electric power in his eyes. I was fascinated by the power of a person who could shine a light from their eyes like that, and I caught glimpses of that in the corners of my own eyes as I lay in bed at night. After my father would turn off my overhead light, I'd slide my eyes quickly left or right, and flashes of blue always appeared.

They were beckoning me, even though I couldn't explain why. And so I kept them secret. Maybe they were friends of Great, maybe they were signals to me. But I couldn't see them clearly enough to know what they wanted me to do. It was an alluring feeling, and confusing. A hazy blue place I wanted to find but didn't know how to get to.

I had been watching Great moving through the house during the week she'd come to visit, and I kept my distance, but I began following her, quietly. There was an early morning routine I had observed, where she took a deep breath and closed her eyes as she sat in my father's big chair in the little living room. I saw something misty rising from her chest as she exhaled; it was a shadow, but beautiful, warm, like the sun that seeped in through the blue curtains behind her. I noticed a slight smile on her face as she would move her lips, like she was telling me something, like she knew I was there. It always made me feel stronger and taller, as if she was assuring me that we were together, watching over our family.

Now that I look back I think Great was saying don't be afraid, everything here is settled. The sky would broaden behind her, the clouds of those Kentucky mornings would fade, and any bad dreams or apprehensions I had about the little sister I was getting used to would vanish, as Great opened her eyes. She'd stare softly into mine and I knew she'd been listening to my thoughts, to my fears of the changes to our family. Her eyes would close again, and I'd hear her voice in my ears saying, go back to sleep for a while Ben, everything is fine. Your mother will be up soon, and we'll have toast and eggs for breakfast.

Then I'd pull the covers back over my face on those chilly mornings, and Great's calm words would rise quietly in my ears. It felt like she was standing right beside me, a warmth I began to accept as her without her body. I would imagine her smiling down at me, and even with my eyes closed, a feeling of strength would settle over me like a comforting blue quilt, letting me drift back into a happy dream.

I was sure that Great saw things I couldn't see.

A few months later we were taking a train to Delaware, and it was noisy and smelly, and everybody smiled at my sister and me. We were moving and my parents wanted to see a house in Hockessin, Delaware, and maybe put an offer on it. My father had been excited earlier that week and I was under a small table as he towered over my mother and said he had great news. He'd gotten a new job at DuPont, and we'd be moving. My sister asked me if the elves under the refrigerator would be coming with us. She was almost three by now and I was tired of trying to explain everything to her.

When we got on the train, Daddy said it would be a long ride, so we'd sleep in a private berth. My mother and sister were on the lower bunk of the small train room we were in and I got the top bunk. I woke up in complete darkness. I heard my father snoring in his chair and the train began to hiss as it slowly rolled to a stop beside a platform. There were low mens' voices shouting up toward the train as people moved along the hallway outside our room. I climbed down from my bed. The steel-colored shadows and gentle rocking of signs in the wind made me curious as I noticed a brilliant blue light on the floor at my feet. I slid the cabin door open and saw more of these bright blue lights. They were the size of eyeballs, and they'd lead me to a toilet I hoped. Then a man in a shiny black hat slid the door of a bathroom open just as I was feeling lost. "Right here, sonny," he said.

I had my butt on the toilet seat when I noticed a mirror in the dark. The face in the mirror wasn't mine, so I stood. It was rounder, and blue, staring at me from the blackness of the mirror. It was veiled and one blue eye shone back at me like one of my father's flashlights when the batteries are dying. It had a mouth, or maybe it was just an expression, but I realized it was a reflection coming from the window behind me, and I turned just in time to see Great. She raised her veil just like she had on that cold day, and she was faded blue, like old soap. I heard my thoughts say, "Thank you. For asking me if our hands were cold."

It was a gruff voice, but not scary; more like she wanted me to hear her through the window, and I did. Then some red signs flashed and a whistle went off and the train began to start and stop and move again and my pajamas were wet now. I'd missed my aim I guess, and I knew I was in trouble, and I wondered if maybe I'd wake up and it would all just be a dream, but I followed the blue lights back to my father, and as I pulled the cabin door open, he sat up fast and said "Hey, Buddy-Row, where were you?"

He didn't notice my wet pajamas, and by the time the train was going really fast, we were all awake, pointing at horses and towns as the racketing track rumbled us over the Ohio River. I didn't talk about what I'd seen in the bathroom window, but I was sad that Great never got to see our house in Hockessin, Delaware. She was ninety-six when she died, and my mother said she'd left something for me. It was in a little white box. Wrapped in tissue paper was a glass marble, as blue and bright as a flashlight bulb as it makes one last thrust into the darkness of forever.

Once we got to Hockessin, I was almost six and I was a big boy; at least, I had two fake rifles and a plastic cap pistol, and climbed trees and threw rocks at things. I never told anyone that I'd heard Great's voice in my head, or that she'd stared at me the way she had.

I didn't look for blue faces or anything that was veiled with a blue eye looking into mine as I lay in my bed at night. In fact, I always let Pup Pud sit on the walnut dresser beside me, just to be on the safe side. I had the sensation that just having his loyal presence that close was smart. But almost every morning he'd be there on my pillow, his orange head facing the window that looked out into the woods beyond the Hockessin house, as if he'd sensed something approaching. I didn't tell my parents, especially my mother, about things I couldn't explain. I'd already been accused of making things up, and my mother said if I lied, I'd get in big trouble.

If there were any blue shapes or shadows with flashlight blue eyes guiding me through my elementary school years, I kept them at a distance. I imagined them as odd visitors and remanded them into the cells of what I couldn't comprehend. My mother would not have a liar in her house. She said having an imagination was fine but that I wasn't allowed to mislead people.

It would be years before I realized that I held the keys to free the very deepest parts of myself; where my past lives and disparate incarnations entwined to make me who I am meant to be. Always blue, my favorite color, even when I couldn't understand the blessing of their guidance on my spiritual journey.

CHAPTER 17

NEW GUYS (1983)

*The road out there
only goes so far*

"Haven't Met You Yet"

There were at least 150 different movers in and out of the Big Boy basement every year. We kept their names in a yellow spiral notebook. Most were regulars or friends of regulars, so we usually had some sense as to how they'd handle themselves. But it's not like rock and roll, where you can tell if somebody knows how to play in thirty seconds. You can't size a mover up by what he looks like or sounds like over the phone, so our policy was that if they showed up, they had the job, at least for the day.

The entertainment factor was beyond measure, as if the groupings of some movers on a truck was living theater. Except it was often tragic comedy that involved fistfights and violent verbal exchanges in front of audiences who had not paid to be so inappropriately entertained.

I'm reminded of Todd, a clownish motorcyclist with an albino rat that rode in the pocket of his leather jacket. Davo fired him because as the crew was loading the truck at the pickup, Todd kept carrying things back into the house; thinking they were unloading at the drop-off. If your brain is a chalkboard, PCP is the diligent sponge wiping it clean.

Gino came from a family of nine boys and one girl. In

1983, when his brother Bradley got out of jail for burglary, he came to live in the basement. Just for a while, Gino had promised. Let him sleep. When Bradley woke up two days later, he bench-pressed three hundred pounds, drank some day-old cold coffee and burped "fuck yes," when I asked if he could work. He was a strong addition to the second crew we were running, as was Tombo, who had spindly legs, a pizza face, and broken front teeth. He wore his baseball cap backward and had arms that swung like twisted steel from his sleeveless shirt. He was twenty-one but had the confidence of a forty-year-old bouncer. He'd shout things at attractive women from the truck. "Nice anus!" was his favorite. I told him if he ever shouted that again, he was fired.

Tombo and Dave R were a team. Dave had done time in Lorton Prison—he was quite reserved but threw monkey strong punches when he snapped. Dave R thought I didn't do shit. When I asked him to monitor whoever sat in the back of the truck, afraid they'd fall out, the cords in his neck ratcheted up. He said if I didn't trust him, he would "go home right now." Said he didn't "give a fuck." Once he'd loomed over Billy in the basement office, drunk, insisting that his pay was short. I stepped in, he slugged me, and we wrestled to the floor. I straddled him, but as I raised my fist, he blurted "I give" in a pleading voice. I let him up.

Tombo and Dave R lived in Pimmit Hills, established in 1952 as housing for WWII vets. It eventually became the home of a motorcycle gang, the Pagans. PCP had long been manufactured and sold from this neighborhood, and many of our hires were raised there. They all knew each other, and often had children with each other's women. I quit asking about police records; my Pimmit Hills renegades were natural born movers, and a criminal past hopefully meant they'd learned their lessons.

Every morning Pimmit Hills would arrive in the Idylwood Presbyterian church lot. Their voices would call out to each other as they approached the trucks parked at my house. Always asking, "Who has a quick?" As in, a quick hit of whatever drug they had in whatever pipe they'd brought along. I would always hope that it would only be pot in that pipe. I would admonish Pimmit Hills, yet I seldom got complaints that my movers smelled like weed. Because I outfitted every truck with mouthwash. It's cheaper than a ticket for a DUI.

Pimmit Hills was the incense of cigarettes, farts, last night's beer, and cold pizza. Pimmit Hills was the thudding up and down my basement stairs, whooping about somebody's hangover, always letting doors slam behind them. Pimmit Hills was always waiting at the trucks while Davo lay passed out on his platform bed.

"He's lillying," Gino would remind me. Davo's mother used to say Davo was in "Lily White Land" when he slept. Finally, in the racket of trucks starting and me pounding on his door, Davo would appear, hat yanked down over mongrel hair. As he backed the F truck out, he'd give me a pilot's thumbs up, unlit cigarette dangling from his lips. From the passenger seat, Pimmit Hills would crane its neck, hoping to catch another glimpse of Bobbi Jo in the open window of our bathroom shower.

By mid-afternoon, everybody was usually back in the side lot with the six-pack tip they'd gotten from the last customer. The rear doors of the trucks would be thrown open, guys would fold pads, grabbing pizza from a box on the back bumper. I'd get the checks or cash, read the paperwork; see if there were any damages. Sometimes there'd be a handwritten note, thanking me for sending such efficient young men. Other times there'd be a terse request to call the customer about an issue with the crew. I took things personally.

Then came Little James. He'd claimed he'd worked for other movers and knew what he was doing. He had taken the metro in from DC and no social security number or last name was given on the application form he'd signed at dispatch. He'd brought a dark blue ditty bag with him and made a bed for himself in the back of the truck, using the folded bag like a pillow. It was a hot morning, so the rear door remained open, and he and another crew member rested on moving pads until the job began on a Saturday in July on Capitol Hill.

At noon I got a call from a very calm client who said that he'd taken out his garbage and as he was dropping the bag into the refuse bin in the alley beside his house, one of our movers had shown him a dark blue ditty bag wedged behind a DC recycling can. Inside it were several cameras: Leica, Canons, Hasselblad, top of the line. Being a professional photographer, our client knew his equipment well, and in fact, he told me his initials were still inked on the cameras. He placed the ditty bag in the trunk of his car, locked it, reentered his home, and called the Metropolitan police.

When the officers arrived, they asked Little James to step outside. They showed him the dark blue ditty bag which he admitted was his. He was handcuffed to the iron fence that surrounded our client's row house. "But I didn't steal those," he said, as he was guided into a second squad car which had arrived. The cameras were inventoried by the arresting officers, photographs were taken, our witness mover was interviewed, the stolen property was returned to our client, and Big Boy Movers was asked to leave the job immediately.

When the client called me, we both expressed remorse at the horror show that the move had become. I was able to find him another local mover, and he agreed not to press charges against me or Big Boy Movers, saying he was just glad to have all his cameras back. So was I. Those cameras and custom lenses were worth almost 200K, and I doubted Big Boy had the insurance to cover that.

I never heard from Little James again, but the mover who'd alerted the client told me that Little James had gotten out on bail and was looking for payback. The witness said he'd heard that Little James blamed him for the felony charges, and that he was the reason that Little James's daughter wasn't going to be able to afford the operation she needed to replace her kidney. "I'm out," he said when he quit Big Boy Movers. "He knows the trucks."

He told me that his cousin drove for a delivery service in Baltimore that was hiring. "Once Little James is locked up," he said, "I'll be back."

About a month later, I heard about a knife fight on a delivery truck up around Baltimore. It was at a gas station, during a drop-off. A short guy had climbed into the truck, in the dark, beefing that one of the movers had been having sex with his sister. By the time the police got there, it was too late. The mover who bled to death was the witness who'd once worked for me.

The fingerprints on the bloody knife that was left behind led the cops straight to James Littleton, out on bail for grand larceny down in DC. My ex-mover's family sued the delivery service, expecting compensation for the loss of their son, who was also a father to four children. The court claim hinged on a simple fact, that the delivery company had allowed a confrontation to occur while goods were under their care, custody, and control. The death that resulted during that time was work related, but there was no workman's compensation in place. There was no personal insurance, no business umbrella policy, and the owners of that Baltimore delivery company were forced into bankruptcy, selling what little they had to settle the case out of court.

Meditation helped dilute the bile that Big Boy Movers wracked from me. And sometimes alcohol. But there was no consistent cure for persistent anxiety; I was shouldering a high-risk business. I made light of it with friends, shared stories with owners of other moving companies, and made daily deposits at the bank. The only thing that successfully calmed me was my certainty that the Universe was delivering exactly what I was meant to receive.

CHAPTER 18

SPRAY TAN VETERANS (1986)

*Temptation's bound
to follow you*

"That Dangerous Thing"

Bobbi Jo made it all the way to the final auditions for the Washington Redskinettes and didn't break down until she flopped onto our bed and told me she didn't make the squad. "Not even as a backup," she sobbed.

I held her as she recounted how hard she'd worked: studying revered cheerleaders, perfecting the singsong voice, mastering the makeup to appear as innocent and as tempting as possible. The spray tan veterans who had made her believe she was going to make the cut seemed like witches casting spells to remind Bobbi Jo she was still just a country girl from a poor family, raised on some scrap of land that Lord Fairfax had granted the McCalls in 1754.

I hoped she'd tap into the sustenance of her heritage. Birth new dreams that didn't involve her genetic good fortune. Her people had used their imaginations to survive; they'd built up a seven-generation family farm, raised goats and chickens, and made their own moonshine from peaches and honey they'd nurtured on a twenty-acre island in the Potomac River, co-incidentally known as Mason's Island. They'd survived the floods of 1935 and 1936 that had taken the life of Bobbi Jo's grandfather, and they'd had the sense to use ladders to get all the goats onto the roof of the farmhouse they'd built in 1847, when the flood of 1935 took everything but what remained of the old homestead. They made adjustments. Through craft and ingenuity, they tailored an agricultural fabric which allowed their family to survive, even after nature's devastation had stolen everything they owned. Certainly Bobbi Jo had that same belief in herself.

But every creation starts with a dream; an idea, a vision of what might be possible. My father would tell me: "You can draw that, you can write that, you can do that." He was my iceberg of power: little display of bravado and assertiveness in view but infinitely powerful in the depth of his own belief in himself, and in me. Join a rock band? Sure; and if you need to quit going to college because of your performance schedule, I understand.

Daddy always trusted my decisions. He made sure I knew how much he supported me, as I failed and succeeded. I wanted to offer the same committed support to Bobbi Jo, but every time I did, she brushed me off, saying she'd be fine. That familiar refrain struck me in deeper ways than I could process at the time. I hadn't yet come to terms with my own need to recreate the trauma of living with a woman who was elusive, and often unavailable emotionally. Whenever I tried to help Bobbi Jo articulate all she might be able to do, she shut me down. But I made excuses for it. That distance felt familiar.

Perhaps Bobbi Jo was too proud to talk about her dreams, and too emotionally invested to stop following them. Silently she stripped, meditatively chewing gum. As she blew a bubble, she examined her perfect body in our full-length mirror. All that astounding sunset hair. All that endless satin white chocolate skin. Those rose-colored nipples. And those breasts that always seemed to be as perfect as a rising pair of moons.

"I'll be okay," she said. Maybe her allure was just too powerful to ignore and had to be spent before it withered.

I pulled her close on the deck overlooking the pool we had installed. Its crimson lights attracted bats that caught insects above the water. Cave blue shadows in the deep end made Bobbi Jo look like a silvery seal as she dove into it. In one deep breath, she swam the length of the pool. I wondered what thoughts or words or screams were in the bubbles that rose to the surface as she glided by. I wasn't meant to know what Bobbi Jo was washing off, or if she was even capable of knowing that sadness could be washed away.

The spell of the cheerleader auditions weakened when Bobbi Jo started working for an entrepreneur who produced lingerie modeling events. I was in the front row for her debut, held at a swanky hotel. The audience was mostly men, but there were professional-looking women present.

I was proud of her bravado, weaving casually past the runway lights, wearing just a black jock strap with a lacey top curtaining her delicate parts. I sat with her afterwards, as fellow models gathered around us, robed and primped, bonding with nose crinkling smiles and stage-whispered compliments. Boyfriends and husbands exchanged looks that said, "Are you okay with this?" I caught a few raised eyebrows and wondered if they were also concerned about where this runway was headed.

And yet it was like I was seeing her for the first time in my little attic room, her emerald-green thong now replaced by what she so confidently wore in front of all those eyes. But there was also a burst of fear. What if she's as generous with her favors now as she was with me that night after the Crazy Horse? I didn't like the mild burning that hit my gut. I chalked it up to one too many vodka and tonics, crossed my legs and smiled at the people who caught my eye. A sleazy lyric in my head teased me with its insistence. "Hey, I'm cool. I'm proud of my girl, and if you want to stare at her, cool. She's really worth staring at, right?"

But every part of that sensual equation was fouled by an axiom nobody knew about but me. Bobbi Jo had a wild streak. If impulses are X factors and desires are Y factors, X plus Y seldom adds up to logical. But that's just on paper I reminded myself, as I noticed Bobbi Jo accepting a business card from a guy who looked like he lived in a gym.

"There will be another showcase next Thursday evening," a well-dressed Middle Eastern man announced, handing Bobbi Jo an envelope which I assumed held payment for the event.

"Thank you, Essey," Bobbi Jo said demurely.

As we drove home, I noticed Bobbi Jo smiling to herself. "Maybe I can open a modeling agency like Essey," she said.

I was still pondering what she'd pulled from that envelope. Two hundred seventy-five bucks cash was generous pay for parading around in a teddy for an hour. At the next light I asked her, "What was Essey telling you and Miranda over in the corner? Just before we left?"

"Oh, that, well, there's a higher pay scale if we do private shows, but I don't know. Miranda's husband kind of freaked out after she did one last weekend."

"Did what?"

"Well, Essey had security set up, so when she went into the bathroom with the client, it was real safe. And she made big bucks."

We slid through the intersection. She'd wound a finger up into her hair and was braiding it thoughtfully. I asked, "Do you want to do that?"

Bobbi Jo rubbed my knee with her bare foot. "No," she

laughed, "good Lord!"

"Seriously, how much money?" I asked, needling her to get to the truth behind the laugh. "Six hundred, seven hundred, in a bathroom? And there's no sex, right?"

She sat up, eyeballing the taillights ahead. "You think I'd do that," she huffed.

"No," I said, "I'm just curious if you ever thought about doing it."

She yanked her foot off my knee. "Well. If you must know, I kind of already tried it, and I don't think Essey should be getting half for what you have to do."

"What? You did what?" The air in the car grew thin.

"I helped somebody out, but we didn't really do it, okay? It was just, you know. Hey, I made four hundred bucks!"

She eased down and laid her head in my lap. I couldn't stop a familiar habit, and my fingers wandered, making her squirm. She shrieked, "Hey! Not while you're driving, mister."

I kept it between the lines. But my fingers stuck to the wheel the whole way home.

CHAPTER 19

WHY MUST WE STRIKE EACH OTHER OH LORD? (1986)

*My Bible's in my pocket
as I fix my bayonet*

"Sweet Virginia"

Gino had a helmet of hay-colored hair and biceps so freakishly large, he cut off the sleeves of his Big Boy Movers T-shirt. He was brazen and brash, but quick to shut down and get defensive. He reminded me of rock star types I'd had to learn not to crowd when there was a problem. If something was happening that made him look bad, he'd been known to walk off the job. I'd never had a confrontation with him when he was drinking; then he was just playful and silly. But right now he was wound up like we'd just been booed off a stage.

An hour earlier, I'd gotten a call from this move. Both husbands were on the line, and they were so angry they were hissing. My movers had arrived, and one of the Big Boy trucks had sideswiped a parked car and left the scene: "Your driver was giggling, like he was high on something." I told them I'd be right there, but they'd already hung up on me.

I still couldn't fathom how quickly this move had fallen apart, so I took a walk around the C truck, looking for any fresh body damage. "Your new truck looks good man," I told Gino.

"No shit, Sherlock," he said. Maybe the tension of me having to come down to the job was punching his buttons, but I had to know.

"So, where's the E truck?" I kept my voice flat, and in that heat, I said it like we all deserve a break, but he turned dark.

"I had nothing to do with that shit, man. Tombo was driving. And anyway, I didn't see it." He was pushing dollies toward the garage, but I kept trying to get answers.

"How's the move going? Any damages so far?" Maybe Gino was too wound up to answer. Maybe he didn't know. But at least he hadn't walked off the job.

I grabbed a hand truck and followed him toward the shade of the apartment building. We were both headed up to those angry husbands.

The F truck was at the entrance of the apartment's parking garage. The radio said 96 degrees, but it felt like an oven inside that truck box. Something transparent, following, as cool as Great Lakes blue, chilled my shoulders as I squeezed past the steaming metal.

We walked a hundred yards through the parking garage and took an elevator to the fourth floor, the top level of a 1950s-era building. We followed a maze of hallways until I saw padded shapes. Our dollies. They were loaded with four-drawer lateral file cabinets that were still full. I'd instructed the clients to empty file cabs, but now, laid on their sides, with the contents stressing the flimsy tracks of the drawers, they reclined as future complaints to resolve. And they still had a twenty-minute commute to the truck.

I rang the bell. A pinch-faced man opened the door, extending some fingers. He implored, "I guess you heard? Jimmy," he called out. "Sorry. He's on the phone; please come in."

The entry area was all boxes, inscribed with phrases

like "Fire Island Honeymoon," "super-heavy/careful," and, "Jimmy's geodes." So far, no gashes on the plaster walls.

In the main room, Davo and Billy were leaning over a dining table, rolling dishware and crystal goblets in unprinted newsprint. Davo's nap had fortified his focus; he was all business. A couple of new guys slid by with loaded hand trucks, nodding as they aimed for the hall. Billy pulled me aside. "That's Chad and Todd," he said. "They wondered if they could get cash today." Chad and Todd were homeless, Georgetown University dropouts, from well-heeled families in DC. They survived the winter hidden in a cloverleaf beside the Beltway, living on whatever they shoplifted. They'd built a cozy lean-to out of plywood and tarps, tucked inside a woodsy thicket, but had lost their shelter to hardcore drifters. They moved with determination now, as if to prove their mettle.

"Who's packing the trucks?" I asked.

"Rider's down there," Davo said. "We're loading the F truck, then the C." Nobody mentioned the missing E truck. Dave R. and Tombo don't have pagers, and even if they did, there was no working phone in this apartment. They had to have known they'd left the scene of an accident. That's a hit and run, and a felony in DC.

A composition pulsed around me. Five movers in harmony in different rooms. I heard the popping of protective bubble wrap, the metallic clack of hangers sliding into wardrobe boxes, the percussion of tape guns securing carton bottoms, and the thudding load-up of small bulky things, like shoes and sturdy collectibles. A sonic disparity connected it all, like improvisation between musicians.

An impatient soloist interrupted from behind a bedroom door. One of the husbands. I caught agitated descriptions of the hit and run. Apparently, our driver gave somebody the finger.

Client Jimmy emerged. We were introduced, and he ushered his husband aside. In the mirror I watched them nodding, pointing toward the street. It wasn't their car that was damaged. Down on the corner, the DC police pulled up. An officer looked up toward the fourth floor, interviewed a man walking a poodle on the sidewalk, and returned to his squad car. Case closed.

Tensions lifted in the apartment. I lingered long enough to help tilt the grand piano up on its side, remove the legs and pedals, and strap it to the piano board and dolly. I didn't ask to play it this time. I was composing myself for another performance. In the elevator, I hoped for an indigo presence to accompany me toward Virginia.

Hours later, I found the E truck in front of Roy's Place. It had a shattered headlight and a gashed-in fender. I parked my Corvette behind it. I was two guys and one truck short, and that DC move was still going on at eleven at night. `

I told Dave R. to hand over the keys. He swung the driver door open and lurched out, fisting my keys up like a prize. Tombo's eyes bugged out. "Oh shit," he chortled, "here it comes. Told you, Dave."

I'd been in bar fights; I'd been in fist fights on school yards; I was jumped by two men on a country road one morning. Whenever I was caught in that sort of chaos, I always told myself to stay calm but I never could. A familiar feeling came surging through my hands as I balled them into fists, knowing I'd need them like tools. I was scared because I knew I was about to go over a waterfall. But I didn't care if it hurt.

Tombo launched himself out of the passenger side. A Pimmit Hills redneck, standing six foot two, ready to rumble. In the parking lot light, his eyebrows appeared to have been scratched off.

A slur of footsteps rushed from behind me as Dave R bellowed, "Alright, here's your fucking keys." He wheeled in fast with a sickle right, over my head. I caught the glint of something sailing up and into traffic beyond the lot at Roy's. My keys were now in the lanes of Route 7 on a Saturday night.

Riled voices and commotion engulfed me as I tried to make sense with drunks, asking them why they did it. "Did what, asshole? We didn't hit nothing. Who said that? No man, somebody hit us."

The bar patrons gathered, leaning on cars, watching the chaos build.

Dave R. fumed and rapidly turned sober. "Hey asshole."

I lost my words. I hocked something up; and as I let it fly toward him, somebody hollered, "Fuck him up."

Tombo said, "Okay, keep it clean."

Spitting out words about what a shitty job this was, and how much money I owed him, Dave R. shoved in closer to me, mocking my flowered shirt. "You're nothing but a total pussy and you don't work."

I tried to get him to back away by raising my hands, but that invited him closer, and some guy on the hood of a car said, "This is gonna be a short fight."

Dave R. narrowed his eyes and grabbed my shirt. I braced, but his uppercut missed, and he swore, "Pussy musician, you think everybody likes your shitty voice and you're some kind of star . . . and you get paid for that bull shit?" His crosscut left hit me hard in the throat. I grabbed him, and his greasy hair was in my mouth as he butted up against me, pushing me backward. I lost a loafer, but I yanked him down with me, elbows first onto the pavement.

Sitting on me, he was a raving monkey, teeth bared, grinning like he expected something like this, coasting in for the kill, chopping me in the face, drawing blood, enjoying it. My legs felt like rubber. Spinning, I wrestled him off—no clean break now, and he jumped to his feet, throwing a good lick on me with a pair of jabs. Half on the pavement with my cheek split like a melon, I launched fast and hit Dave R. dead center under his chin with the top of my head. He turned green, then white, reaching feebly for his tongue which lolled like a piece of bloody spam between his lips. I came up under his chin again, this time with the force of both my fists, and he looked like he was trying to hold on to something, but his head snapped back, and his heels were rocking. In the agony of exhaustion, he half slapped at me, just as my right knuckles found his face and I tore the button off it. Blue light settled over me. I backed away.

I found my lost loafer and pointed it at him. He winced. I was so tempted to kick him in the ribs like on TV, but what was the point, I needed him to drive next week. I pulled him to his feet and dug the spare key out from under the twin I-beam. Tombo stood aside, silent for once. I rolled open the rear door and he and Dave R. flopped into the box.

It was a fifty-degree midnight in Pimmit Hills. Country music and rock and roll tried to get along. Blinking street lights cast a movie set glow on lawn ornaments collecting like shrines in narrow yards Three minutes later, in front of a squat little house, Dave R. and Tombo soldiered out, cigarettes ablaze, signaling that they couldn't be broken by some pussy musician in a flowered shirt.

Our incarnations are like the clothing we wear. What's visible is always temporary.

CHAPTER 20

LOBSTERS AND MOBSTERS

(1986)

Time shoots faster than a gun

"The Imperfect Crime"

A compelling fantasy plagued and inspired me. I still had thick hair, worthy pipes, and my 130-pound frame. But my appearance was not what made me want to preen on stages and hear myself attempting to win over a room. That charm might help me get bookings, but I wanted to get back on stage because I had been writing songs since I was thirteen. It had been four years since I had been actively performing, but I was more in love with that adventure than ever. Now, at thirty-five, the dream that my songs would lead me to some vein of radio gold had faded, but the thrill of digging deep for powerful lyrics and melodies had not. While I fantasized that I might break into the Top 40 charts, the payoff I got from doing a new song and getting a positive roar from a small crowd of strangers meant more to me than it ever did when I had a record deal.

I knew I was born to write songs. They were my first children. And in order to raise them, I needed to give them all homes in the minds and hearts of whoever came to my gigs—at least, for a night. Then I'd pack them back up in my leather satchel, the yellow legal pad sheets with lyrics and chords and notes written above each line, stapled to pieces of perfectly cut cardboard forming a supportive skeleton for each body of work.

I'd been practicing at my bedroom piano for years, letting those sounds inspire me, but I still missed the applause. I missed the playful taunts from audiences and the way someone would tell me their romantic fantasies over a beer. Mostly I missed the spontaneous affirmations as audiences applauded the pain and the joy that was born from my life. Moving a china cabinet without damaging it was powerfully compelling, and it paid the bills. But moving furniture would never make strangers cheer for the work I was doing.

I went to New York City and had publicity shots made. Working on new material two floors above the beat of moving crews coming in and out of the basement kept me vigilant. My fingers had withstood all the furniture I'd lifted, and my voice felt stronger than ever. My gear was smaller now—setting up took thirty minutes, not three hours. I imagined the noise below as an audience, and it inspired me to rock my portable keyboard and land a dozen gigs a month around the DC area. Bobbi Jo was supportive; in fact, she suggested a place in Chestertown, Maryland, and we made a romantic weekend out of that gig.

I split the performance at that little bar with Pete Kennedy, a guitarist friend, who was in-between tours with two nationally known female country stars. The audience didn't know exactly how lucky they were to hear him zinging his hot licks over my piano chords, but they cheered and were quiet as I sang my confessional and often bawdy lyrics. I felt comfortable, in the arms of that listening audience, holding me as I occasionally stumbled, forgetting a lyric that might have been just a little too new.

There were also unplanned moments of harmonic mystery, as the overtones of the real piano I was playing and the serpentine gems from my friend's guitar wound together. There seemed to be a newfound sense in me that I was listening more clearly than I ever had before. Perhaps the break from touring and jet engine stage volume had allowed my ears to grasp a healthier level of sonic balance.

Music is medicine. Songwriting, performing, being on stage; it's all medicine. And people need it, even when they don't realize they do. I had to remind myself not to take it personally when crowds talked through my songs. I'd hear my ego telling me that I'd been blessed with the ability to give the most to people who deserved it the least. Maybe. But I saw a lot of smiles, and some misty eyes as we finished our first long set and took a dinner break. We were hours from Falls Church, but the warmth of that fellowship of listeners surrounding our table made me feel like I was home again.

Pete had dinner with Bobbi Jo and me, and as we were about to return to the stage, we were approached by a man who introduced himself as Doctor Willy. He wanted to hire us to play his 60th birthday party up on Long Island, offering to fly us up and pay for our hotel rooms. He got my phone number and Pete and I finished out the night, doing soulful guitar/piano duets of songs we had each written, as well as a classic rock medley that lasted at least twenty minutes. It was always invigorating to play with Pete, and his guitar prowess is internationally revered. Our history as musical friends goes back to the early DC '70s scene, before either of us had record deals. I think the crowd picked up on our homegrown connection.

When Bobbi Jo and I were in bed in the Victorian house that we had been offered as part of the gig pay, she said I'd never sounded better. Having her heartfelt appreciation spoke deeply to me as a songwriter. It took years to reach down into wherever my songs came from, and our partnership was strengthened by her channeling into the passion of my writing. Almost as if she knew she was sharing me, and yet loving that she could also be my muse.

When we got home, I bought an eight-track Teac recorder and a twelve-channel console and turned my upstairs office into a recording studio, complete with multi-voiced keyboards, outboard effects, and a drum machine to create more radio-friendly songs. But I became so obsessed with how each track should sound that within a month, I'd lost touch with my songwriting. So I returned to my Knabe spinet and wrote on legal pads, notating melodies above the lyrics I sang at the piano. I would occasionally cook up songs on the electronic machines in my studio, but the spirit of what I was trying to express would often be overwhelmed by the infinite choices that multi-tracking offered me.

When I was in a band, I measured the power of songs in a different way. How good they sounded, and how they were produced, indicated healthy creations or deformed ones, and the writing was just part of those musical bodies. As a solo songwriter, I strove to find my truth, digging deeply for the treasure that lay hidden within me. That search was personal; machines and players in a band rarely guided me toward what I wanted to say and sing about.

I wrote about my spiritual awakening, Bobbi Jo's unaccountable love, civil war history, UFOs, lost tribes in Africa, betrayal, and intelligent possums. I wrote whatever came out of that fire hose that God had screwed into my mind, body, and spirit.

The current of those performances lifted me out of the

riptides of the moving business. I'd have to remind myself where I was sometimes, holding a long note, focused on just how I wanted to carry the musical vowel I was forming. I'd feel like I was flying, touching down as the crowd began clapping.

My rehearsal time increased, knowing I had a special performance coming up. I'd worked up a song request that Doctor Willy had made, learning "Paradise by the Dashboard Light." It had been a long-winded hit by Meatloaf, and really wasn't my cup of tea, but it had grown on me. I was still running the song around in my head a week later, as I was helping Bobbi Jo zip up her pink suitcase. We were about to leave for National Airport to jet to that sixtieth birthday party for Doctor Willy. He'd booked a waterfront restaurant out on Long Island and had requested that I play a 1957 white grand piano in the main room that overlooked the Hudson River. I'd been thinking about the set list, my tuxedo, and the limo that was being sent for us at LaGuardia. As Bobbi Jo and I scurried about, I'd also been replaying a conversation in my head, when the doctor had told me that he'd delivered babies for famous Mafioso. John Gotti, the Teflon Don, was a neighbor of his, and he'd be there, and that other big money gigs would come my way. He'd warned me not to approach anyone at his birthday party, that bodyguards might be rude if I got too close to his guests. No problem I told him, I own a moving company. I deal with tough guys every day.

The show went smoothly. I did cocktail treatments of my own songs on that incredible white grand, Bobbi Jo learned some Italian expressions, and our hotel bedroom had a heart-shaped Jacuzzi. Lots of champagne, lobsters, and mobsters filled the lavish ballroom. Every table blossomed with tuxedoed and tight-suited hard cases, adorned with women as gorgeous as money could buy. I was just one of a dozen performers on two stages under a hyper light show as the Doctor, appearing to be on mood-elevating medication, commandeered the dance floor. Slinging his jacket with one hand, he spun shirtless; a clutch of plastic glow rings around his neck.

I was used to seeing steely-eyed businessmen enjoying themselves. In fact, I had played in bands in bars in DC that were owned by what we used to call the DC Mafia. They ran numbers, they "rented out" waitresses, sold hard drugs in back offices, and had done time for tax evasion. I knew them personally. We became friends. And as a band member I was witness to their lifestyles, in their clubs and in their residences. And all the owners of those clubs either ended up in prison, disappeared, or owed us gig money that we never received.

The bar business is not for the faint of heart. The mafia types at Doctor Willy's birthday party just looked like typical club owners to me. But at least I got paid.

CHAPTER 21

BEAUTIFUL MISTAKES (1986)

*I got to where I am
by screwin' up*

"Beautiful Mistakes"

My song "Beautiful Mistakes" always feels pacifying whenever an unexpected damage occurs. Though it remained unfinished for several years, living that song in real time was horrendously painful, especially when my heart had been freshly broken. I'd put it aside, but eventually it was polished, and every time I performed it, I experienced the healing paradox of life. Life is beautiful. But it's also very fucking breakable.

I began writing the song in 1983 and it became a touchstone for me as I built relationships in my world which included people whose belongings had been broken by Big Boy Movers. One lyric in particular made sense over and over again. "Move between the lightning, feel the earth that shakes, we learn this dance of living by making beautiful mistakes." I eventually recorded "Beautiful Mistakes" with my old friend Steuart Smith. He's the lead guitarist with The Eagles and his impeccable playing is a highlight on my album "Flesh and Bone".

It felt therapeutic, as I began fixing everything Big Boy Movers broke, except the mental construct of those who believed they'd paid for perfection. It is a concept that is never measurable. There is no exact science in the moving business.

It's chaos, held in check by the laws of chance.

And when the chaos of a move is in full swing, when the changing of life's patterns becomes too unpredictable, as always happens during a move, a damaged item becomes evidence of betrayal. The company the client has hired to guide them safely has let them lose their way, and the cracked tabletop, or the splintered arm of an old chair is proof that Big Boy Movers didn't care enough to keep that injury from occurring.

It becomes a personal affront, and I got very good at knowing how quickly I needed to arrive at the scene of that accident. Just my being there, on site, was often enough to neutralize some of that chaos. Just the sight of me with my black suitcase full of artistic repair tools was even more compelling proof that I gave a damn. And if there was a calm in that storm, as the glue was drying and the lacquer was setting, or the skim coat of drywall was waiting to be sanded, I might take note of a piano in that newly imperfect world.

And when calm began returning to the new space, I might ask if could play that piano. I'd noodle around a bit; see if the customers were listening. If they were receptive, if the move seemed to be back on track, I'd let the sounds of that piano wash over the new space. We'd hear it together, for the first time, and usually, there would be a sonic baptism, a blessing if you will, of all that had been fervor, noise, and disruption. And the song I'd sing would always be "Beautiful Mistakes."

On the other hand, nobody wanted to hear me crooning poetry when granny's dresser had a fresh gash in it. So I'd always do my artistic repairs before any music began.

My father had taught me to improvise. I'd watched him fix things around the house with whatever was handy: pencil and crayon shavings, sawdust, glue and string. Daddy was a fine watercolorist and I wish I'd inherited more of his patience and calm perspective. He knew when to walk away. He always said it takes two people to paint a picture—one to do it and one to say you're done. He believed in letting the viewer remain curious by what he would imply with his soft water-infused strokes. He was self- taught, and his confidence encouraged me to take on projects that I often faked my way through, perfecting as I improvised.

Doing repairs became its own kind of art to me. A bad gouge would be filled with two-part epoxy, sanded, and then color matched using a mix of lacquer powders. I used a technique known as French padding where I put graining liquid and finish on a soft cloth and with one finger, I rubbed a combo of colors into the fisted pad, swinging it like a pendulum. Reds, browns, oranges, and blacks mixed together on that pad would cover the repaired area, which had been sanded smooth to match the existing level, and then, once the colors were right, I'd use a brush to add grain lines of dark brown or black, top coating all of it with a pre-catalyzed lacquer to match the existing patina. I'd spread the area of repair out to integrate it with the surrounding surface and mist it with a clear coat of satin lacquer. That would usually be all I needed to do to make the damage literally disappear. I could fabricate shapes, corners on nightstands, spires on a Thai prayer house, and the filigree that runs along the edges of gold leaf mirror and picture frames. I'd match those colors as well, employing blues, greens, yellows, whites, whatever, using brushes and sometimes a soft steel wool. I used ultra-toxic glues that bond instantly, like ethyl cyanoacrylate. If I didn't wear my chemical mask I'd get a buzz like I'm drinking moonshine.

I saw these repairs as my karma. Even if some mover I barely knew had screwed something up, it was my cosmic duty to make things right. And not knowing exactly what I was doing made each repair an artistic adventure.

As I perfected my repairs of drywall, furniture, artwork, floors, tile, and landscaping, I'd appeal to my long-haired pirates to be more careful. But I'd become that office guy behind a desk, being served lunch by a redhead in a string bikini and sunglasses. What did I know about moving furniture? They'd stay for a day or a week or for years, doing things their way; checking out Bobbi Jo washing her Porsche; nudging each other when they thought I wasn't looking. But I never discouraged them from hanging out after the moves were done. And they often sheltered in my basement like soldiers after a firefight.

I wasn't sure what the movers knew about what had gone down at Roy's. Dave R. and Tombo remained on the crews, but they seldom came into the house. The talk I overheard in the basement was that chapter had closed, with me having gained respect from the guys who'd seen Dave R.'s swollen jaw, black eyes, and bandaged nose.

The moving business wasn't all numbers and formulas and graphs. I was finally learning that the guys I hired were not like hand trucks and dollies. And they weren't roadies, working because they loved being part of my stage show. They had bills to pay, and Big Boy Movers was how they survived.

Everyone knew I'd hired a bad apple here and there. Thieves, liars, and in one case a homicidal maniac who I justifiably had fired. I had sufficient insurance to keep us in business if the god-awful unforeseen ever happened. But some mistakes require preventative action. Nobody deserved to suffer because of my miscalculations.

We'd moved a Maryland State trooper, and he'd asked one too many questions about the origins of the mystery

rental truck. He kept saying it had a very "familiar looking profile." Felonious intent or not, too many people and
families depended on Big Boy Movers. And with business
running so smoothly, the liability of that mystery rental
truck had to be erased completely.

The C and the E trucks were used as barriers to cloak the
operation which would happen in the side lot. Davo arrived
with his brother's five-foot acetylene tank, blow torch and
masks, and he and another guy cut the F truck into pieces
small enough to fit into wardrobe boxes for solid waste trash
day. We sold the axles, rear end, engine, and front seat. We
torched the doors off, broke the glass and sliced up the twen-
ty-four-foot-long frame, including the heavy-duty springs.
The gas tank, muffler, and exhaust system were traded to
a friend for a bushel of crabs, and the tires fetched us fifty
bucks each in the Want ads. We moved the twenty-four-foot
box behind my garage and painted it to look like a metal shed.
The door still slid up and down, giving us a place to store
packing supplies and moving equipment. I was lucky to have
discreet talent around me, and I gave them a bonus for the
speed of the demolition.

Within a month we found a replacement for the F truck, a
twenty-four-foot GMC freight body, which we named appro-
priately, the G truck. We now had a major chord in the C, E,
and G trucks. At last, everything was in harmony.

CHAPTER 22

MY CURRENCY OF FAITH AND TRUST (1986)

Every time you drift away

"The Other Side of Love"

The relationships I built with my movers and every client on the phone were underwritten by a currency of faith and trust. In Buddhism, it's best to address anything that would devalue that currency; to transform negative actions; to illuminate them. Illumination was my desire to fill the garden of my heart with the light of the Divine. Bobbi Jo's secrets were weeds I couldn't control.

I accepted business conflicts as karmic debt I was paying off in this incarnation. It was unavoidable. But wanting Bobbi Jo to tell me what was going on inside her head was a karmic conflict I couldn't make sense of as easily. I knew she was hiding something broken from me, and I began to wonder who might be repairing it. But how could I transform a negative action if all I had to go on was my intuition?

Illumination would bring us closer, and prove we had faith in us. Makeup sex in the dark would never light up that part of my heart. But it always kept me from asking hard questions. And my erections always gave Bobbi Jo the answers she thought I wanted.

The weeds kept growing, though, until I couldn't resist

their power. I surrendered at Giant Food, as I watched a dark-haired woman untacking a Big Boy Movers card from the community bulletin board. She was Florida tan, and wore the tightest, whitest pants I'd ever seen. Her name was Gina.

I invited her to the double garage to buy packing supplies. She was moving back to Fort Lauderdale, and needed materials that night, so here she was, bending over to see how deep the picture boxes were. "Are those eighteen-inch wardrobes?"

I remembered Bobbi Jo giggling into her pink phone, telling me she wouldn't be home until three am. "An Algerian soccer team is having a bachelor party at Maxims," she'd said. Earlier that day, I'd pulled a corner of the carpeting up to see why we had ants in the bedroom. I'd found a disc of birth control pills, with two weeks' worth punched out. We never used contraception. Bobbi Jo wanted to get pregnant. If she was constructing a life separate from mine, at least she was being careful.

"Those are twenty-four-inch wardrobes," I replied, as Gina's red-nailed fingers held up a roll of yellow strapping. Her white pants drew my gaze again when she faced me.

"Hey, what's this do?" Gina asked.

The mysteries of Bobbi Jo's motivations vanished under the carpet as I kissed Gina. Her lips had a mango taste, and I told her so while we spread out moving pads in the back of the E truck. I hadn't been pushy, but, after I'd loaded a dozen book boxes and packing paper into her car, she'd started asking questions. "What's the inside of that truck look like?" she'd wondered; pointing toward the three behemoths in the darkness. "Which one," I'd said, and we hugged tentatively, her white pants resisting my wandering fingers. Her pants remained immaculate as she unzipped them in the moonlight and folded them like a priestess might handle a sacred robe. We kept our tops on, though hers was pulled up to expose a pendant that said "Dang It" resting casually between her breasts.

I felt the need to lift her and make sure she was properly wrapped. I tucked her body against a stack of pads as I entered her; I reached for the wall of the truck, grasping the straps that hung in place on either side of Gina. I turned her abruptly one way and then another, measuring her strength against mine, kissing her as if my mouth was my way of telling her how fragile she felt, protected now in the embrace of my arms and hers. Tan limbs were measured and spread, and her back rose and arched, free from my chest—more padding was shoved into place to support the load that was coming to join hers, the sounds of our moving in sync with the squeaking of all fourteen feet of the aluminum box of the E truck. It consumed every part of us until finally, our gasping ride delivered us to our destination, her southern voice noting something about a moving experience, the weave of our tongues silencing her words.

Hours later, I could still taste the mango candy that had been Gina as I stood at a bedroom window. It was five am. I'd heard the phone ring once around three, but when I picked up, the line was dead.

Headlights cut through the curtains. A large car eased into the driveway. I saw the driver's melon head, and Bobbi Jo, opening the passenger door to exit. I caught her hand wave and lip pucker. The car backed away as Bobbi Jo shimmied toward our rear gate. I heard the key in the door, the toilet flushing, water running, and with one eye open, I watched her strip, unsure of what to ask first. Shivers of guilt felt like Gina's nails on my skin and I stayed silent, wondering if Bobbi

Jo was feeling that same guilty after pleasure. That stimulating curiosity rose when she climbed into bed. Did she sense anything different about me?

But she began purring that her stupid battery was dead, so David had given her a ride home. There was whiskey in her kiss as she wound her legs around mine. I nuzzled her tempting bonnet of hair. She had something slippery in her hands. It was warm and scented but I asked her, "Who is David?"

"Pennsylvania David," she moaned, "the office in Pennsylvania. He picked me up at Maxims."

Sometimes after encounters like these, she'd remind me about her next weekend trip to visit auctions or estate sales. She'd begun storing boxes of "inventory" in the basement, saying that someday she'd open a high-end gift shop. These trips always brought her home after midnight. Antique French dolls or Belgian carvings would triumphantly pose on our dining table. Then a loud car would rumble past outside; I'd ask, "Did you hear that?"

"Nope," she'd say, examining a doll's face in her hands. I wondered why these friends she traveled with never entered the house to meet me. I asked her this. "They're shy," she'd say. Or, "He's harmless," as I was clearing my two am pizza box full of beer cans from the dining table.

I had an unfinished portrait of Bobbi Jo in my mind. She was smiling proudly; a striking work in progress, testing her entrepreneurial talents with a variety of influencers. That they were all male, and that I hadn't met them was perhaps just coincidence. Her efforts to expand her business world did not include me, and that actually seemed healthy. I had my enterprises; she would have hers. I didn't want to take away her power, but I did feel like we deserved a break from our lack of note comparing.

Illumination might not be finding the dark corners of our

relationship at the moment, but that didn't mean we couldn't put on wings and let a grand adventure unfold between us. Rather than confront her, I suggested a getaway from our continuing distance. To Europe.

CHAPTER 23

OUTLAW PUSSY (1987)

*Don't put no price on
your green skin*

"Reptile Boy"

A week later, I woke from a nap to find Bobbi Jo bouncing on the narrow bed beside mine. It was sunset in Paris. A bottle of wine stood on the dresser next to baguettes and a plate of olives. "Look," she said, and up above her new fishnet stockings, I saw a most unusual jacket. It was completely covered with small plastic gumball charms from the 1950s. She had an eye for whimsy, and I told her I loved her. In that little room on Rue Jacob, I mentally forgave Bobbi Jo for all her inexplicable actions. And silently thanked her for the songs she'd inspired.

The wine glasses on the dresser glowed like her platinum curls in the mirror. With her rear end to me, she adjusted her garter belt and smoothed her stockings. "Somebody named Gina called you before we left . . ." she said casually.

I noticed a small tear of lace running down her thigh. "I don't know any Gina," I said. My meditation that night was fraught with guilt. And infinite, blue-lit forgiveness, reminding me of all I had yet to learn. And lose.

For five weeks, thanks to a profitable summer and Billy's managerial skills, Bobbi Jo and I wove through France, Belgium, and Italy, between the snowy thighs of the Alps, across the belly of Switzerland, and into Germany. The Autobahn tempted me to drive at speeds over ninety miles per hour, as maniacs passed us going over a hundred and twenty.

We entered Belgium and on a still October morning, a ferry at Ostend carried us across the channel to Dover, England. The white cliffs gradually appeared, and I leaned over the upper deck rail, humming Neil Young songs, fighting off the urge to hurl my croissants into the sea. Thoughts of my ancestors huddling below deck on Atlantic crossings humbled me as I imagined them at sea for weeks, with little to hum about and much to fear.

Our first day in London was nippy. We window-shopped in the neighborhood by our hotel, and that night we went to a rock and roll club to hear my friend's newly-signed band. Doors opened at midnight.

Bobbi Jo wore a new luminescent green top and a matching mini skirt. She'd gotten most of her hair lopped off at a salon on Kings Row, but she was ravishing and she knew it. Smiling coyly, with her eyes enlarged by eel-colored mascara, she looked like a mermaid on nitrous. Her silver boots were laced thigh-high, and her wrists were aflame with glowing coral bracelets.

We exited the taxi amid fog and diesel in the air, and the hooting of barges from the Thames. In a crudely lit alley, a girl with a safety pin driven through her nostrils took an indeterminable admission fee from the pound notes in my hand. People holding clove-scented cigarettes let us pass into a vaulted room booming with bass drum and low E string hemorrhage. High on a red-lit stage, a loin-clothed trio beat a minor chord to death. A psychotic elf bounded into the spotlight and pointed directly down at us: Rolf, my ex-bandmate from The Infernos in Annandale. Death had taken most of the guys from that band, but Rolf seemed to be aging backwards. I could still feel our competitive kinship in the grinning glare he aimed at me. I hadn't laid eyes on him in ten years but in our last phone conversation we'd guffawed at what today's rockers were doing on stage and I'd hung up, amused at how he'd described this dumpster fire I was seeing now.

"Motherfuckers, welcome to the end of the world," he wailed, comically preaching from his perch on the mic stand. I put my hand across Bobbi Jo's leather miniskirt as she bumped her hip into mine. "He's good," she shouted. The bellowing chorus of: "Fuck you, Fuck me; Fuck us all," enflamed the bacon-scented crowd around us as they bludgeoned each other in front of the stage.

"God Bless Rolf and his determination," was the silent mantra that kept me from fleeing the sonic anger that made every note a nail, impaling the flesh of listeners as it pummeled us with volume that forced me to shove spit laden napkin bits into my ears. I offered Bobbi Jo that solution, but she waved me off, smiling like she was listening to the Infernos, when happy little songs about falling in love with a flower girl was all a crowd needed to become charmed by the music.

I had to admit I was just plain jealous. Rolf had gotten a major label record deal. He'd said he needed two more songs; something "quirky." I'd gotten my hopes up when we'd talked by phone, but now I was dismayed at how out of touch I felt as the crowd worshipped what I considered primitive noise. Still, one of my tunes might be a golden ticket, a lighthearted gem shining through Rolf's hard rock screamers. And hit song or not, I could write this trip off, as my musical endeavors fell under the corporate umbrella of Big Boy Movers, Inc.

I spied Bobbi Jo at the bar after the set, her shimmering green back to me. By the slight shake of her shoulders, I could tell she was laughing. Rolf smirked as he sketched something on a napkin. He had a silver chain roped between his nipples, and an unlit cigarette in the corner of his mouth. I gave Bobbi Jo her distance for a few minutes and then I put Rolf in a friendly headlock.

He freed his little bald head and pushed a beer my way and we screamed salutations at each other over the racket vomiting from Club Zero's speakers. Teasing me, he let his hand wander, until elfin fingers traced familiar circles on Bobbi Jo's leathered derrière. I grabbed his left ear as Bobbi Jo giggled and excused herself.

Rolf grunted, "Apologies, mate. You brought music?"

I handed him my work. "Here's your quirky songs," I reminded him. Songs like "Reptile Boy," about a mutant carnival couple who raise a son with green skin. "Mama don't you know he'll never be a normal little cub scout. When he wears his uniform all the other boys make fun of how his tail hangs out." And "Mambo Genesis," about a crazed man who takes a baby possum hostage and eventually flees to Graceland. "They'll chase my car to the highway through the field, but the cops will never shoot me with my possum at the wheel." Mambo Genesis is the name of the baby possum. It ends happily by the way.

My demo sat on the bar while Rolf stared at his drink. "Sanctuary's telling me to call the record *Outlaw Pussy*, and Bobbi Jo's it, okay?" He shoved me what he'd been drawing on a napkin. I said "Rolf. Cut my songs if you want. But putting a cowboy hat on my girlfriend sitting naked on your grandfather isn't going to happen." Not at two am in London, England.

Bobbi Jo and I flew home in November. The Virginia colors were still peaking, and we found everything in order at the house. The pool was clean, and the boys were truly happy to see us. We drove out to see Bobbi Jo's parents and were met with more welcome embraces. But even while we showed our European slides to family and friends, our separate lives unfolded again. It was impossible to measure the distance between us, smiling under a mackerel sky, with the Mediterranean behind us. And even on that bright screen, our wonder seemed dulled, like the camera had captured the shallowness beneath our surface.

The day we returned home and unpacked, I asked Bobbi Jo about the box of scented lubricant I'd found in the closet behind her suitcase. It was brand new. She turned her back to me when I told her it had come from someone in Pennsylvania. When Bobbi Jo and I both answered the phone that night, a man's voice said, "Wrong number." It left me wondering if our travels had driven us too far apart.

CHAPTER 24

WE MAKE OUR OWN LUCK (1987)

*This sleepy thief won't rest 'til
I've stolen my last breath*

"Narcoleptic Kleptomaniac"

Sanctuary rejected "Mambo Genesis" and "Reptile Boy" as too milquetoast, so Rolf asked for something "a bit more bizarre." I sent him this:

> *"Maybe I'm the monster, ever think of that? I eat your love and patience and then I pass the hat. / Maybe I'm the angel who doesn't know where to land. I make a parachute and jump the plane and end up in your hand. / I can't get no distance from you with your body in my fridge / I lost my appetite for looking, I'm taking off my bib/ Don't need to chew your heart / I look better thinner/ Give me space, give me space . . . Space . . . that's what's for dinner."*

Rolf went nuts. And so did Sanctuary. But he wanted to rewrite the music. I said "Sure, man, whatever." Luck in the record business wasn't a shot in the dark, it was trusting a conference room of blind people to point you toward the target.

One day I met some musicians who actually were famous, and that surprised me, as they were three unflashy guys who were making ten bucks an hour working for Big Boy Movers. They were a heavy metal threesome called Strangle, and they had a mega following in Europe. I'd heard of them but wasn't a big fan of that type of edgy music, though they were excellent players. For about a year, they'd leave every three months and go on the road for six weeks. They were humble about it, but they had a record deal and supernova stardom seemed imminent. *Billboard* magazine tracked their international sales and I wondered why they needed to be humping furniture. Apparently, their enslavement to the label was so long term that it would take a decade of touring to pay back what they owed on advances and studio time. Bad business aside, they were gentlemen, even with purple eyeliner and multiple tattoos, and even better movers.

I thought about the opportunity Strangle had been given. If Primadonna had toured Europe, scored long-term label support, maybe I wouldn't be in the moving business. But the die had been cast, and I was still making music, just not counting on it to pay the bills. And freakishly, I'd stumbled onto a stage where what I did wasn't rewarded by encores and blow jobs, but by spendable payments that went into a bank account, payments rendered by satisfied people who even tipped me and the other movers for sweating on this newfound stage. Big Boy Movers felt like a band that was finally getting top dollar for what it provided, and it was more satisfying than bowing to audiences of strangers awash in a tide of alcohol and smoke.

The guys from Primadonna still felt like brothers to me, and I was glad that they were employed and seemingly happy to be out of the music business. Three had gotten married and started families. One had become a male stripper but all of them were sober. And none of them sounded jealous about my success. But the call of the wild, the longing to go it alone, had not struck any of them as deeply as it had me. I'd offered all of them a chance to join me six years earlier when Primadonna had disbanded, but who wants to load heavy objects into a truck. That torture was one of the agonies of the business we were disbanding.

Back when I was twenty-five, I dreamt of finding a home for my songs, a place where the world would gather around some cosmic radio and adore what I'd written. I never imagined myself finding success by any other means. But it was a giant leap for me to imagine reaching that goal without a band of musical warriors around me. My movers, even the ones I fired, gave me the camaraderie I'd taken for granted in the groups I was in. They were a constantly changing band of thieves and saviors, of strangers and friends, who gave me the freedom to go it alone when I felt the need. It was liberation I hadn't foreseen; if I wanted to do a solo move, I could. If I wanted to continue my dream of being alone on a stage, I could.

Sometimes my movers would appear at one of my shows. They'd throw darts or bottles, fall off bar stools, and be escorted out by bouncers. I'd tried getting them up on stage to sing backgrounds, but that was like expecting howler monkeys not to use their jungle voices. Their efforts always rattled a room of bar flies, and after the sarcastic applause died down, I'd remind the crowd that Big Boy Movers would offer a discount to anyone who'd witnessed our rehearsal.

One Friday afternoon, I let a couple of movers help me load my gear, and that old appreciation of roadies filled my heart as big speakers and anvil cases were hefted into the E truck. Primadonna load-ins were always grueling, and varied logistically, depending on the entry to the stage at any particular venue. We didn't always have roadies, but load-ins usually averaged about three hours, not including our sound check—when cascades of pink noise would flood the speaker stacks and monitors as our sound man adjusted the frequencies for the room. Once all that was set, we'd do the drum check; I'd hit each drum as sound man Joe would tweak levels and effects for my snare, toms, bass drum, hi-hat and cymbals. It was a tricky mix to get right because I had a vocal mic that picked up everything I played as I was singing. I learned to avoid cymbal crashes and heavy rim shots while I was on that mic, but sometimes my enthusiasm overtook me, and I'd get a hand signal from Joe to lay back. I know I bugged him. One time I asked once too often if my vocals were ok, and he wrestled me down behind the soundboard and said something like "What? You think you're the only guy up there?" It ruffled my feathers, but a waitress took me aside and consoled me. As we left the bathroom, she said, "Call me. But don't during the day. My husband works night shifts." Memories. Sometimes I barely recognized the guy I was back then.

I still knew a lot of hungry musicians, so I had few regrets about leaving the full-time performance world behind. But later, as I carried my piano to the E truck, I found my glass-framed publicity shot ruined by a fist-sized smash to my black-and-white face. That's what my movers thought of my "side job."

CHAPTER 25

EMMA MORGAN (1988)

Ethereal with an attitude

"Emma Morgan"

"It has to be broom clean."

I'd never heard that expression before. "It has to be what?" It was a dark Sunday morning. Bobbi Jo pulled the blanket over her face as the voice continued.

"It has to be broom clean; we don't want any sign of anyone having lived there. It's got to be done today. You work on Sundays?"

"Yes. Of course, sure," I said, pulling this together. It was Randy from the law firm of Howell and Jewell, saying he'd called last week. Dim recollection, but I got up, bumping my head on the ceiling of the attic nook. I'd gotten in from playing at the Round Table in Georgetown just four hours earlier.

Randy went on. "Usually, we get the family to act on this, but they want nothing to do with it. And they don't care what it costs. It's a 1950s bungalow, right off MacArthur, NW, DC. Six rooms total. Everything to the curb, you can do it?"

"On my way," I said.

Bobbi Jo sent one leg out into the light and rolled over, bare ass in lavender shadows. She'd come in late as well, smelling like African cigarettes. Her French Algerian friends were in town. As I was leaving, she gave me a smoky kiss and reminded me she had some business with her new friend, Jasmine, kind of a seminar, she added. It sounded a lot more entertaining than a six-room solo move on a frozen Sunday.

Coffee, a broom, gloves, donuts, a full tank; ready, I crossed Chain bridge into light Sunday morning traffic. How hard could this be? I promised myself that I wouldn't go nuts, wouldn't hurt myself; that I'd do exactly what the lawyer said. Take everything to the curb and sweep the place clean.

The little white bungalow sat alone on a shallow rise, a dozen feet up from the street. It waited cautiously as I approached the porch where a key lay under a pot on the right. Dull glass windows watched me mount the peeling steps, and something moaned when I pushed the key into the brass face of the worn doorknob. A sudden breeze urged tree branches against a gutter.

I stood in the silence, listening. Remembering details the lawyer had told me. No one had been inside the house for nineteen years, since the deceased, Emma Morgan, had walked away from it on a spring morning, telling her family in Brooklyn, New York, that she was on her way to see them. She'd made it as far as Wilmington, Delaware, which wasn't bad, considering that she was walking.

Emma Morgan was a schoolteacher, born in 1902. She'd saved every page from the book of her life, and most all of what every student had allowed her to keep, from her thirty-one years of teaching seventh grade. There were newspapers, magazines, and calendars dating back to 1912. Loaded scrap books, faded WWI and WWII posters, colorful corny greeting cards, holiday newsletters, wedding and birth announcements, dance cards and personal diaries, stacked neatly, filled every inch of flat space, be it a floor, tabletop, or shelf.

In the kitchen, a bright blue breakfast plate sat askew beside a crumpled red napkin. An encrusted cereal bowl nudged a still upright box of Wheaties, the juice glass standing moldy beside it. The sink was full of her last dinner dishes, and an apron hung from a kitchen chair, with a note in one pocket, listing the items she'd need at the grocery. I stood in the tiny kitchen and counted the boxes stacked to the ceiling. Each one was labeled with the year of its collection. I quit counting at fifty-three.

The dust was beautiful in the morning light; silver, gold, and iridescent, it had settled and then risen upon my entry, almost excited, as if finally something living had arrived. I sat down. This was going to take all day, at least, maybe longer. But there was no way I was going to simply shove this stuff out to the curb for the trash pickup. I opened a kitchen drawer. There, beneath a purple felt cover, lay a dozen sterling silver spoons, nested like shiny fish, waiting to be discovered.

Emma Morgan had never married, but she had been in love with a man named Joe. Joe didn't have a last name in the letters. He'd met Emma at church and worked as a Navy orderly down on the Potomac. She'd been a nurse during the war, and her letters to Joe included an accounting of her studies, and how much she wanted to serve, to go over there, she said, to help the men who needed it the most, not that her hospital rounds weren't important. But she'd been rejected, she declared stoically, because of her bout with pneumonia and her bad back. She'd stay stateside, and her letters talked of weekends with the girls, dancing at the Bayou and Glen Echo, and missing Joe, who by that time had been sent to the Pacific on a sub chaser out of Miami. They must have kissed or gotten intimate before he'd left because in the letters between them, they refer to missing each other in terms of "grunts." He'd sign off "14 grunts" and she'd write back, "Miss you, 9 grunts."

I opened box after box. Baseball cards from 1934, the

year Freddy claimed he was born, autographed playbills from a Louis Armstrong show at the old Ambassador Theater, colorful French postcards from 1899 showing two men "charming" a naked woman, a typed resume describing Emma Morgan as age 42, 5 feet tall, 138 pounds, with glasses, and willing to work for $45 a week and traveling expenses. I found a 1949 program from the National Theater featuring Spike Jones and his Musical Depreciation Revue; a lock of hair apparently from President Wilson's head; an aluminum Merry Widows condom container, still intact, with the words "for Joe" taped across it; Japanese bills from 1944, and a War Ration Book, number three, with only one row of ration stamps removed. I put them aside and kept working.

By noon, the truck was almost loaded. Not with trash, but with items to be returned to my house, where I could cull through the collectibles, and see what was worth saving.

I discovered a closet full of 1942 nurses' uniforms decorated with blue, gold, and red pins marking Emma's accomplishments, and six fancy hats in boxes, 1920s Flapper style. A trunk under the bed held a stamped set of Newcomb pottery vases, each one worth over five hundred dollars. Above the fireplace, I found a key in a lacquer box, and used it to open a small door hidden behind a dresser in an upper bedroom. My flashlight shone on the green Army footlocker inside. I broke the padlock in the afternoon light of the bedroom, and drew out a short-barreled derringer, pearl handled, wrapped in a newspaper from 1846. In a large manila envelope were several black-and-white pin-up pictures, showing a stocky woman gazing at the camera as she reclined on a couch, her glasses off, a full-lipped smile, her body hidden from the waist down by an American flag. The signed papers of some legal brief were at the very bottom, and the words "Adoption Declined" were bold and stark in the empty room. I looked at the moth-eaten teddy bear in the white crib beside the window. A halo of twinkling dust rose from its head as I picked it up. When I set it back down, one of its button eyes appeared to wink toward the closet behind me.

Something fell solidly, thumping the floor below me, and with it came another sound that made no sense. I rose, as quickly as I could. What would make a giggling sound in an empty house?

I should have remembered there was no electricity, but still, I ran my hand over the light switch in the darkening kitchen downstairs. The back door had blown slightly open, caught by a winter breeze, and the broom, leaning against it, had hit the floor with a musical splatter, wood playing the linoleum like a marimba. I stood it back in place and kicked the door closed.

Back to work, I thought, keep moving, not much left, the truck is almost loaded. I was halfway up the stairs, listening to the shuffle of my feet on the hardwood, when I stopped and whipped around. My broom lay on the floor in the kitchen. This time it was directly perpendicular to the back door. But, the head of the broom, a yellow weave of fibers drawn tightly by a piece of canvas banding was split in half, the fibers forming a radical V shape. I don't remember using it like that, I thought, but it was getting cold, and things do stiffen up. Had I heard a breathy conversation a few moments before?

I looked at my hands. I wasn't allergic to anything, not mold, not dust, but still, I felt hairy all at once, scratching my legs, pants pulled up at the ankles, looking for insect bites as I ran my fingernails over bare skin. Everything itched. Fingers, eyes, elbows, ears, stomach, tongue; yet I could find nothing.

Old houses were like this: full of crazy little mites or fleas, what did I expect? That's why they wanted it broom clean.

The pink afternoon light through the windows darkened, and a deep mauve settled over the glass. Impossible; how had I lost track of time?

The truck was loaded, well, almost full. I circled back through the empty rooms, and tried to recall something I knew I'd made a mental note of earlier. Had I noticed a door in the floor? I'd gotten a blurry glimpse as I cleared the rest of the heavy boxes out of the kitchen. Why was I so foggy? It had to be the dust. And the colors, I'd seen them in the light; that dust was almost twenty years old. Bacteria, God knows, some kind of toxic stuff must have been stored in the house, and I was breathing it. That made sense. I shined my light out onto the dusty patterns on the floor around me. Why would there be a door in the floor?

A cough rose in my throat. I struggled to breathe, and imagining dark fresh air, I reached out for the doorknob, but the room wobbled, and the old brass turned worthlessly in my hand. Behind me, shadows of my effort to escape wavered in windows and doorways. My stomach had become so nauseated that it made me squint. I slid to the floor. A playful green light kept running in thin shafts through the kitchen. What was that? Was it a car? I needed to get out of here.

Overhead, I heard the dull thunder of wheels rolling over a floor and above that, the sprinkling of tiny wood chimes, like freezing snow falling on tinfoil. Leaning against the door frame, I pushed myself up to my knees and I crawled toward the stairs. Something on the floor above me was moving back and forth, I was sure of it, making the floorboards whimper as it did. Mice, rats, possums? I put one foot on the step. "Who the fuck's up there?" I shouted. Nothing came back to me until a sound I'd never heard before began at the back of my head, and grew louder, until all I saw was fast white lights, and then I slept.

I woke up with my face flat on cold linoleum in Emma Morgan's kitchen. I must have fallen hard. I had no idea what time it was, but a frozen moon stared in at me from a cloudless sky.

But my head was clear now. And when I shined my light on the floor, the edges of a trap door appeared in the corner, where the boxes had been stacked. A ladder led down into a cellar. I went down the metal rungs into dead silence.

I stood on concrete. Inches above my head, ceiling rafters ran the length of the small rectangular room. On a cot in the corner, my light found a blanketed shape. It was baby-like in size, and the head of the body showed it to be a doll from the 1950s. It had on blue pajamas, held in place with buttons, and cowboys on horseback galloped across the faded color over its chest. There was a wristwatch on the arm: a Timex, and still ticking. The time read one thirty-five.

My light revealed stacked canned goods, a tank marked "water", and a thick manual inscribed with the words Defense Department Procedure, Fallout Shelter. There was a Bible, a dozen encyclopedia books on shelves, and a calendar with the year 1961 in bold red letters at the top. Beneath it, "June 23, Daddy comes home!" was written in neat blue ink. A framed picture on the cinderblock wall beside it showed a man in dark bell-bottoms and a white short-sleeved shirt, holding the doll I'd seen on the cot. The edges of his white naval cap caught the sun. I looked down at the doll and smoothed the blanket back up over its face.

Then I started up the ladder. Four or five fast steps, a panicky grasp, and I was pulling myself through the opening. I slammed the trapdoor hard and made for the front door.

Something in that cold little space had touched me. It had happened so fast, the gripping and the letting go; slippery, like the time some kid grabbed my ankles as I was climbing up the ladder out of a swimming pool. The feeling around my ankles again, and the unmistakable sound of a murmur.

I left Emma Morgan's house broom clean. I locked the door, then turned to my truck. I didn't want any part of whatever was in her boxes. It took me over an hour to unload, but I put everything that was in my truck back on the curb.

The first shades of dawn were washing over the sidewalks on MacArthur Boulevard, as I turned the key in the ignition. I was exhausted. My headlights caught a small shadow at an upstairs window—the narrow shape was distorted by the watery colors of morning but I saw it up there. It held something. From the wheel, I realized my fingers were lifting, waving goodbye.

CHAPTER 26

A DREAM IN GOD'S EYES (1988)

*All we are is streams
of dust from stars*

"Everything's O.K."

It was seven in the morning when I eased the E truck into the lot on Rudyard Street. Davo was folding pads in the G truck, on time for once. He'd brought a friend, a beefy-nosed guy he introduced as Mungo. "He's a good man," Davo said, "knows trucks and can drive anything. You alright?" Davo stepped closer, patient concern in his voice. "You look messed up, boss." My pants were ripped from the shins down. There were scratch marks all the way across my ankles and my face was bruising where I'd fallen.

Bobbi Jo appeared and opened her car door, all coiffed; her green leather jacket hugged her hips. She gave the boys a gloved wave as I approached her.

"Who's that?" Mungo asked.

Davo pushed him toward the G truck. "Come on man," he snorted, "we're burning daylight."

Bobbi Jo lowered her shades and stared at me. "Holy shit!" she said. "What happened to your shins? You get in another fight?"

We had a rule about scenes in front of the guys, so I just shook my head and said "I don't know, I can't . . . " Every image of what I'd thought I'd seen in that house clung like cobwebs across my eyes. I wiped my hands over my face and heard Bobbi Jo say, "Aspirin, on my nightstand." I'd lost my words but as she swung her legs into her Porsche, I saw a flash of pink lace on milky freckled skin.

"Okay," she said, "I'll be home for lunch, around one. Meet you upstairs?" I nodded, thinking, *sleep.*

As I lay in the little room, the house quieted. I was drifting in slow motion, but I could still feel the rough skin of the scrapbook I'd left on the passenger seat in my truck. It was the only thing I'd taken with me from that house. Her family would surely want it. Her name was delicately inscribed in childlike script on the cover. Below it was a date, 1908, in faint black letters. Morgan was a common name, but I remembered a postcard that had been sent to her from Allentown, Pennsylvania. It was signed Robert Morgan. I'd start there, and I'd be able to find out what happened to her. The lawyer had given me very little information, but I knew she'd never have left her house if her family hadn't reached out to her and asked her to visit them. Her life had been so well preserved, all of it, compressed so carefully in that pale green scrapbook. Her people would have her history to pore over, with eyes and hearts that would see beyond what was between its covers.

I pictured Emma Morgan, locking her door for the last time, hiding the key, walking north toward a family who never offered to pick her up. Her mind had directed her along highways until it left her staring at a ceiling in an institution in Wilmington, Delaware. Now landfill dirt would cover the evidence of her life, and grass would sprout from her memories, only miles from where they began in 1902. I imagined the satisfaction of finding her family as comforting blue light washed over me.

I was out cold until Bobbi Jo came home for lunch and woke me up with an exasperated question.

"Hey, did you know the power went out?" she asked. "There was a blue flash." It had come from upstairs, she said, but the lights were all back on now.

That was when she saw my shins. They were unblemished, almost as if they'd been sunburned and had returned to their normal state. I rubbed them and flexed my ankles, not feeling any pain where they'd been scratched. "That is so weird," she said softly. She pulled the sheet back and took a good look at the rest of me. "Now roll over," she commanded. She gave my butt a playful whack and said, "No more solo moves for you, Mister."

Over the next few days, I called the Pennsylvania telephone information center to get listings for a Robert Morgan in Allentown. In fact, I called several major cities throughout the state, and asked for the phone numbers of people named Morgan. I could only get a few at a time, but I amassed over eighty numbers and made calls for about a week. Nobody knew of an Emma Morgan. I even spoke with men named Robert Morgan. And none of them knew who I was talking about.

But she was so vital. I felt like I knew her. And I sensed she realized why I'd been going through her things that day. That I'd appreciated her life. As I'd worked, I think she made several efforts to introduce herself, but maybe what I'd encountered wasn't her. Maybe it was what remained of her dream of children. An incarnation unrealized. Reaching out from spider webs and silent dust to tell me something, to inspire me to find Emma Morgan's family, to offer them the gifts she'd left behind, the treasure that had been buried in plain sight.

That energy didn't appear like my blue-lit guides, like my angels of mercy who were connected to me in ways I couldn't describe to family, doctors, or even to myself. I just let that grace find me when it did, and it was always for the best of intentions. That day had proved otherwise. They hadn't kept me from encountering that presence that physically wounded me; perhaps that's how desperately Emma needed the father in me to act. So I did. I went searching for the family of a lost soul, a child of God who walked away from her own safe place to find people who she believed would father and mother her. But they let her remain un-adopted. They let her wander. Maybe Emma was still traveling. Adrift in the blue light of that endless ocean of Divinity. And perhaps that was her choice. If family hadn't cared enough to come for her, she'd remain free in that place where flesh and bone don't exist. Maybe she had healed my wounds. Maybe she'd wanted to touch someone who appreciated how she'd spent her time on Earth.

And yet it hurt to know I would never find her people; to let them know how rich a life she'd had, how much hope she'd had to have a legacy for her own children. And in the end, how hard she'd tried to leave her legacy to them.

CHAPTER 27

THE KING OF THE BASEMENT
(1989)

*Deep and dark and
dreamless sleep*

"Carmelita"

"I got to do what I got to do," Davo said, wet-lipped and belching; the beer can shrinking in his big paw. "California. Man, the solar business is boomin' out there." We'd had a decent day; it was parking lot talk. Just Davo and me; everybody else had left for Saturday night socializing. I popped a top as he handed me the paperwork.

"Where's the check buddy?" I asked, and as if he'd read my mind, he dug into the back pocket of his jeans and pulled out a crumpled trio of hundred-dollar bills. "Paid in cash," he said, and "oh yeah, Gino dinged the dresser with an ice skate Tombo threw at him. I knocked fifty bucks off the bill so everything's cool." I took a calming swallow and said, "Solar huh?"

What a paradox. I'd met Davo at Annandale Plumbing supply, and they were training him to be their lead solar panel salesman when he'd taken a cigarette break and sold me on hiring him. And now, seven years later, he was on a break again; touting a business opportunity he'd once rejected.

His ambition was infectious, but like this truck lot conversation, it always involved the future, dramatically outlined, and as solid as smoke drifting between beers. I'd revered his enthusiasm early on and had given him free rein to move in and expand the confines of my house and my business. We both had a passion for finding solutions. We both believed we could do anything. And I'd let him try.

By beer number four we were laughing about how he'd drawn workers in with his big brother party animal spirit. The basement would be full of new recruits, all friends of friends of Davo's and the party would continue into the wee hours, and onto the trucks the next day. But we had an abundant supply of labor because new guys didn't want to be left out of the party gang that Davo was running. Not my style of socializing, but Big Boy Movers had no shortage of labor once Davo had become king of the basement.

Davo always thought I should have made him an equal partner, pointing out all he'd brought to Big Boy Movers. But I'd shaken his shoulder one too many times as he drifted in lily white land, while crews and customers waited. Davo believed everything should move at his pace, that it would all get done. I always told him he was like a top-of-the-line Cadillac—but he kept losing the keys to that car. He would do a wonderful, perfect move one day and the next day, he'd misplace the check for the job. The customer would put a stop payment on it, I'd drive to DC to get a new one, and two days later, I'd find the lost check under the driver's seat in the G truck, in a brown paper bag from Dixie Liquor. Check and job performance report, right there in that bag.

Every time I tried to talk to Davo about my misgivings, he'd agree, and promise it wouldn't happen again. But it always did. Customers loved him. Crews loved him, and he and

I were friends. He was always a cheery light when business intensities pulled me into my shadow land of worry. It hurt to admit it, but I'd lost confidence in his ability to be the best he could be.

And I needed Big Boy Movers to be the best it could be. In many ways Big Boy was me, which made me abrasive and domineering at times and some movers found me tough to be around. But the jobs got done, and the company grew, because my standards were rarely compromised. We worked for our customers. Making Davo my partner would have made it impossible to oversee him—one doesn't monitor a partner. I wouldn't want to be guiding someone who was my business equal.

Davo handed me another beer, grinning like he was reading my mind. I knew he was taking Gino with him. "It's gonna be alright man," he said. "You still got Billy. And Mungo's coming onboard."

Bobbi Jo pulled into the lot as the sun settled and our last cans were emptied. She waved as if she knew what kind of a meeting we were having. But we all knew it was time.

I wished him luck in California. I asked him what he wanted me to do with all the stuff he'd left, items clients had given him after a successful move. Things like three barber's poles, a dog de-skunking harness, the motor scooter, and a fish tank full of prosthetics. "Sell 'em, man," he grinned as he pulled away. "They're worth bucks!"

Davo's tender side, his humor, and his lightness of being always offset the weight of problems that Big Boy Movers faced. I just hope Davo knows how grateful I am for what he brought to the company, because the good far outweighed the bad.

Ben at Home desk 8/23

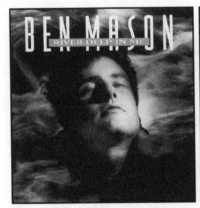

Albums:

River Deep in Me (1991), 48 States of Love (1998),
Loveland (2005), Flesh & Bone (2017-2018)

Art:
Ben's mixed media constructions

Artifacts:
Pamunkey (Native American Artifacts)
Found on Ben's property (Rappahannock)

Before-After:
Ben's Artwork "The Nest"; exterior of Home Studio

Ben and Family

Ben and Love:
Fan love note, Performing with Primadonna, loving couple (1978)

Ben Performing:
8/23 at Gadino Cellars in Washington, VA

Current portraits by T.J. POPKIN, 8/23

Ben Primadonna:
Performances 1976-1980

Early Years:
Ben with mother (1997), Mother dancing (1940s)

Family:
Ben, Henry, Arlo, Susan 2021

House:
Rappahannock (front and rear)

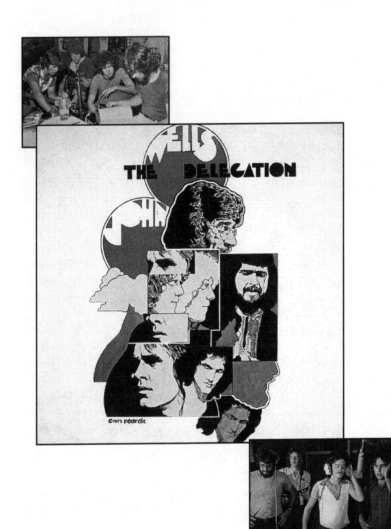

John Wells Delegation Album (1975),
JWD Album,
Recording @ Hit Factory in NYC

JWD: Evolution of the John Wells Delegation 1967-1976

Rites of Spring:
Mixed Media Construction of found objects on Ben's property

River:
Ben in Thornton River, summer & winter

Solo 90s:
Ben's 1990s performances incl. Rolling Thunder before 110,00 people

Trucks:
Big Boy Movers (Ben's Company in Falls Church, VA)

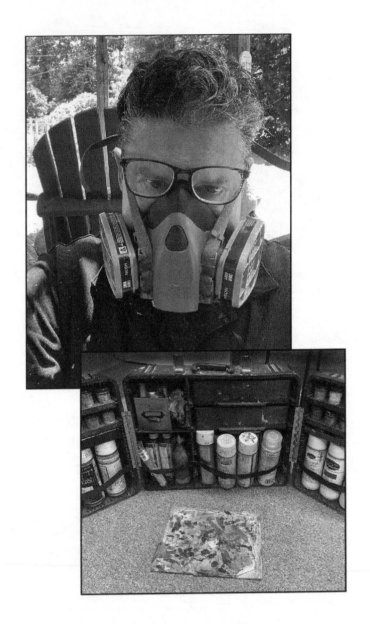

Work:
Big Boy Repair (Ben's Company)

JASMINE (1988)

I don't know you,
you don't know me

"You're a Secret"

Two days later I answered my front door, and I saw a face that made the blood rush to my head. I was nursing a hangover and at first, I thought it was just that, or the afternoon sun that was burning behind delicate eyes which now bore into mine. I said, "Hello," but the face remained impassive, and I wanted to ask, "How have you been?" Yet my mind silenced me.

The black-haired beauty stared through me and asked, "Is Bobbi Jo home?" The face began to grow hard and I felt scorn I'd long forgotten; I said, "Sure, she's here somewhere." Bounding giggles approached from behind me, and our smiles remained frozen as Bobbi Jo introduced us, joking that I was meeting "another loser from the Redskinette auditions."

But I already knew Jasmine. Sheltered in Bobbi Jo's happy hug, her eyes never left mine. As hard and black as coal in a bucket, they looked as dead as they had on the night I'd seen her last.

It had been over ten years ago, back when I was selling Native American jewelry: turquoise, red coral, mother of pearl, silver; all real, mostly. I'd play in DC bars with the John Wells Delegation, finish at two in the morning, and then offer my inventory to club owners, strippers, and massage parlor girls.

I'd met Jasmine at a club owned by Jimmy Jolson, an ex-Hells Angel whose little finger sported a massive diamond ring. Three fingers of that same hand were paralyzed in a gnarled fist; he'd broken them, killing the man he'd struck. Jimmy had done time for manslaughter, but he got a break because the guy he'd killed had chained JJ to the back of a Harley and dragged him a mile down a gravel road outside Omaha. "Be nice or you won't get any cookies" was tattooed on Jimmy's left bicep.

Back in his office, I opened my case. It was lunchtime, and through his two-way mirrors we watched businessmen tucking folded bills under dancers' G-strings.

The sounds of ZZ Top quaked the concrete bunker of JJ's office. He offered me a short glass with brown liquid in it and pointed at the top drawer of my open case. "How much for that squash blossom necklace?" It was Mexican silver, strung with teardrops of blue Kingman turquoise, and beads of black onyx and fire opal. We agreed on five hundred cash and my pick of any of the dancers working the lunch shift.

JJ introduced me to Jasmine after her shift, softly saying, "Remember what we talked about, Jasmine?" She'd nodded then, and with her hands in her raincoat pockets, and her shades perched on her regal nose, she reminded me of a librarian on lunch break. She looked at me with stubborn disgust, which I accepted.

Now I remembered attempting to kiss her, and how she'd stared up at the ceiling as she gave herself to me. At some point she'd spoken in a language I had never heard before, and when I asked her if she was ok, she calmly said, "What do you think?" I'd listened hard to my heart for an answer, but I felt so hollow inside that all I caught was the rustling sound of our breath. It had drawn me to the edge of somewhere I'd never been, where all I could see was cold blue emptiness.

In this dizzying moment, I saw a weaker me. I had taken part in the wounding of an innocent woman. Jasmine had been treated as property, and I'd let that secret be a shadow over the man I was. And now she was Bobbi Jo's friend. What a perfect paradox, that life would deliver this awakening to my own front door.

The silence felt heavy, outweighed by the mystery of why our paths had crossed again. I believe the Universe wanted us to heal. The truth had been in some dusty file cabinet that I'd locked up and vowed not to open. Now I was poring through it, reliving the lust, the fervor, and the ice-cold touch of her hands on my back. I still don't understand what drove me to take advantage of such a vulnerable spirit, doing something demeaning just to pay her bills. I felt myself asking for Divine forgiveness; I knelt like a pauper in my mind before some goddess of all that is pure and innocent. Jasmine was flesh and bone, but that goddess was within her, and I felt small in her presence.

I closed the front door and suggested that we go out to dinner. Bobbi Jo was excited and wanted Jasmine to be her maid of honor at our wedding.

Bobbi Jo and I were getting married in four months; doing the right thing. But had guilt convinced me it was the right thing to do? Did I feel some obligation to some legacy I was bound to continue carrying forward? My parents were still married; Bobbi Jo's parents were still married. Marriage was a promise engraved by sacred trust, born from faith in commitment. And yet I knew there were typos in that inscription and flaws in the terms of what we would be appearing to uphold. I wondered if I was being honest with myself.

We were on different spiritual paths, but the Divine had brought us together for a reason; I was certain of it. Bobbi Jo had wandered away from me at times, but the troubles I'd gone through to understand her had opened my heart and had made me more forgiving of her, and of myself. Some things had hurt, but the breaks in my heart had let more light in, and I wasn't as afraid of the wild unknown that Bobbi Jo seemed to attract into our lives.

Forgiveness was a flickering candle at our table. I saw it glowing in Jasmine's eyes as the girls discussed wedding details. By the time we'd finished eating, our candle had melted, but one blue flame refused to surrender, as persistent as the hope I held in my heart.

Jasmine and Bobbi Jo were in their own little world as I followed the stumbling turns of an old jazz standard from a piano in the next room. The girls lowered their voices as if a secret was being shared, something about that "David guy" who had introduced them at the Redskinette audition. "What a hound dog," I heard one of them mutter. Then they both laughed, and I caught a raised eyebrow from Bobbi Jo as if she had more to tell Jasmine later. In the candlelight, they glowed like roses, and whatever I had hidden in that dusty file cabinet inside myself remained as a distant memorial.

Yet as I handed the waiter my credit card that evening, I wondered what other debts would surprise me. The weaker me and the stronger me were bound together, and each would reap what the other sowed.

CHAPTER 29

RIVER DEEP IN ME (1988)

*Father pours and
mother stirs*

"River Deep in Me"

Bobbi Jo and I celebrated our wedding mid-May at Selma, a Civil War-era mansion north of Leesburg, with satin, black-suited waiters and caterers, and a seven-piece rock band. My parents were beaming, but as I looked at myself in the bathroom mirror, a wrinkled baby blue face appeared behind my own. It was Great. I was in her baby carriage, ushered toward where I was meant to be. A sense of obligation twinkled like diamonds in my eyes; there'd be no turning back now. Whatever missteps I'd made lay like gentle hands upon me.

My stoic expression wavered in the steam as my razor, catching a cheek mole, sent my blood trickling.

Though I hadn't finished shaving, I closed the bathroom door behind me, Great whispering, "Hard times, never broke you down enough to keep you from getting up." But maybe that was just me, rehearsing lines for a song I'd written for the wedding, "Thank God for Hard Times":

"Thank God for hard times; they made you the girl I love."

Bobbi Jo's family thanked me with tears in their eyes. It was hard to deny my sense of obligation, and even harder admitting the doubts that came with it. Those were my "Hard

Times" . . . a song I wasn't yet ready to write.

"Life is just a drink, Time is just a glass, and we all need re-minding not to drink it down too fast"

"Love is how we taste it and we taste what we deserve, and we vow to share it all, every blessing, every curse"

We had ring bearers, bridesmaids, and sushi I'd rolled at 3 a.m. Big Boy Movers ferried guests up to Selma from the parking area. Big Boy Movers delivered ice to oak barrels filled with beer. And then they pissed behind boxwoods like this event was just another fucking truck lot party.

Bobbi Jo was Bohemian regal in an Art Nouveau gown of chiffon and lace. Jasmine was an exotic maid of honor in a pink leather mini skirt. Everyone smiled at us so proudly, even the dozen ushers, all movers, all shit-faced in stiff tuxedos, reminding me how I'd arrived at this sweltering mansion. At one point, Dave R. fainted in an aisle. He remained in a snoring heap as we led everyone outside to eat at white-clothed tables and admire the views cascading beyond Route 15. Two hours later, over two hundred guests followed us down Selma's cart-wide lane, anointing our union with flowers and bird seed.

We had open door sex in the Stingray behind our honeymoon hotel and flew to St. Maarten at sunrise. I shared song ideas with my bride on a nude beach, and as we ate crisped sea scallops on the French side at La Vin en Rose, Bobbi Jo told me she was pregnant. We intertwined fingers and I asked her if she was scared. I felt shivers of tension; maybe that was fear; maybe it was shock. In a way I was cornered, as some giant new life bore down upon me. I envisioned life without performances, applause, or albums. But my smiling wife pushed dessert around her plate, and we sat united in silence. A child was coming to show us who we were born to be. I could do this. I knew that somehow, the truest love of all would be that of a child. But it was hard to wrap my arms around that feeling as I imagined the strength it would take. I barely slept that night.

But Bobbi Jo wasn't pregnant. She just wanted to know how married we were. She'd wanted our honeymoon baby to unite us, but the truth was born a week later, with her lie wrapped in an apology. I couldn't find the words, but I was angry, and though I didn't want to admit it, I was disappointed too. The loss was confusing. I held on to the image I'd had of myself as a father—that guy lived inside me, and I caught glimpses of him in the maze of emotions that surrounded me, until the savage face of betrayal was all that remained.

And that just made my songwriting dream kick harder inside of me. I'd been keeping track of my inner growth, and a slew of notebooks with scribbled gems and drunken screeds lay like a dry stacked wall on my piano. My dedication to my craft, and my pride in what I was writing, created an irresistible image in my mind. I was not too old to do this. I was singing better than ever and as everyone knows, hits are all about The Song. And I was certain I had more than one hit. My connections in New York and Nashville would grace me with a phone conversation, maybe even a face-to-face meeting. But I needed to be able to deliver the goods. When we returned home I found an experienced producer in John Jennings. He was also producing Mary Chapin Carpenter's first album, and we worked well together. I finished a song called "River Deep in Me". It would be the title of my first album.

"*Father pours and Mother stirs . . . the mix they make is a mystery to me . . . so I swim down in myself, to see this thing nobody else can see . . . river deep in me.*" Maybe the father I'd seen wandering in that maze of emotions was my musical self, searching for what I'd been creating since I was thirteen years old. Everything and everyone had been created by the Divine. Bobbi Jo had given me an opportunity to accept what The Divine had created. And every growing pain was as perfect as what was born with it. Because rock and roll would soon be bounding through my house again. It would spring from my heart, from my seat of wisdom, and hoaxes would be trampled into dust by its truth. My baby was on the move.

CHAPTER 30

A FATHER'S LOVE (1970)

I watched a sheriff hand me the phone

"Tough Love"

My father lost his mother when he was thirteen. Minerva died of an infection in her right eye. This was in 1933, before the discovery of penicillin. Daddy's father went on to marry again, twice. He was a published writer, a photographer, an engineer at the Norfolk shipyards and the editor of "Whitelaw's Guide to the Eastern Shore." He was always writing or lecturing or traveling to give talks to ladies' clubs who'd invited him to be their guest speaker. His second and third wives also died, and my sense is that my grandfather comforted himself by constantly working. My dad said my grandfather sequestered himself, even during vacations, writing or photographing birds, wildflowers, and colonial churches, all of which he wrote books about. My own father was his opposite.

Daddy made himself available to me, and my younger sister and brother. He was an illustrious storyteller, a tenor guitarist, and an entertaining extrovert; prone to breaking into song. He was whimsical, silly, and playful while still being what I considered a serious person. He dispatched his advice with certainty, but what my father said to me as I came into my late teen years was his boldest message. He told me that I should get married and have children as soon as possible. That essence settled upon me in all our talks, and I wrote it off as an intoxication that satisfied him. That gave him a chance to say what his father had not.

But now I'm certain that the shelter I gave my movers later, my patience with them and the financial assistance that I provided them, was my way of being a father. This was apparent when Davo would call me Dad, and obvious in the long talks and second chances I offered them after they'd "misbehaved." My role model was ingrained in me. I had experienced a patient, loving father who bailed me out of trouble, even after he'd been so lenient that he'd lent me the family car, knowing I was heading to Ohio in it with drugs. Much as I had let my movers "borrow" one of my trucks, knowing full well that they might misuse that privilege. And they did. But like my father before me, I trusted them, and I was willing to let them make mistakes, knowing I could usually bail them out of their dustups with the law.

But I had escape clauses in my agreement as a surrogate father to my movers. I had insurance, and I could fire them. I didn't have a genetic responsibility to them hanging over my head. My father wanted to give me every chance to find my way. He wanted to let me make my own decisions. There was no artifice. He was simply present, and never behind some closed door writing a book about the native ferns of Virginia. But I do wish he'd laid down the law, as I did with my movers, when it really mattered. I still can't believe he let me use the family car, after asking me if I was taking that "leather bag along." He knew it was full of drugs. He should have crossed the threshold and did what I did when my movers were too drunk to drive: asked for the keys, until he knew I was making a sober decision.

Four days later, both of our decisions changed my life

forever. I was eighteen years old.

I'd been asleep in my father's station wagon, stretched out on the back seat, still half-tripping on the LSD I'd eaten at a Chicago concert in Cleveland the night before. Up front, frizzy-haired Frank was driving, his girlfriend Lynne beside him, both still tripping on whatever they'd ingested.

We got pulled over because Frank was going 13 mph as we passed the Pennsylvania State Troopers' barracks outside Somerset. I remember hearing panicky distorted sounds, and I woke up as Lynne said "pigs, spanked by pigs. Red bacon lights. Sausage hot behind us."

We were rousted from the car. I was bent over the hood, a gun held to my head; told I'd be shot if I resisted. The leather bag of drugs I'd slid under the back seat was raised up like a trophy by a crew cut trooper in the six am sunlight. My navy bell-bottoms and jean jacket were pulled off me as we were handcuffed and loaded into separate squad cars.

The troopers said I'd be making my phone call when we got to the jail in Somerset. They led me across the town square in my underwear, sock-footed and chained on a Sunday morning. I staggered up some worn steps into the magistrate's office as churchgoers passed by. It was spring-time, and birds flitted between the red buds. Someone's mother said, "He's a hippie, don't look." I was shoved into a chair and handed a phone.

I never saw Frank and Lynne again. I was the one in trouble as my father's name was on the vehicle registration. I was the one who had heroin, needles and syringes, LSD, a hash pipe, and MDMA, all in that smooth blonde leather bag. This was a Class One felony and would send me away for thirty years according to Trooper Crew Cut.

After three nights in jail, and some chili and stale

crackers, I was released on a fifty-thousand-dollar bond. I drove for three hours and parked in my parents' carport in Annandale.

My mother was drinking bourbon at eleven in the morning and as she hugged me, I felt her shaking as she sobbed.

My father beckoned me over to where he sat at his desk, an old postmaster's desk that had compartments he'd labeled with phrases like "bills," "funnies," and "kids' notes." I noticed his glasses were taped together in the middle, and he looked like the actor Gregory Peck. His shirt was plaid, he had his ink pen out and he used it to point at his bank balance in a dark blue check book. I thought I was about to get a scorching lecture. But he was calm, cool in a way I hadn't seen before. He got right to business.

"It's going to be alright," he said. To bail me out, he'd taken out a second mortgage; I could use my paper route earnings to pay him back. I slumped into a chair beside him, feeling like I'd woken up in a movie starring my dad. He went on. "I got you the best lawyer I could find."

He'd called a neighbor, a local attorney who'd referred him to a venerable lawyer in Somerset named Archibald Matthews, who had a long-standing relationship with judges who'd allowed moonshiners to supply hideaway bars in that part of Pennsylvania.

Archibald Matthews' steady requests made sense. I was to get clean and keep my GPA up. I registered with the Fairfax County drug rehabilitation clinic and joined The Group, a circle of addicts who met three times a week to garner leniency from the Virginia court system. Every Monday, Wednesday, and Friday I urinated into a plastic testing cup in the men's room. I swore I was not going to use again. But Reggie, The Group's leader, said I was an insect, and that was why I was in The Group.

Suzanne, the bellows-bodied brunette who monitored us, told everyone I was the only one who was still clean since joining. "Not a single positive," she said, laying her hands on my shoulders. But I was still using. My junkie colleagues in the district had told me to drink a hot mug of Real Lemon juice after I shot up, and it would wash away the quinine and morphine. I was still an insect, but I was to all appearances, a clean insect.

I'd been doing heroin for over a year at that point, and still not disgusted enough to go cold turkey. I reached that point on the way to a Santana concert at the Baltimore Civic Center. I was driving my 1960 Mercedes four-seat sedan. My new girlfriend Laurice and her two friends were in the car. A mile from the Civic Center it hit me. I'd shot up too much heroin. I began retching out the driver's side window.

It snaked down the door of my grey Mercedes in full view of fellow travelers whose windows were open. I remember parking and following the girls inside. Seated front row center, I stretched my limp legs out, and let the seat of the chair be a pillow for my back. A security person paced by as I sank lower toward the floor, until my arms crossed over my chest as if I were a corpse. I was warned to "sit up or get out." I tried. But even the bombastic rhythms of a two-drummer band and the undulating wail of Carlos Santana's guitar couldn't keep me awake. The warmth of my own urine finally snapped me into place, and I remained on high alert, stiffly upright, unwilling to let anyone see that I had pissed my pants. I had on a new shirt with the sleeves rolled down to hide my needle tracks. If I'd had the energy, I'd have torn off that vomit-soaked rag and shoved it into a trash can.

I quit heroin that night and never went back to The Group. For the next three weeks, I stayed in the Falls

Church apartment I shared with Laurice, sweating and trembling as the poison left me.

As I kicked, I had nightmares about the felony charges. I could do nothing but stay clean and keep my grades up. My parents checked on me, calling often. They came over with a steak. My mother knew Laurice was a vegetarian and she worried about my diet. During that visit, my father took me aside and told me that after a dinner party at our house, he'd told the six couples present, all my parents' best friends, about what had happened to me.

"Everyone knows," he'd said calmly. But this was not conveyed to make me feel guilty. My father just wanted me to know that I was loved, and that everyone was aware I was looking at thirty years in the federal penitentiary. We had friends who were that close to us, and they appeared in my mind like family I didn't realize I had. I imagined my mother's face as he'd told them; sensed the tears she'd held back. I couldn't find the words to tell him, but my father had been my shepherd, and pride flickered in his eyes. I'd gotten clean, and I was safe, surrounded by people who might have gone through worse terrors.

Four months later, on a morning cloaked with ominous dark clouds, I sat in Somerset Courthouse with my parents and Archibald Matthews. I was in a suit, clean, straight, and ready to receive my sentence. I stood up to hear the cold hard facts of life. When the judge declared that my charges were being dismissed due to "an illegal search and seizure," the Pennsylvania State trooper with the crew cut charged toward the seated judge. "Look at this!" he cried.

In his outstretched hand were pills of heroin and my syringe. "He should get thirty years for this," he shouted, as my father ushered his family toward the exit. I'll never forget how a magnificent blue sky appeared like an answered prayer as I hugged my dad on the courthouse steps.

So I tried to be that man to my movers now, and my business child was thriving. Even without Davo and now Gino, who'd also moved to California, shortly after the wedding at Selma. In the week before he left, Gino had totaled a Korean minister's car with the E truck, walked off a move while tripping on mushrooms, and made it clear that he hated me. I wrote him a letter of recommendation but tossed it; remembering that he had once slept on hay in a horse stable, and that I had given him a job and a rent-free room in my basement. He was one of our best movers, ever. And I was just another male figure of authority who reminded him that a man had gotten his mother pregnant ten times, and that a man had created the math that robbed him of the attention every child needs.

Real love is what we are. A spark of The Divine within. Maybe Gino needed to escape the shadow I cast over him to see that light.

CHAPTER 31

MOVING THE MARSHALS (1990)

They took my name, took my face, say I'm free

"Dead to You"

Billy was at lunch and I was manning the basement office phone when the US Marshals Service called. A flat foreign voice said they needed a discreet moving company, who could relocate thirty offices in unmarked trucks from a clandestine location in Tysons Corner mall. "Could I give an estimate?" he asked.

I followed the directions carefully. I was to enter the mall, find Pet World, and knock on their stock room door. The voice had said: "Tell them you need cedar chips for your hamster cage. They'll let you in. You'll see an elevator. Press the button with the smiley face on it."

I did all that, descending slowly until I stood under a wash of fluorescent light. A thick-browed man in a gray blazer filled a doorway down the hall. He waved jerkily, like a salute he'd given up trying to perfect. "Ben? Over here, I'm Yuri, welcome to US Marshals Service."

I got frisked in Yuri's office, where a somber wall plaque was emblazoned with the words Polish Strip Search Academy. His garlic breath suggested the new kabob place next to Pet World. He made copies of my Virginia driver's license and Big Boy Movers' insurance certificate. "Okay, fine," he said, throwing a silk jacket over the cattle prod attached to his belt.

His bald spot glowed confidently as he led me through a subterranean maze. He'd tap on a door, and a dimly-lit office would appear. Conversation would end, a phone would be clasped, and a handlebar mustache would track everything I observed. A vintage revolver in a holster slung over a chair would catch my eye, and I'd write down desk/chair/credenza/four-drawer file cab on my inventory pad. As Yuri closed the door behind us, I caught a voice drawling, "He's got tits now? Go pick that fucker up."

This underground workspace was all sharp turns and shadows, but an iron cage filled a brightly lit area Yuri called the museum. Thick worn bars stretching twelve feet long and six feet high were mounted to a western-style wagon. It was the Marshals' original portable jail, which carried prisoners to trial before the railroad was built. "Don't worry, you're not moving that," Yuri said dismissively.

The genesis of frontier justice, hidden in this crypt, posed as unceremoniously as a priesthood of lawmen walking incognito through a shopping mall. The roots of their service appeared as silver stars stabbed into black leather vests, cowboy boots resting on worn desks, and in the head shots of criminals, with sharpies marking them captured or dead. But in a crowd they all just looked like regular guys who liked to work out.

At a metal door Yuri said, "Can't stay too long in here." He fingered a set of keys and wiggled one into the lock. Shoving the door open, he said, "WITSAK room." Witness Protection files, all in 1.5 cubic foot cartons, clearly labeled with names/aliases and addresses. Yuri said, "Seven hundred twenty boxes here," and I imagined the weight of all those new identities, and maybe new fingerprints, courtesy of Uncle Sam.

I left with a legal pad of notes: thirty workstations and over a thousand boxes, though the Marshals would pack themselves. We'd need ninety four-wheel dollies; we'd rent them. Yuri said no security clearances, he didn't want a paper trail. He said not to wear shirts or hats with Big Boy Movers' logo on them, and that all movers must sign a release stating they understood that violating or stealing US Marshal property was a federal crime.

The relocation was scheduled for a Tuesday night, between 10 p.m. and 8 a.m. when Tysons Mall was closed. Each twenty-four- foot truck could hold six offices; for thirty offices we'd need five rental trucks. A sixth truck would be used just for boxes. We'd flat load everything, float it on, and dolly it off at the new location which Yuri said was beneath a suburban retirement home. We'd use eighteen guys, three per truck, with the Marshals providing security during the long carry to the loading dock. I called my connection in the President's Honor Guard at the 8th and I barracks in SW, DC. A dozen Marines would join our six best movers on Tuesday evening.

Strategies left my mind that night as a lacey thing landed on the pillow next to me. The sun was teasing the curtains as a silken rump bent to get something from a drawer and I caught what looked like a hickey on the back of Bobbi Jo's neck. She turned around. "I like that new song," she said. "Is it about me?"

Reflexively I answered "Yep," because the lyrics spun like a roulette wheel, and the blur of where our hearts would land was the essence of the song. As I toyed with the melody, I forged a sensuous blend of strength and patience and burnished it with minor chords the color of hickeys and bruises. Lately my inspirations had come from meditations on acceptance of who I'd married. Bobbi Jo's hunger was insatiable and reminded me of a stove arriving before me still warm, yet carelessly scented with the sweet fury it had created elsewhere.

I tried to practice detachment as I undid snaps and zippers. Under a waterfall of auburn-streaked tresses, our secrets were like altered identities in the WITSAK boxes.

CHAPTER 32

DANNY (1990)

*You were stronger
than I ever knew*

"Hard Times"

I talked to Danny Casolaro every day, for years. We amused each other, agreeing that everybody had a job, but we didn't. We were self-made men, without bosses, who harnessed our skills for putting words together. We were both songwriters, and I wanted another record deal, but Danny had a different plan. He was writing a book, *The Octopus*, an idiosyncratic account of murder, international espionage, and government theft. I'd seen his handwritten outline. His chapters and photocopies of "evidence" spanned the globe. The names of political figures and three-letter agencies were wound together in a ball of corruption, more dense than any one man could unravel.

And that's why Danny told me about it, in details so involved, that I began taking notes. I was rooting for him to get that big publishing deal, for the world to meet the complicated mystery he called *The Octopus*, whose relentless tentacles stretched all over the world. Danny had woven the Japanese Yakuza, Israeli Intelligence, the BCCI and Iran-Contra scandals, the CIA, the Bay of Pigs, Allende's Chile, The Heritage Foundation, the American Mafia, and a Cabazon Indian reservation in California into a body of work as a solo, independent investigative journalist. And hence, he was vulnerable to the reckoning which followed the invariable death threats he'd gotten.

He talked to dozens of characters, many in different time zones, and would ask for my sense of where this monster was leading him. Our conversations were too colorful to remember and too unbelievable to repeat. And we agreed that whatever he said, and I heard, stayed on that phone line, between us. But I wrote everything down.

I'd mentioned at some point that Big Boy was relocating the US Marshals. I never said when. I never said where. And I never said how bizarre it was to see their clandestine operation not three miles from where I lived. But after it all went down, I remembered Danny's visit.

He'd dropped by to use the hot tub, and in the glare of the February sun, we'd sat outside, sipping coffee at a patio table. I'd had the business phone and Big Boy Movers schedule book with me. I got up to take a leak behind the boxwoods that sheltered the pool. When I came back and settled into my chair I saw that I'd left the schedule book open. In black ink was my bold script. "US Marshals Move 10 pm, Tuesday, February 11. Tysons Underground garage."

I'd closed the book and asked him how the writing was going. He described a new contact, somebody that knew where the "money was coming from."

"I'm a bad hombre," he'd laughed when I reminded him that this same source was involved with a Mexican cartel.

"And the death threats? They still coming?" His housekeeper, Inga, had told me she was very worried for "Mr. Danny."

He didn't answer right away, but with a bathrobe on and a towel around his neck, he looked like the boxer he'd once been. "I just tell 'em to make it fast, brother," he'd said. Then he wanted to know if I had any Irish whiskey. "I think that stolen PROMIS software is being sold by a Black Box inside Justice. To that cartel. The intelligence veneer lets Justice track the cartel. And the cartel gets to launder its money. And the Black Box buys off whoever is sniffing around."

I tipped the bottle into our mugs. A shot or two apiece, it was the end of a quiet day. Nobody had called threatening to kill me. But some hard-bitten lady did complain that one of my movers had really "stunk up her powder room." As I watched Danny thinking, I forgot all about what he might have seen in my schedule book.

At ten o'clock sharp that night, we slid the six trucks into the underground garage at Tysons Corner. Yuri met us at the dock and collected driver's licenses from all eighteen movers. Including me. Inside, he gave everybody a quick tour, and by 10:15 pm we were rolling. Every office was a two-man slam dunk of one desk tilted onto a four-wheel dolly, with file cabs and boxes leaned into place on hand trucks. Chairs and odd-shaped items like gun racks were padded up and nested on the remaining four wheelers. Chatter was kept to a minimum, and the watchful eyes of various US Marshals oversaw all interferences as doors, tight corners, and elevator entrances were abated by helping hands or stern directives. Movers chugged water occasionally, but all thirty offices were emptied at breakneck speed.

The WITSAK room was wall-to-wall boxes, all labeled, and in that gloomy space, shafts of leaden light fell upon us as we worked. We were told not to read what was written on these labeled cartons, but that they were to remain upright, with labels legible on the front side facing inward. "That way we can restack 'em like they are now," Yuri said as he held the door for the hand trucks that our drivers pushed. "Only your top guys in the WITSAK room," Yuri had ordered.

The rumbling floating of dollies and the stacking slam of boxes against truck walls was finalized by the snap of the nylon strap that held each layer of the load in place. We didn't want to stack the load any higher than how it had been rolled onto the truck, as we could then disperse the load out of each truck just as it had been inserted. The only catch was that these floating sections needed to be padded tightly, assuring that they would not rub against each other, creating damages. I had been warned that we would be docked for scratches or breakage that occurred. And that I would never be allowed to return to the premises of the drop-off after the relocation was completed.

This solemn atmosphere spread throughout each area of the move, but about halfway through the load-up, the energy lightened. I caught some banter between the movers and the blank-faced Marshals that had to have seen the darkening sweat on the fabric of the plain white T-shirts I'd instructed the crew to wear. Somebody handed out sandwiches and Gatorade around 2 a.m., but conversation was still kept to a bare minimum. I heard the words "Thanks," and "Would you like some champagne with that?" but otherwise, the mood was all business. I noticed Yuri checking his watch, and we crossed paths several times, as both of us attempted to be everywhere at once.

Around 5 a.m., I heard Mungo shout, laughing, "Yuri, thanks for the new dudes. Wish they spoke better English." Mungo had been a silent blur up until now, and I was surprised to hear this change in tone. He'd been the lead man on the often-crowded dock, directing movers as they queued up from inside the building. He'd been overseeing everything that was floated on and fit into place, in command of all six trucks, winching straps tighter, and adjusting pads as necessary. Yuri was standing next to me, pointing to emptied offices on a diagram when he heard Mungo shout. His eyes snapped toward Mungo's voice. He shoved his clipboard toward me. "Take this," he said. His radio was barking when he jumped off the dock. I followed.

There had been little talk on the loading dock, no sounds, just the scudding thud of items finding their place inside the trucks. The light was quicksilver smoke, unpredictable in how it shifted as I ran. I could feel the quiet shattering around me, no one had directed me to follow, but I knew there had been a break in the security of what I had assured Yuri, and I wanted to be present; to take responsibility if we had breached the sanctity of my promises to him. I saw his broad back, and the ink of an ornate tattoo as his jacket and shirt lifted. He was sprawled over, peering under the last truck on the dock. Papers were scattered in its shadow, and he used one leg to drag them toward him.

A black van sabered past. I heard a shout—or was it a laugh? Then a rising curse and a zapping sound, and the echo of doors slamming. I followed Yuri back onto the dock where a mustached man in a leather jacket was wrapping plastic ties around the wrists of a mover squirming on the cement. Another mover lay in a fetal position, his mouth open in a silent scream as a Marshal held a booted foot to his neck. Three WITSAK boxes lay on their sides, their contents broadcast between the edge of the dock and the pavement beneath it. Some papers had fallen behind the truck, but Yuri grabbed them and shoved everything back into the open WITSAK cartons. As he closed them up, two movers I'd never seen before were jostled into the black van. I had no idea who they were, and Mungo, addressing a cowboy-hatted man in a suit, said, "Hey, I didn't know they were going through boxes." Tires squealed as the black van shot out of the tunnel. The compromised cartons were examined by a third man, a kneeling Marshal with a silver cattle prod.

He held it like a sporty baton, tapping the labeled boxes as he drawled, "Cali Cartel, Yuri, how'd they know we were moving?" He holstered some blinking device and gave me a hard look like I wasn't supposed to be listening. But I'd seen the words "Escobar/Wilson" on several papers Yuri had scooped up. I wondered if that connection of names would find its way from this move to save someone's life. Or end it.

I regretted telling Danny that Big Boy was moving the US Marshals. I'd tossed it off as idle drunken talk; easily forgotten. But I felt used. And the danger he was racing toward, and the breakneck pace at which he kept it up, made him reckless and foolish.

I recalled that he'd bragged that he discovered how one of the tentacles of the Octopus slipped out of a black box in the Department of Justice, straight to Mexico, into the cocaine highlands owned by the Cali Cartel. Danny had been wrestling this monster for three years, but this Cali connection was new. "And it's irrefutable proof; Pulitzer Prize stuff," he'd said.

I'd warned him, "Don't mess with them." But by the mess I'd seen on the Marshals' loading dock, Danny already had.

When the WITSAK move was completed, Yuri sat with me in an unmarked van as the six trucks began to leave. He never said a word about the two errant movers or the compromised WITSAK boxes. And the nursing home residents had no idea that they had new neighbors beneath them. The US Marshals entrance tunnel was concealed behind the refuse crematorium outside Green Springs Manor.

I got the check two days later. Made out to Big Boy Movers, Inc. Five beautiful figures, and so far, not a damage claim to blemish them. I gave bonuses to everybody who'd made the move happen. I told Billy he could leave early.

Then I went upstairs and read the note Bobbi Jo had left on my pillow. "Won't be home 'til Saturday, David needs me on a project in Pennsylvania." The little note looked like a happy butterfly with an erection. There was a lipstick smooch above Bobbi Jo's signature.

The US Marshals track down criminals all over the world. But there's no law that says your wife can't go three states away for what she calls "work." I released the butterfly into the toilet. I had a birthday party to plan.

CHAPTER 33

THE PARTY (1988)

She can walk her tightrope,
I won't be the net

"Running and Reckless"

Bobbi Jo is turning thirty. I'm writing a song for her, naturally, in the key of B. There's a diminished chord (C# E G A#) in the bridge, hinting at the strain in our eight years together, but the verse chords are strongly wrought, C# m to B to A, to portray her patience as Big Boy Movers matured in our basement. She's the only female in this rumbling house of men; a sexy den mother to the movers who push through the side door and catch her at the sink in the kitchen. She's always ready with iced tea or water, and I know she's amused by their clumsy flirting. I mean, she's right there in her sheer bathrobe or jeans shorts and I'm proud of how she keeps her cool. "No, I won't stir your tea with my finger," I heard her say last week. "We have sugar, right here."

Her beauty makes me feel like I deserved her; that I'm being rewarded for building this new life, with her in it. I'm hammering out deals, doing business with bullies and freeloaders, but she's my foxy counterpart, and I'm impressed with how rarely she rolls her eyes. Last night the guys slammed the side door and thundered down the basement stairs. A long move, but not too late for a wolf whistle and an off-color joke about redheads. It woke her up. But I saw her grin as she stood at the sink in her shorty pajamas.

And if she sprays Gino, who keeps leering at her orange bikini as she washes her Porsche, that's another flirty scolding from his den mother. This familiarity doesn't bother me; Big Boy Movers is all about close quarters. It helps me know who's working for me, and this growing family of worthy dudes is a huge reason we're successful. And it's not Bobbi Jo's fault that she's the best-looking woman in our commune.

The song is called "I Can't Make You Do Anything." "You are like an ocean, always moving, always open. You are like the currents of the sea. You are like the seasons, always perfect, always leaving, and I can't change what is meant to be."

The lines arrive as if I've already written them. "You're just beyond my reach, but I learn what love can teach, it's everywhere you and I have been."

Bobbi Jo and I have been all over the DC area, in rooms luminous with truths hidden under shiny outfits. Perhaps our party spore still sparkles in the night, glistening amber-like in the cracks of more than a few strangers' hearts. Like sumptuous imprints of sculpted flesh on expensive hotel sheets. The fabric of our social life is a colorful weave of models, ex-cons, White House appointees, photojournalists, hillbilly poets, fruitarians, punk rockers, and even a national news anchor. One night he snorted his cocaine and tossed his empty brown vial under my English boxwood, where I weeded it out, spoon and all, still the color of his camera-ready skin.

Some of those characters may show up at the surprise party I'm planning for Bobbi Jo. It will not be a party I'd invite our families to.

• • •

I was in bed, leafing through mental images. I saw faces, but

I was having a hard time remembering the names of Bobbi Jo's friends. With the help of a worn phone book, I was making progress. I was up to about ninety people when my wife came home early—David's Pennsylvania project had been cut short. She discovered her birthday surprise as she rolled naked over the guest list on the blanket. An ink-sodden piece of paper, infused with sweat, really does leave a tattoo on bare skin. "Don't invite her," she said, pointing at a name on her left thigh. I made a little pun.

"I barely . . . know your friends," I said. Actually, I realized I really didn't know her friends.

As I reached for the fallen invitations on the floor, I felt Bobbi Jo's fingers on my shoulder, making sure I wouldn't slip away. How do you tell someone that holding on is getting harder to do? The air wasn't filled with words, but I heard each of us reminding the other that we were still trying.

Bobbi Jo's birthday was in March. On the brittle morning of the party, I swung the leaf blower over every surface where bare feet might wander, dumped burnout in the hot tub, heated the pool, and set out the good towels. I opened cases of frozen cheese and meat triangles, pita pocket melts, champagne, and wine. I hired two movers to hang twinkling lights and ice the beer kegs, and I set up my airbrushed drums and piano in the basement. We cleared the lot of trucks, and closed the office at noon, to give us some breathing room before our six o'clock appointment with 120 guests.

By sundown, Bobbi Jo was flushed with expectation. Squeezed into her birthday mini kilt, she looked wide-eyed and flawless. At six sharp she was in the foyer, welcoming people to what was obviously an already spoiled surprise party. Outside, snow rustled down like feathers from dark blue pillows hanging over the house. Inside, champagne was flowing. Three movers in rented tuxedos masqueraded as waiters, offering party favors from cardboard trays made of folded book boxes. Guests tucked Big Boy Movers T-shirts and ball caps into gift bags as sparkling ice struck windows like albino gnats in flight. New arrivals inspired giggling bursts from Bobbi Jo. I heard whispered invitations between guests as doors closed behind them. I hovered discreetly, wanting the party to be about the birthday girl and her freedom.

In back porch shadows I took off my pants. Guests were slipping into the warmth of the heated black pool. I joined them in water that became a misty cloud, but I stared up, the snowflakes tickling my face. It reminded me of a March night in 1979, when I'd driven twenty-three hours straight from Panama City, Florida. Snowflakes had welcomed me then as I walked toward this very house, expecting something wonderful to embrace me. But what I had witnessed had crushed my heart. It felt like centuries ago. I was not that man, not that reckless musician, angry enough to risk arrest. If Divine providence had steered me, it was to be here, in this womb-like water, grateful for a rebirth, grateful for the perspective I had now.

Shadows of blue light settled over two women embracing, locks of hair entwined like seaweed. Somebody hooted and they separated; I saw the silhouettes of their breasts. Revelers splashed around me, like so many caimans, carelessly playful. But I was invisible.

My consciousness rose over the pool, as I retraced my path from the band truck to the window, turning the whisper of snowflakes into a Fever Tree song, "San Francisco Girls." I held my breath and went deeper, letting the weight of forgiveness overwhelm me. I apologized to lovers on my bed. In my mind was an ethereal voice, saying give and receive only love.

I rolled into the hot tub, resting my chin on the cool slate. Someone brought their mouth onto my neck; a tongue as tender as boiled okra swept my lips. Flesh and bone are made of stardust and light, and I tasted both as someone said my name. Jasmine had arrived. Forgiveness became a feeling as she took my face in her hands. There were no words; just the silence of that innocent kiss, as I felt both of us letting go of the past.

What happens at our parties is performance art. It grows like a tribe of nomads; feasting on a carcass of fun, as we urge body parts into its greasy openings, and there, in our fiery cave, under a pagan moon, we make love to it, and smear it all over ourselves until we pass out. And the performance ends when you leave the party.

I made my way back inside. The heat felt good, and I caught sight of Bobbi Jo and Jasmine slipping into a bedroom. I was wrapping a towel around my snow-soaked head like a turban when a hearty voice rang out. "Benjamin!" It was Danny Casolaro.

Finally, someone I could talk to, and gently interrogate. Danny raised his beer; "To Bobbi Jo," he grinned. Danny, the bulldog blonde Italian. "I'm a bad hombre," he'd always say.

"Danny," I said, "Cut the crap." I told him about the WIT-SAK papers strewn around the dock and the fake movers. I reminded him about our afternoon beside my pool, and I wondered if he'd snuck a peak at my schedule book.

He admitted he'd been trading information with someone who knew someone in a Mexican cartel. "A legit source," he said as he popped another Olympia beer. And he might have let it slip that the Marshals were moving. Might have said Big Boy Movers. Maybe the witness protection program had come up. He frowned. "What? I didn't say when the move was. How would I know that?"

We were in the midst of a birthday party. I wasn't going to let my anger show. But he deliberately manipulated our code of secrecy. I never told anyone what he told me. I assumed he respected me the same way. But he'd picked up the scent of what lay in the bowels of some building which he described as a black box within the DOJ. "The very heart of the beast," he'd said. So I listened as he took me aside and told me what he'd done.

He knew it could cost him his life. He'd already been warned not to go to a certain red brick three-story townhouse on Jackson Place near the White House. He'd been warned by the people who'd invented PROMIS software and who believed they'd sold it to the DOJ. He'd been warned that it was a sensitive building used by Justice, and probably where PROMIS software had been manipulated. But he'd gone there, alone, full of bluster. Even though he never made it inside, there'd been a car chase, and the death threats had intensified.

Under Danny's bluster was a trusting soul, meeting with psychos playing on all sides of the law. I knew the details of the death threats; the whispers of professional ghosts tailing him. Of course I worried about him. But he was a torrent of energy, unstoppable, and who was I to thwart his plunge into the dark water where the monster he pursued lurked; multi-faced, decades old, and wealthy beyond measurement. I'd had a firsthand look at his outline of *The Octopus*. He had the goods. At least most all the goods that mattered. And that damning treasure was always with him, in a reddish-brown briefcase or stacked against a wall in his basement bedroom in Fairfax, Virginia.

I trusted Danny's sense of duty. I didn't trust his sense of danger. I prayed that God would protect him, but the words in my head sounded like fruitless murmurs. Danny was bound for divine illumination. That was his destiny.

CHAPTER 34

TOO MUCH STUFF (1988)

*Ever wanted more, when you
knew you had enough?*

"Lovin' the Truth"

Cleaning up after the party took days. Maybe it's still going on in some space time continuum beyond this one, where Bobbi Jo's party has become boundless, spilling into our future reality, creating what people call déjà vu. Or maybe these metaphysical musings are only possible when one is hungover while reaching under the marital bed for what turns out to be a crumpled napkin with a magnum-sized condom in it.

During the party, an old friend, Coach Bob, had asked if he could film people as they entered and exited, especially his wife, Nina. I'd known why he was doing this as he spread his tripod like the cold legs of the woman he still slept with.

At some point, Coach went mobile and people quit noticing him. When he invited me over to watch the video with him, I understood: He'd aimed into the blur of Bobbi Jo's thirtieth birthday party, but he'd captured the clarity of my marriage. Secrets, and risky thrills. Beautiful people; beautiful emptiness. I kept thinking I'd see Bobbi Jo but she was behind a closed door. I could hear her laughing in the video. Coach gave me a look. He'd heard his wife's giggle as well.

He didn't have the heart to remind me of our similar marriages. A year earlier, he and Nina had thrown a party and

I'd returned at dawn, wondering why Bobbi Jo hadn't driven herself home. I had quietly let myself in and found her in an upstairs guest room, in bed with a guy I'd never seen before. Bob asked why I didn't slug him. "He was passed out cold," I told him. Coach nodded. I didn't want to go into details, but Bobbi Jo had her shorts on inside-out, and tried to tell me she was too drunk to drive. I think Coach and I both knew we'd never tame the wild beauties we'd married. I wondered if partygoers noticed those secret dalliances, which weren't always very well hidden. Entertainment, on a stage that Coach and I didn't want to be on.

After a few minutes, Bob's camera moved down two flights, through snatches of conversation. "Fuck off Coach," was a constant interjection as he entered the haze of basement bong hits. A perfect pair of breasts appeared across the screen, and then another jiggled in. It was Nina and Jeanette, brunette and blonde: they flashed the camera and disappeared up the stairs as Bob recorded his mumble, lonelier than a whale song from an ocean too deep to carry it.

Bob said, "There's something else you might want to see." On his screen I saw the Big Boy office. Movers had gathered and were commenting on a photograph laid across Billy's desk, some naked woman smiling up at us from a red checkered tablecloth. Her delicate fingers held a big wooden spatula which she was using discreetly.

Coach Bob circled, catching different angles of this chef on the desk, when somebody blurted out, "Shit, that's my aunt."

I overheard mover Rider shout, "Hey it's the Maryland dudes. How's my Suburban?"

The guy grabbing his aunt off the desk replied, "It's running strong." The Maryland dudes, I knew, had bought

Rider's beat Suburban, which always sounded like a jet landing on Route Seven just a mile away. Rider had needed the money. He'd been using a dead license he'd gotten with his birth father's last name, which had cost me 486 bucks when the DOT guys pulled him over in the E truck. I'd fired him when he threw his clipboard at me. But a month later Rider was back. With a good license.

The camera kept moving. Somebody asked the Maryland dudes how they like working in Virginia. "Good, I guess," one of them said.

"Big Boy Movers," snorted another. "Guy that owns the place some kind of wimp? He got bucks, man. Any you fucked his wife?" Hoots and giggles became a pot smoke coughing fit.

A falsetto voice warbled, "In her ass," and the camera shuts down.

"Jerk offs," said Bob, as he flipped on the porch light. We rose from his Lazy Boys, lightheaded. Like we'd just surfaced from underwater caves filled with corpses of people we thought we knew.

Midnight. Home from Bob's; half asleep, I heard a car in the driveway. Bobbi Jo had left the morning after her birthday, on a two-day business trip. She crept onto the bed quietly. I wanted to know how she and her friends liked the party, but she was already passed out, snoring softly. I wanted to ask how she liked her white-leather-seated, walnut dashed, XJS Jaguar I'd paid twenty-three thousand bucks for, but I eased off her stiletto heels and covered her up.

What kind of husband looks in his wife's purse? Its black maw mocked me from her nightstand. Shiny things peeked out, all corners and folds. Bent truths and twisted secrets were just inches away, as she snored under silk sheets.

I couldn't help myself. I plucked out a temptation and

unfolded it in the bathroom as I squatted on the toilet. Hotel stationery from The Greenbrier, in White Sulphur Springs, West Virginia. A name, "David," and a phone number. "We're on," was scrawled in black pen.

An angelic blue presence hovered over the bathmat at my feet. I felt it like an inhaled prayer, inspiring me with peaceful focus. I put David's note back in her purse. I thought of my legacy. I'd founded Big Boy Movers in this house by myself. It was pulling in six figures and yes, Bobbi Jo had been here while that had happened. But as I imagined a child unborn, I realized I couldn't have that with Bobbi Jo.

I lay down beside her. Nothing's perfect, I thought; nothing's perfect but happiness. And even that looks ugly sometimes.

CHAPTER 35

SCENTED, EMPTY, AND LOST
(1988)

Are we never or forever?

"Kiss Me Like a Waterfall"

Thanksgiving morning. I was writing two songs at once at my piano: about lies that blossom from torn hearts and desires that ripen like peaches. I spread my ears to catch melodies and chords as they fell in that orchard in my mind. The music helped me sort out my thoughts. I always assumed I'd remember what came to me as I was half asleep; the notebook I kept on my nightstand proved otherwise. I didn't resist the nature of these truths, some fruitful, others, gibberish. But what I collected in that orchard of paper was often very prescient. It was like I knew things that weren't ready to be revealed until darkness and silence allowed them to become visible, and by the light of my nightstand I'd scrawl lyrics about what I hadn't realized, or yet seen. I learned to get out of the way of all those precious answers, worthy of song or not.

Bobbi Jo had left with Jasmine at ten, reminding me about an estate sale they had to get to. She'd traded her Jaguar for a 1975 Silver Shadow Rolls Royce—David had made her an offer she couldn't refuse. She blew kisses and said she'd be home "by three." At four the phone rang with a West Virginia area code. I answered. All I heard was the scratchy sound of electronic breathing. By five thirty I was headed for dinner at my folks' house in Annandale. At six, as I sat down at a lavish table spread for eight people, I knew Bobbi Jo McCall would be missing another Mason Thanksgiving. Nobody asked me about her, but I explained that she'd gone to West Virginia to be with a sick friend from work. Family members read each other's faces. I didn't have to explain.

I got home about nine. There was still no word from Bobbi Jo as I stepped through my partially open back door, and a sudden panic of footsteps answered me. "Who's there?" Meezer meowed and the kitchen door slammed across the room from me. I saw cherry tomatoes scattered all over the floor as I sprang forward. A wooden spear from Samoa, which hung on our kitchen wall as a decoration, became my weapon.

Out the side door. I beat my way down deck steps, under streetlamp shadows, stiff new loafers slipping off; I pushed between pine branches into the church parking lot toward the roaring of an engine. Then came the scream of tires, screeching in a victory cheer, we got you wail.

Barefoot, cursing, I threw my spear. It fell short. A beat-up Suburban rocketed onto the road, fishtailing, as gears caught, loud as a jet, and I remembered the Maryland dudes I'd seen on Coach Bob's video. How polite they'd been, asking about my collections and the art and antiques and what it was like to find those rare dueling pistols. I'd practically given them my insurance inventory.

They were haphazard burglars. Every nude photograph of Bobbi Jo was gone, but they'd left the original Rembrandt, *Death of the Virgin*, and the Albrecht Durer lithographs. They took half my coin collection, a silk Persian runner, our racing bikes, and the video camera with private home movies in the case—but I found a mound of leather jackets, a pile of shoes, silver candelabras and the English tea service, electronics, jewelry, alligator purses and real furs, all abandoned on the floor.

I called 911.

Hey Bobbi Jo, I thought, *you ought to see this. Police are here. Two in the living room, writing in little notebooks; scattering black powder on the armoires.* "Fingerprints," *one says, as he stains our Oriental rug. Another is examining your panties, the ones we bought in Paris.*

Someone was at the deep end of the pool, poking a long rake into the water, fishing around for something. Somebody asked if my wife was home, and since her underwear was all over the place; they asked if she had a gun. "No blood, so far," somebody said.

The burglars had climbed to the second story. They'd gotten in through a window above the back porch. *How'd they know I wasn't home? Bobbi Jo, did you hide behind the two-way mirror in the bedroom?*

I reached into the great beyond. Nothing there, but one detective kept pushing me. "Did your wife leave a note? Did you have a fight, she say where she was going? She receive any threats?"

Twelve hours ago, I'd thought I knew, and I remembered Jasmine's wave. "She went somewhere in West Virginia," was all I could come up with. "And she's not with her family; they called earlier to wish us Happy Thanksgiving."

I caught words as two raincoats came in from the sleet. The tall one holding a paper cup said, "Nothing in the pool."

But an image tormented me. *It's Bobbi Jo. She's in the deep end. Even with her black bra on, even with hair crossing her purpled face and hands bleeding from fighting burglars with car keys, she hides from the cops. Maybe her corpse is* weighted under murky leaves, or maybe she doesn't want to be interrogated. Maybe she wants them to leave her out of this. Another image: she's on top of somebody at the Greenbrier, pumpkin pie and whipped cream on a nightstand, with jazz radio muting that whimper she always made. I saw David's cigarette and his coffee.

The detective rested his foam cup on an overturned chair. "I apologize," he said, "but was she seeing anyone? Someone who knew she owned that car you mentioned, what was it, a Rolls Royce?"

The stench of policemen's indigestion lingered after they left. I had the detective's card, and promised to call as soon as my wife contacted me. It was three am. "Have you seen a pattern like this?" I'd asked. "A burglary that's also a carjacking and kidnapping?"

His thin lips barely moved. "Number's on the card."

Sleet beat on windows like my coin collection rattling the counter of a pawnshop. I fell asleep with the lights on. I dreamt the Kleenex I held was a ransom note. Somebody wanted a hundred thousand dollars for Bobbi Jo, and I dreamt I paid it, but all they sent me was a pink fingernail. When I woke up, blood had drenched that note in my fist.

I vacuumed and put things back in place. My parents came over. Cool Shoes Jeff appeared; Billy, and a few movers gawked at the crime scene. It was like there'd been a yard sale held by people who hated me, but loved my stuff. I got a check from the insurance company for about eighteen thousand dollars, but how do you put a value on a 1923 silver Peace dollar that your grandmother gave you?

The scented box that held that coin was empty. And I still hadn't heard from Bobbi Jo.

CHAPTER 36

WHAT'S WORTH KEEPING? (1988)

*It comes through us
but not from us*

"River Deep in Me"

I hadn't seen my wife in two days. I still had on my Thanksgiving clothes, as if I was trying to hold on to those moments of pandemonium so I could expose them to her when she got home.

Detective thin lips hadn't called.

Lifeless silence filled the house. But I was waiting. For what? For Bobbi Jo to call? For the burglars to return? I couldn't let go of Bobbi Jo's last wave, and why she just happened to be out of town while we were invaded. The November moon made the living room windows burn like burglars' eyes in the dark.

I'd been bundled up in a blanket on the Victorian sofa for hours. I was sick of being pursued by images of smug renegades ripping rooms apart, stealing my sense of security. It was two in the morning. I threw on a black jacket and got into a white van we'd rented for a pack-up.

Even if he knew, Rider would never tell me where the Suburban and those Maryland dudes had gone. Why would he? Or maybe it was a different crew, and not the same car at all; I'd seen it under adverse conditions. Pine tree branches had kept me from reading the tag, and in the broken light of the church lot I could barely tell what color the vehicle was. Still, I imagined it under a tarp somewhere, a secret burglars could lean on, as they shared a joint and passed around naked pictures of Bobbi Jo.

I eased through Pimmit Hills. Every hulk moored in a side yard got a once over as I followed narrow channels lined with tagless heaps. No beat-up Suburban. I had no idea where the Maryland guys lived; but this reconnaissance might give me something to tell the cops.

Rider's house was under a watery streetlight, so I parked around the corner. A donkey brayed on a television from inside, and Rider was visible, rasping into his phone about a "sweet deal." Smoke fluffed out an open window. I didn't see any Maryland dudes, but Rider's leg was in a cast from the knee down—did he jump off my porch roof?

I had a history of violence with Rider. We'd come to blows the day he'd thrown his clipboard at me and said he'd "fuck me up." But tonight I left as quietly as I'd arrived. I didn't need to have a trespassing charge mucking up my burglary investigation.

Bobbi Jo's Rolls was in the garage when I got home, its rear window broken out: a gaping mouth; too traumatized to tell me who'd assaulted it.

I ran my fingers over the warm Silver Shadow. Opened the rear door. Reached between seats. I hit something—a soldier's ring, solid. Absolutely one of the items I'd listed as stolen. As I held it under a blackboard of chalky stars, I felt the weight of its history and closed my eyes. A foreign sounding sentence appeared that made little sense, but every word was blue: The Optimality of a Certain Type of Optimism In The Face Of Uncertainty. My confusion faded as a command rang in my ears: In plain English; smile, because she's going to lie.

Bobbi Jo greeted me with whimpers, her face buried in my chest. "I tried to call you!" Our losses sent her through the house, returning regularly to where I sat, watching her performance.

She'd left with Jasmine, she said, and ended up spending Thanksgiving with friends in West Virginia. And their cabin had no phone. But she'd tried to call me. She didn't know when the Rolls had been broken into. But some car had trailed them from the estate sale. All the way to the church parking lot.

I showed her the ring I'd just found in the Rolls; one I thought had been stolen. How did it end up in her car? Someone had given me that ring on a beach in Florida when I still thought I was a rock star. There were skulls on it. It was too revolting to wear. Why hadn't I gotten rid of that thing? "They followed us," Bobbi Jo sobbed. "They had on masks."

She was grasping, exhausted. She went to bed, unable to answer me.

A week later, my Vedic astrologer said I was under the influence of a Saturn Rahu; "Think of him as a playful demon," he'd intoned. "Surrender. He'll leave." I paid ninety bucks for that insight.

Surrender? I held on to things, and people. I believed Bobbi Jo could make peace with where she came from, and that all our inexplicable disconnections could become as innocent as what I sensed when we shook hands at that Burger Chef six years earlier.

I gave Bobbi Jo a sheet of paper and asked her to write down everything she valued about our marriage. The paper remained uninscribed on the nightstand, and after a week I threw it where my playful demon could wipe his ass with it.

• • •

I needed a break. I loved moving furniture, and it would take my mind off of things I couldn't wrestle into place. The guys were amused, and as I backed the truck out of the lot, somebody said, "You sure you remember how to do this?"

We were moving a senior from an elevator building in Annandale to a high rise in Chevy Chase. I joined in, padding glass-fronted chests, and pushing dollies of furniture. I tore my hand on the sharp metal of bird houses I carried from a balcony. In the Annandale breeze, my blood fell as I emptied a box of dried leaves over that ninth-floor railing.

A door slid open behind me. "My leaves, no, not my leaves," a voice wailed. The wind tossed them playfully as I restrained the frail senior from the railing, her legs sagging; one hand reaching into the abyss. "My leaves. Goodbye, my loves, goodbye," she cried.

The tomato soup on her stove and her Joy perfume were the incense of anguish. But the prayer that had followed her leaves to the ground redefined the sound of sorrow. Afterwards, she'd held out her arms to receive the empty box. "I'll put this in their new room," she told me, cradling it to her bosom.

I stopped the truck in Rock Creek Park and we filled her book carton with the prettiest brown and red leaves we could find. Two hours later we were done with the move, but I couldn't write up the receipt with my bandaged hand.

"Here," the old woman said, "I'll do it." In her shaky scrawl she inscribed her name, and the words, "Thank you, Benjamin, for my new tree babies to love and cherish!"

If only I could have let go of things that easily.

CHAPTER 37

FRANZ (1989)

*What you don't know
won't ever hurt you*

"Lovin' The Truth"

Franz's application had been awkward, the way he'd said: "I want to . . . come . . . and work for you." But he'd managed a store somewhere, lived nearby, and his voice sounded confident, so I agreed to meet him. Billy had set a high bar and had rarely asked me to help him lift it. Or hold it. His decision to go back to the University of Virginia made logical sense; he'd done all he could do at Big Boy Movers. He needed to apply his brilliance to get that engineering degree he had been talking about for years. I was looking for that same kind of intelligence in his successor, and Franz had impressed me with his curious enthusiasm. I kept an open mind. To some extent, I knew Billy was irreplaceable, but if I could find another energetic savant, perhaps he would blossom in the management position as Billy had.

The large hand that extended from Franz's raincoat and through my open front door was mollusk- like, its sticky appendage certain to make purchase with opportunity. His face had a crumbled Ritz cracker over bone look, and, as I was telling him he had the job, he pulled a bottle of Tums from the pocket of his Dockers. It went into the top drawer of Billy's old desk and was still there the day I fired him.

Franz had little bullet eyes and a turtle smile. He was married, and his wife might have been pregnant on the day she dropped Franz off. I saw how delicately he ruffled the fluff on his boys' heads; his voice reached my open window. Closing the door of the red minivan, he said, "This is Daddy's new job, you be good for Moo Moo."

I trusted Franz to interview and hire movers who responded to our help wanted ad, and we started getting more bookings, but I couldn't read anything he'd written in the schedule book. The jagged slices of his pen marks were unnerving. Franz's words bore so deeply into the paper that they tore through, and I'd have to decipher what was on two pages instead of one.

I asked him to print in block letters. I calmly explained that I'd need to read what he booked, if someone called in to change an inventory or confirm a move date. He stared at me like a box turtle I'd once held up to my face. It had bitten me on the nose.

Franz was gregarious on the phone, though, and I appreciated how he extolled the virtues of Big Boy Movers in a hearty voice. As with Billy, I left him alone, but he went out of his way to engage me. "Got something to tell you," he'd say, and boundaries crossed, he'd appear upstairs.

He was fascinated by my decision to start a moving company and wanted to know all about my previous career as a rock musician. He asked to see old pictures and kept probing me about the tours and the women. He was sure I still had what it took to make it. At first it was flattering, especially coming from a younger guy. But I had to focus, and I needed my own space to do that. It was getting harder to tune him out. "Wow," he kept beaming, "wow, you stayed where in New York City? The Essex House, and Miss Florida was in your room, with the whole band?" He reached for his Tums, and I noticed a plate of enchiladas in the drawer behind them. "And you're telling me you guys didn't bone her? That's bullshit, man. But okay, if you say so," he said, as the business line lit up. He gave me a theatrical wink, and as I left, I heard the sound of his enchilada drawer closing.

Upstairs, I was in my own turtle shell, inching closer to finishing "River Deep in Me." I didn't want to distract Franz, so I wrote after hours, at the upright Yamaha piano my mother had bought me. I sang my revelations with purpose, using gut support and not just what I could wring from my throat.

Part of me was sure that Franz was right. That I still had the talent and the appeal to stay in the spotlight, and that my newfound humility would only make me more approachable and genuine. I wasn't over the hill, in that way that rockers retire. Perhaps the music business had rejected me. But I hadn't quit doing what I loved; I still wanted to share my creations.

We are creative beings. The Divine created us and in doing so, that undying, infinite energy will always be our lifeline; our means to recover, survive, and teach our children how they can do the same. Whenever I was in my stillest place (usually as I lay in bed before falling asleep), I would see my purpose as God's gift to me. And at the heart of that gift was my songwriting. I'd been at it since I was thirteen. Decades later, it didn't matter that I'd been in *Tiger Beat* magazine. What mattered most to me was that I still measured my success by the growing list of songs I'd written that I was most proud of.

Songwriting is a little boy's tears that tell of the heartache he'll mend by forgiving some parent who hurt him; songwriting is a bizarre account of a narcoleptic kleptomaniac, who wakes up wearing seven pairs of polyester slacks, songwriting is the mental equivalent of scaling Mt. Kiliman-jaro and not caring if you reach the top. The adventure is so satisfying in your ears, that it fills you with sonic vistas from every elevation on your piano keys or guitar strings. Paying gig or not, I'm going to enjoy it until my body tells me to stop. During my solo acts at clubs, a few women had given me pho-tographs of themselves with contact info attached. Nothing kinky, just savvy women sharing what they'd sent to *Pent-house* or *Motorhead* magazine, perhaps hoping I might know someone in the entertainment business who'd appreciate im-peccable breasts and buttocks. I never showed these photos to anyone, but I did save them in a shoe box in my upstairs closet.

I'd forgotten about the secret shoebox in my upstairs closet, until I went looking for an old diary one afternoon and pulled out the naked girl envelope. I opened it. De-lightful curves blossomed from lovely photographs, but the last one I'd never seen before. It was a Polaroid photo of a whale-bellied man, his face hidden by a shower cap, mastur-bating toward the camera. A mollusk-like arm was holding an anonymous penis, but the jaw beneath the shower cap looked just like Ritz cracker over bone.

The next morning, I got up early to meet Franz in the kitchen. I heard the grind of a key in the dead bolt, and then his muskmelon head appeared. Seconds later, out of their shell, the turtle eyes glinted, as if he'd just remembered he'd forgotten to tell me something. It was wet outside and we had no trucks out for the day. He closed the door.

"Franz." I slid the masturbating guy onto the counter, a joker in a game I didn't want to keep playing.

Franz swore he had no idea who the naked fat man was. I followed him downstairs. He was really moving, a runaway truck, weaving in the lane in front of me, his briefcase swinging like an errant trailer. I let him settle into his chair, then set jerkoff man on his desk. The words, "For My L.L., love, Karl," were written on the back of the photograph.

The Tums came out. He bent the gooseneck lamp closer to the picture. We were both sitting, but I kept my eye on his hands. He'd taken his silver wedding ring off and was itching his knuckles. "I don't like how you're looking at me right now," I told him. He swallowed something, words rumbling in his chest. Thunder hammered on the windows and the fluorescent flickered over his face.

"You did something to me," he said. "Remember when I asked you about your band? Primadonna? My Uncle Karl used to see you guys at the Crazy Horse. He saw you at the Bayou. He hung out with your lady working the lights; called her his Light Lady." He pointed at the photograph. "Everybody knew he loved her, everybody."

I said, "Franz . . . she was my girlfriend. She lived in this house. With me."

A black-and-white love letter. I knew who he was posing for.

Franz fingered the photo, his eyes squinting turtle red. "I called him Uncle Karl. But when my mom died, I found out he was really my father. He came, he left, my mom was gone a lot; okay, maybe he was my stepdad. I don't know, I was fifteen."

Lightning stabbed the basement windows. I studied the photo. The beached whale body; the bandage on one arm. Franz saw what I was noticing. "Oh that," he said, his voice hardening. "Uncle Karl got that from a radiator burn. Skin graft went to shit. You know how bad that smelled? He got sepsis; went to his appendix. We lost him. Last Christmas."

He looked up. The brick wall I'd smashed into when Karl was here, was right above us.

I tore up the photograph and let it fall into his trash can. Outside, morning rain was spitting pink and lavender in the sunlight. "I'm writing you a check," I told him.

He stared into the trash. "Dad must have given that to her. How'd you get it?"

At this point the crazy bell went off in my head. I sure as hell didn't put it in that box. Then I remembered. I'd come home one afternoon and as I came in the backdoor, Franz had appeared from upstairs. I'd given him a look. "Oh, hey man, I just wanted to see where you practiced. That's a cool old piano."

When I went upstairs my closet door was open. And the shoebox full of naked girl pictures was not shoved deep in the shadows. It was in full view, its lid on backwards.

Franz went on to start his own moving company, and we crossed paths a month later at a light in DC. He was behind the wheel of a big yellow truck, all wound with black stripes, like the body of an insect. A phallic stinger painted across the back door aimed at a phone number. Black letters across the yellow body proclaimed: "Big Bee Movers! Save Your Money! Call Us Honey!"

Big Bee Movers did not survive. I saw Franz's yellow truck with something taped across its window in a parking lot—a For Sale sign. But I couldn't read the number slashed across it.

CHAPTER 38

THE GRAVES OF MY GOODWILL
(1990)

I woke up naked on the floor

"That Dangerous Thing"

The upper crust homeless guys, Chad and Todd, returned, pushing a loaded shopping cart. They showed up at noon on a hot Saturday and said they were ready to work. But they looked like they hadn't slept in days. They'd caught a ride to the church lot from a landscaper they'd worked for in DC and everything they owned was in the back of his pickup truck: the cart, sleeping bags, canned food, tarps, wet clothing, and plastic jugs of water. They smelled like sewage and couldn't stop thanking me for "giving them another chance." Chad said a storm had washed away the lean-to they'd built under a pedestrian bridge in Rock Creek Park: bamboo had kept them hidden and Todd wistfully described how it sounded like humming when the wind blew. "We cut a little winding trail through it, so nobody ever even saw us," he added.

I asked why Chad had a ragged bandage on his hand. On their last night in DC, they'd been digging through a dumpster and a maintenance man had chased them away. He'd come at them with a machete, and they'd run, but admitted they'd returned later and tried to set the dumpster on fire. The lid had slammed down on his hand as Todd was lighting the matches. "Bad Karma," Chad admitted.

They'd been asleep when Rock Creek had risen and come through the cinder blocks, carrying away the plywood and even the bicycle they'd been using to get around. "We weren't meant to be there, I guess," Chad said, looking at me with his mouth open, as if I had an answer to fill it with. I didn't have children, but the helplessness of these two grown men inspired me to tell them they could stay, but I needed them to understand how that was going to work. I didn't bother to do any inner accounting; how could I calculate whether I'd be giving as much as I'd be getting? I just knew I'd feel guilty if I didn't help them. They weren't slackers or freeloaders; they'd been accepted back into Georgetown University but couldn't adjust.

I'd made some wrong turns in my life, but luck, providence, or the Divine had led me back onto the path. So I made it clear that they could stay, but that I expected them to be on a crew. Everyday. They could use my hose to shower, and they could pitch their tents back in the woods behind the house. "Until you get on your feet," I said. In the garage I handed them a shovel and a roll of toilet paper for bathroom use. Chad saw my grill, charcoal, and lighter fluid. "No big fires," he promised soberly.

A few days later there was an odd occurrence. "Somebody got into my tent while I was asleep and took my cash and my new flashlight," Chad fumed.

Todd was upset as well. He kept saying, "Why man, why?" I'd caught a whiff of something metallic drifting from the woods during the night. There was almost an acre of underbrush and twisted trees hiding their tents, but I had to ask.

"Did you guys see any neighborhood kids in the woods?" They hadn't, but they looked at me like I hadn't warned them about something dangerous. We tossed it off as fumes from nearby roads as I pulled out my wallet and advanced Chad twenty bucks. At least they smelled better, but their faces bore frown lines that were still encrusted with dark scum.

Todd's Georgetown Hoyas jogging shorts had been pulled off him while he was asleep, and his iced tea was gone from the stump outside his tent. I advanced him a twenty as well. Maybe some doped-up neighbor kid had been the culprit. Weird. "Keep your eyes peeled," I told them.

It rained for two days, so I let them sleep in the E truck. They hung their wet stuff in the trees to dry, and nothing went missing. They made good on their promise to be on the moves, every day, and I was told they were as efficient as they'd been before they'd disappeared a year earlier. I trusted that my investment in them would be repaid. I bought the homeless preppy guys new sleeping bags, and gave them cash advances to buy decent clothes. They took furniture moving seriously; it was the right thing to do.

Evolution doesn't give a damn if we're nice folks. It just wants us to survive so we can pass along our genes. But we have choices in this matter. My father taught me to give people opportunities to succeed or screw up. He had always said that "giving a little boy an apple when he's hungry" was not meant to make him feel dependent, but to teach him to help others. It takes courage to be that vulnerable. Risky or not, the lessons of his generosity helped fill my trucks with movers.

A month had gone by when Chad and Todd discovered that the new sleeping bags I'd bought them and the charcoal grill I'd lent them were gone. "Thieves," they chanted as I added up the losses. But they'd been collecting tips from the moves they'd been on, and by the end of the next month they had re-paid me for the advances they'd received. They both seemed content, and the summertime smell of grilled hot dogs and hamburgers swept through the woods from their camp. I still caught that occasional metallic scent as I heard the roar of vehicles on quiet nights. Catalytic converters; loose manifold gaskets; we were stuck between Route 7 and Route 66. In fact, the Beltway had enough traffic on it to send us that chemical stench, windy night or not.

I allowed Chad and Todd access to the washer and dryer in the basement, and they knocked on the side door respectfully every time they needed to do a load of laundry. But they kept to themselves and didn't take part in the beer and bong fests that happened after the moves were done. Davo gave Todd a mirror, and he and Chad proudly showed me their clean-shaven faces. They'd cut each other's hair, using a plastic bowl and some sharp landscaping shears, but that project had elicited hoots from the basement. They both looked like Moe from the Three Stooges, so they shaved each other's heads. "Now you look like Curly," I told them.

Meanwhile, there were other characters I grew to appreciate. A Jamaican semi-professional boxer, who had Big Boy stitched in gold across the robe he wore into the ring; a long-haired epileptic who got tongue choking seizures; a rock and roll vocalist, whose girlfriend was crowned Miss Maryland, and who left him for Donald Trump; and a quiet mathematical genius named Evan. I'd call during a pack job, and Evan would ask me for the amounts to charge per box. Before I could pull out a calculator, Evan would give me the totals for each type of box packed, and the grand total due for all boxes packed. "I see numbers," was all he ever said.

He lived at his father's house and drank alone in his attic bedroom. One night he ran the G truck through four red lights in DC. The truck was impounded. He called, admitting he was drunk and just trying to go downtown. "I've never seen a naked woman," he said quietly. He asked me to bail him out. I fired him through the static of a jailhouse phone. Then I bailed him out. Good drivers are hard to find.

As autumn began, I stopped at a yard sale in Pimmit Hills, attracted by the sight of a leaf blower. I wandered past card tables of collectibles, toward a rough cardboard sign beside the leaf blower. It directed me toward a pathway into some shrubbery between two houses. No one was present, but I heard hysterical giggles as I entered a clearing strewn with milk crates and open book boxes.

"Everything's for sale," said a voice from under a drooping hood in a green lawn chair. Someone with their back to me was urinating into a pile of blackened refuse. He had on a G.T.U. tank top and when he turned around, zipping up, I recognized Chad. A few feet away was my charcoal grill, and next to that, resting in an open crate, was the new black and red sleeping bag I'd bought him, a ten-dollar sale sign taped onto it.

Chad was drooling as he zipped up. "Todd's dead," he whispered. "Died last night. I don't need this shit."

A hand lifted from the sweatshirt in the green chair. "Sell it, man."

I inhaled something, and it burned my nostrils. Metallic, caustic, chemical; it forced its way into my lungs as the person in the chair blew smoke into my face. Sounds pierced my ears and my eyes quivered as if broken glass had replaced them. Coughing wracked my throat; I was drowning in something I couldn't help swallowing. I aimed for the path, as a hump strap flopped around my neck. Todd and Chad. They clutched me, tickling, scratching; their fingers crawling under my shirt, "We're lizards, man," they kept whispering, as a pinched-faced boy sucked my wallet from my pocket.

"I want that leaf blower", I told them again and again but all I heard was my own monkey voice as my words turned to bloody spit because they kept making me bite my tongue as the noose around my neck became a filthy snake, and then I felt my shoes coming off and I saw the grinning pinch faced boy. "Hey Daddy," he said as they yanked me down. I was naked, twisting, bound by three scarecrows, flat on my back, as feathers of blue light began falling everywhere. I heard my mother shout, "sing that song about dancing on graves, son, sing it, sing for me," and I felt the razor edge of a broken shovel beside me; she wanted me to use it, and I did, swinging it with all I had, howling like a chimpanzee, until there was blood on the leaves, until all three scarecrows screamed the song my mother wanted to hear, as they started chewing what had been smoldering in that fire: hair, their own fingers, paper money, until at last they spewed it out; blackened spit poetry that they scrawled with their tongues in the dirt around me, and then screeching hawks and eagles carried everything away.

I knelt in the rain. Blue feathers drifted into smoldering ashes before me, and rose again, entwined like a mother and child. I found my clothes. A shirt, pants, my shoes gone to God knows where. It was almost dark. I vomited bile but I was alone. I threw my weapon deep into the bushes. I hate PCP. It steals minds and turns men into monkeys.

The homeless castaways had left my car untouched, and it was a warm womb when I crawled into it. The next day I buried the remains of Chad and Todd's stuff under the trees in my woods, where maple and oak leaves would hide the graves of my goodwill.

I accept who I am. Who I truly am, imperfect, and at the

mercy of my own karma. I have no noxious gut churning feelings of guilt or shame. But I must have deserved what happened. I would like to think of myself as an alpha male with heart, but I admit I was careless in my early years. With women and people in general. But I was never cruel. Perhaps this torture I escaped from was my way of settling some debt I incurred in this incarnation or another one.

Jesus said, "I am the Way," and he was right, and I owe my life to the blue-lit grace of the guides who always seem to be exactly where I need them the most. If they are angels, so be it. If they are able to hear me, it would be in the thankful breath I exude now, in my bed, alone, wounded physically but not spiritually, as I forgave Todd and Chad for what they did to me. If my generosity toward them created this, I do not blame myself. I own the courage it took to be vulnerable, and it has led me perfectly in this lifetime. There are no accidents, only the surprises of lessons one never sees coming.

If I could speak to them, I would tell them there is faith and strength in their hearts. And that as they find their way, that is all they need. I want them to know that I am fine. That they can repay me for the way they raped my mind, by seeking the heart-centered way, by going within, where all that is love lives. Maybe someday I'll meet them in another clearing. Maybe someday we can forgive ourselves for all we have done to awaken in the Light.

The cruelty and irresponsibility that these young men brewed in the cauldron of their lives scalded me and it's trapping them in a hellish version of masculinity.

I wish for Todd and Chad to come to terms with manhood that is strong, protective, and kind.

CHAPTER 39

LOSING EVERYTHING I NEEDED TO (1991)

The truth falls out of the blue

"Single Shoe"

One in the morning. A white limo has blocked my driveway. Maybe my wife's hosting a Redskin's victory party. I park in the church lot. I'm home two days early from a songwriter's showcase I played in Asheville, North Carolina. The new songs went over pretty well, and somebody backstage said a publisher from Nashville was there. I sold a couple of CDs; I wonder if they'll find their way to Music Row. I'm not really a country writer, but three chords and the truth can quiet a room. Okay, maybe one of those chords has some pop dribbled on it; I write for me, but a hit song by somebody wearing a cowboy hat might change my mind.

As I find the back door keyhole, a light comes on. Shadows bounce through the window to my left.

And through that funhouse lens of leaded glass, I see a black man's body stretched out on our guest room rug, his legs pointed away from me, his hands guiding a pale pear-shaped ass up and down, onto his penis. Holy shit. I turn the doorknob, step in and flip on the dining room light. I feel no impulsivity. No urgency to ram my truck into the side of this house, no desire to harm whoever is fucking my wife; I stand my ground beside our dining table, as I wait for what's coming next. It's not dangerous, just a smeared portrait of pitiful shame.

Bobbi Jo slips out of the guest room half smiling—light flickers behind her; candles? Lavender, smoky weed. The door closes quietly. "Hey!" she says. I set my suitcase down, take off my leather jacket. I haven't seen her in almost a week; I can smell her libido; she senses my realization pulsing. Her hands fluff the air; she appears to want to take flight. Her hair is sweaty wet. Eyeliner wanders down one cheek. "Hey," she says, her smile tilted, her robe modestly pulled together. She's smoldering, post orgasmic. "I'm so glad to see you?"

This becomes a comedic question as a deep male voice rises from the bathroom, broadcasting "Love you baby, love to love you, baby," as it veers into a Marvin Gaye falsetto, the sonic ejaculation splattering through the sounds of the shower. My wife doesn't know where to stand during this performance, so she gathers up pieces of someone's clothing from under the dining table, and I notice she's minus her wedding rings and naked under that robe.

"Hey, Mister," she says. Bits of pink velvet wink as she chirps, "I waited for you." Behind her, I see the man brushing his teeth, his singing now just a low rumble. He nudges the bathroom door shut. Bobbi Jo opens her robe, her lips a blowtorch at my ear, and whispers, "Don't be mad, I waited for you. Come on. Upstairs."

She smells like a flower truck on fire.

"Who are these fucking assholes in our house?"

"They're guests," Bobbi Jo snaps, "calm down!" But there's no awkward introductions, just the sound of a voice so deep it makes my hair vibrate.

Bobbi Jo smolders. But I'm not melting down with her.

Adrenalin, pot, vodka, lust; all of it is draining from the pores of bodies in my house and rising in this cesspool I've come home to. I will not drown in my own dining room. Not anymore.

I make for higher ground, Bobbi Jo in pursuit.

On the stairs, she squeezes past, her robe open now; her breasts teasing my face. "Benjamin, we have guests."

I'm exhausted. I reach out. She obliges, her ass lifting like the stern of a boat cresting a wave, and I grapple aboard, the deck salty as we pitch forward up the steps.

She says it again. "I waited for you." And she turns, wrapping her thong around my head like a crown of seaweed for a condemned cuckold. From her orange depths, she smears my lips with her fingers. Like bad fish and perfume.

"We're done Bobbi Jo McCall," I tell the perfect bottom on the steps above me.

Downstairs our bedroom door bangs open. Jasmine whistles. "What in the fucking morning?" From the dining room, she frowns up at us. She's wearing a man's dress shirt. Her hair is wilder than I remember. Something that looks like a brown bear paw encircles her waist, and she's drawn into the bathroom.

As that door bangs shut a deep voice sings out, "Play nice you two!"

"David's with her," Bobbi Jo says. "He's a Redskin."

I duck my head and collapse onto the foam mattress in the little attic room.

"Who the fuck is the guy in the guest room?"

"That's another David," she says. "He just got traded to Dallas."

Maybe she had waited for me, whatever that meant. In her own way she'd always waited, for opportunities, for something better, and for this to end. To get that big settlement she always imagined was hers. I was the president of three corporations, and I think in her mind, on paper, there had to be stupid money somewhere. Buried in my corporate accounts. Hidden in plain sight in my file cabinets.

The burglary would have been a natural subterfuge; turn everything upside down and see what falls out. But her infidelities felt more obviously staged, as if she was using her allure to create a backup plan; auditioning lovers to see who would be there if our marriage ended. I felt played, but I wasn't angry at her, in fact, I was still addicted to her sexual power. But like heroin, I had to go cold turkey. Not knowing what she'd do next was the same as waiting for Gordon to sell me some junk that would stop my heart. But that rush, that red-haired rapturous rush, was just a breath away, and I told myself, one more time, just one more time.

In the dim light of the attic nook, she arched her back, and even after all her secrets and misdirection, I couldn't contain myself. I bit her neck. She mumbled words from a language I'd never heard before, syncopated Arabic phrases, and the deeper I went, the more she commanded me to spank her, until finally, as I slid my thumb into her, she climaxed and I followed. Bobbi Jo clutched an ivory pendant around her neck—a pair of white footballs, deflated into the shape of a heart. The words "Washington Redskins" were engraved upon it. A new season was beginning as our old contract disappeared into the sheet beneath us.

Staring wet-eyed at the Indian bedspreads, Bobbi Jo agreed to a payoff. No courts, no lawyers, but she kept raising her number. Unlike players on a football field, both sides won and lost. It took forty grand to end our game.

We divided everything in half, and she promised to leave

my stuff where it was. Over the next week she came and went as usual, bringing boxes to the house from work, taking loads of her things away in her Rolls. I didn't ask her where she was moving, and she wasn't giving me any entry to that question. Conversations weren't warm or hollow, just short pleasantries as we passed things that had once belonged to both of us. I didn't want her movers making honest mistakes so I made a point to tell Bobbi Jo that to avoid any confusion, I'd be setting some personal items aside, in a padlocked closet: pieces of collected art, small curiosities I'd saved since I was a kid, all with more sentimental worth than what they would sell for.

Two weeks after our breakup conversation, I was in Maryland helping on a move when my neighbor Siggy paged me. She gave me the news in a motherly voice: Two rental trucks in the driveway. Six movers and Bobbi Jo. In and out of my house in ninety minutes.

Everything was gone by the time I got home—even the light bulbs were removed. In the beam of a flashlight, I discovered the padlock splintered, the closet emptied. I imagined the brush of a mover's arm, heard the tinkle of things cracking as they were gathered. She'd left my piano and my dresser full of clothes, the Big Boy office stuff, Meezer, and his litter box.

I had a sense of something reaching into my chest, urging me to let go, to rip the cord that stretched from my heart to Bobbi Jo's. To rip the cord that wove through years of family gatherings and trips to Europe, American Samoa, Mexico, and California. To let those memories fall as freely as my tears. As I did that, a parachute of blue light lifted me. I looked down to see that losing everything that filled my house would let me fall softly, into the arms of all that mattered.

CHAPTER 40

THE LETTER (1991)

You're not here,
but you're not gone

"Blue Tattoo"

And I was letting go of blame. Until a letter came. As innocent and still as a newborn sleeping in a mailbox. I felt something delicate tugging on me, urging me to be certain I was fully alert as I peeled it open. As I held it, I sensed that its message would reach into my past, but images of who had written it did not appear. I noticed an artfulness in the way the envelope was addressed, but when I began reading, I felt raw urgency and longing reaching out to me from every sentence. I knew that feeling. Someone was desperate.

Dear Ben,

I'm not sure if you're my father. I had some paperwork and records and stuff to show you, but all that's gone. Bobbi Jo told me you don't want me in your life. So maybe that's for the best anyway. She said you'd be real mad, and I'm sorry if you are.

Mom's not with us much longer. Her illness has spread so I'm taking the bus home today. I'll tell her you're OK.

Some things are better left the way you think they could be, instead of how they are.

Maybe we can meet some other time.

There was no signature at the bottom. Waves of helplessness roiled me as I closed the mailbox. Why had Bobbi Jo kept her encounter with this letter writer secret? Why had she turned her away? As I read it again, I tried to tease out images of what lay between the lines. I inhaled the open envelope, and the unfolded letter that had traveled inside it. Nothing. No familiar scent of a place or of anyone I'd ever known.

I'd once mentioned my trepidation about possibly having fathered a child to Bobbi Jo, but that had been imparted over wine, at a beachside table where she'd kept her cool and smiled as we ordered from a menu. She knew how my anxiety had haunted me. I'd talked to her about it; that in my mind I always imagined that it was a little girl, though it was just a gut feeling. She had interceded, but for what purpose? It felt like an unspoken lie, meant only to benefit Bobbi Jo. This had to be about money. But now we were barely on speaking terms and I wasn't going to confront her with truths I knew she'd never admit. And if I called her, it would only infuriate me, and I needed to stay centered. Calm, so I could sort through recollections from my nights on the road.

How would I ever know who wrote this? I closed my eyes, scrolling through both hazy and vivid memories of women who'd followed the band; and I vaguely recalled hearing about a serious illness one of them had, but nothing solid came to mind. There was no return address or postmarked stamp on the envelope. It had been hand delivered by someone who had been determined to remain invisible to me. I'd spent days using a last name and a state phone directory in my fruitless search for Emma Morgan's people. Yet this mystery held even fewer clues for me to follow.

Back inside the house, my memories gradually turned blue behind my eyes. I didn't regret how easily women had drawn me in; their beauty was a gift from the Divine. But some of those anonymous faces, hungry ones who'd said very little, stared at me like ghosts in my mind. I wish I had been more attentive about who they were, beyond their looks. I wish I had ventured past the heat of our flesh and the urges that melted us together. Maybe if I'd have talked to them, and listened to their words, instead of whatever sounds they made, I might have known if one of them had intentions of becoming pregnant by me. Regardless, if this letter was real, then I needed to do the right thing.

Bobbi Jo had given birth to a baby nine months after we'd split up, but she had refused to be clear with me, telling me: "Don't worry about it."

I had gotten angry with her and said, "If I'm the father of your child I need to know." Doing the right thing was part of my DNA; it meant doing what my father had done for me. It meant opening my wallet, my heart, and my mind—to provide life support and guidance to a brand-new human being. It meant imparting a moral code that would foster purpose and patience, it meant teaching a child to be creative, vulnerable, and to seek strength by letting go of shame and blame. It meant embracing gratitude in this lifetime in the light of Divine Love. It meant more than any words I could conjure up.

Bobbi Jo never told me who had gotten her pregnant, but she did agree to bring her baby to a medical lab where a DNA test had proven that I was not the father of her child. That genetic truth cost me $948.

I was relieved that we had not had a child. A partnership with someone who bears secrets would feel as empty as I had felt, staring out a window and wondering where my wife was at two in the morning. A healthy pregnancy is founded on a steady bond of trust, created between father and mother. It is a blessing from the Divine.

Songs about faulty hearts in need of parts, twisted relationship compasses, and healing kisses sprang from this nerve-racking odyssey, as I took a hard look at how I'd decipher the intentions of women who might tempt me again, dating-wise. I needed to admit it. I had lied to myself.

I was seduced by the beautiful deception that I had manifested. Bobbi Jo was every fantasy I'd had since puberty, from the *Playboy* centerfold to the small-town cheerleader who had fucked two guys in a hayloft. Overtaken by her allure, I kept the truth afar. She was a slammed-shut book, who never let me past its lipstick pink cover. I never knew her and still don't know who she really was. I own my blindness. And my hindsight. I needed to never let myself become deluded by any sort of beautiful deception again. I prayed for the strength to see the truth in a woman's heart, beyond any beguiling costume which surrounds it.

NEAR DEATH IN A DIAPER (1953)

*I heard forever in
my son's first breath*

"The Sound"

I'm sure I was still too young to climb the shiny wooden stairs at my grandparent's house in Anchorage, Kentucky, in the summer of 1953. It was a two-story Victorian, at the end of a long white gravel driveway, proud under giant oaks, with a basement where I saw my first television. The lap siding and gingerbread had been painted white and shuttered dormers jutted out from all sides of this elegant masterpiece. It stood on five acres, with a separate garage and a patio garden that had a trellis over it, and where a welcoming side door opened into a canary yellow kitchen. There was a Steinway grand piano in the adjoining living room, and every wall held artwork which my grandparents had collected on their trips to Europe.

My mother had lived in this house until she finished college and married my father. We visited often, and on this particular day, my mother was probably nursing my sister, smoking cigarettes, and chatting with my grandmother and Great outside on the brick patio, next to a fountain my grandfather had built with tiles he'd brought back from Portugal.

I imagine my mother had asked my father to keep an eye on me, as he excused himself to work in the upstairs bedroom that had once been hers. He'd carried me upstairs and set me down on a soft round rug that surrounded me with colorful circles in the middle of the room. Stuffed animals and some blocks kept my attention as he tapped away at her college typewriter, maybe crafting a resume, or a letter to his folks back in Virginia. He'd just gotten out of the Navy, and our little family was living a few miles away from "Langmuir," this estate blessed with a small vineyard and fruit trees. I'm sure Daddy carried me carefully up those stairs, and I'm sure he had every intention of keeping me in sight as he worked. But as he became lost in his writing, I too became distracted. It was summer, and all of Langmuir's windows were open. I can still recall the scent of something sweet wafting through the room we were in, from the hallway, and from outside.

I was small enough that I could see under the bed behind my father as he sat in a chair, typing. I do remember thinking his feet were really big as I crawled past the soft clatter of his two-fingered typing, drawn toward the whisper of summer noises and fragrant smells coming in through the windows above me. I can't say how I pulled myself up on the suitcases stacked beneath a window, but I did, probably with the help of the leather straps which bound them. Once at the top, I discovered that I could reach out and feel the hard lower ledge of the open window. And this I'm certain of: I was able to stand and push my bare chest against the soft metal screen and I must have been wondering how I could get further out to where loud birds flew, where branches of a willow tree teased me like laughter in the breeze.

My father told me later that he looked up as the screen came undone, reached out as I began falling, and caught me by the back of my diaper. He remembered my pink back, angled, while he wrestled me in, his grip on a fistful of soft cotton, the big safety pins holding, as the screen tumbled two stories down, onto a slate patio that hosted spiky iron chairs and a glass top table.

I wonder what he said to my mother, or if he told her. Apparently I never made a sound, and the screen landed silently on the patio stones, thirty feet below us. He told me he carried me back downstairs and that I was given a treat of some kind. Knowing my father, it was probably ice cream. I was teething, and I would imagine he was as well, chewing on a feeling of helplessness and incredible luck.

The heat of my intensity has always inspired me to push against whatever has impeded me. I'm not complaining. When the band began to fail, I used that fire to start Big Boy Movers, to thrive in glorious ways. There were times when I had fallen into complacency, but more often, I'd leapt into the Great Beyond. There have been soft landings and painful impacts; but I've built a life out of the risks and chances I've taken.

My father took different risks, captaining a subchaser during World War II. His quiet strength guided me as I began a new wifeless life; advising me toward a distant horizon, knowing I'd always had a woman by my side. He'd seen adoring fans handing me notes after my performances. His continuing confidence in me was an unspoken order for me to remain strong, as he had aboard ship, sailing across darkening oceans, knowing there was solid ground and sunlight ahead. He never seemed threatened by his future or traumatized by what he'd seen. Daddy emerged intact, to create family, adventures, and art. I thank him for how he caught me whenever I fell; his shepherd's heart will beat within mine forever.

I began to carry myself more assuredly and was better about leaving water out for Meezer. In my new bachelor life, I was jamming in an empty house to the rhythm of

244 • BEN MASON

connections I'd let go of. I wrote new songs about being fucked over, but I hadn't really been fucked over. I'd been liberated. I wasn't dreaming about applause and groupies and encores. I was living in a new reality of being deeply appreciated, of being paid for services that really made a difference in people's lives. All my fantasies about the luxurious life I'd left behind became party debris, to be swept away, like the charade of my life with Bobbi Jo.

I bought a yellow Indian shirt and decided to book more gigs. I wanted to find out between sets if I could talk to a woman and not think about her being naked. But no matter what color shirt I wore, a woman could see through it, and find that hole in my heart that no one had filled. Yet. Still, I wanted to see if I could be with a woman in public and not care if the people around me were impressed. Did I always need an audience? Who did I think would be watching as I used her as a stage prop? Where was that guy who would connect with her as she revealed her human self? I imagined him as I fell asleep. I also imagined him asking himself if he was finally ready to connect with a woman.

I picked up *The City Paper*, and scouted the section that said "women looking for men." I went on some dates, ordered drinks, appetizers; but those meetings often led back to me being a performer, on stage or as the proud owner of a moving company. I thought I'd learned to listen, but I realized I was still as clumsy in conversation as I was on the dance floor. When I did relax enough to let my dates open up to me, I was always amazed at how similar our war stories were. It was a pleasant way to spend an evening but as I walked them to their car, I avoided any physical intimacy. It had been less than a year since my divorce, and I kept feeling broken places as soft blue illuminations rode home with me, reminding me that I was still healing. Bare flesh wouldn't change that.

Relationship-wise, I was learning not to push too hard against the glamorous temptations that I encountered. I saw that as healthy complacency, and I accepted my limitations. That meant avoiding women like Bobbi Jo. It meant saving myself before I fell from another window in my heart.

I felt lighter. I asked the Divine to help me find my true self. I'd let myself be swallowed, but Lord, let me rest in my depth, in my own blue water, until I drown my desire to blame Bobbi Jo for anything.

CHAPTER 42

HOPEFUL BLUE LIGHT (1992)

We fell to Earth through God's own grace

"Infinity"

Tangerine sunset; Falls Church overpass. Route 66, a serpent beneath me. A song called from the westward skyline that had been writing itself for weeks now. "Give us an answer, some peace to hold onto. We don't need no fancy rhinestone rodeo. Give us palomino ponies, soft as river sand. Let the broken ends of daylight be bouquets in our hands. Let hurricanes and earthquakes be whispers from the Earth, as she tells us to awaken, to be grateful for our birth."

I kept hearing the sound of hooves as my future family rode westward, away from pavement and cement and chaos. I kept digging deeper into my heart for a rhythm that I could share with someone who was meant to travel with me, but the noise of traffic unraveled in my ears like drunks brawling in front of a stage.

Since Bobbi Jo left, I'd had more time to play piano, to study spiritual teachings, and to experience what I believed was guiding me. It wasn't just the blue images. It was a growing sense of a sacrament that previous incarnations were sharing with me. That there was something I wanted and was afraid of receiving. It followed me through dreams and spoke to me without words. I was frustrated, but entranced.

I caught glimpses of it in songs, as I closed my eyes and saw the figures gathering around me. A circle of serenity. Always calm, always insistent. I was to move, I was to gather up all I had creatively, and take it where it would flourish. This included a wife, children. I began to accept that this would come as easily as my waking dreams did, blurry, and then as clear as the broken ends of daylight.

I had only been dating for over a year since my divorce, but I wasn't ready to put my past into perspective. Blame was a word I struggled with, as I knew I had shouldered my share of it with all I'd overlooked in my marriage. Blame only matters if it leads to resolution, and divorce from Bobbi Jo had resolved that quandary.

A statuesque brunette named Susan came to visit me at my house. We were enjoying our third date when she asked where I kept my tequila. She'd recently moved to DC from Fort Worth and could reach my blender on the top shelf without a stool. I'd found her personal ad: she was looking for someone who would be by her side, loyal and strong. I sensed that she had been through her own ordeals, but that they did not define her, or cause her to seek me out to even some score with men. Her intelligence was understated, and she dealt it toward me gracefully, allowing me a chance to consider what she'd laid out before me. Stability was in the way she moved, an effortlessness that I found sexy. Ivory-skinned and ravishingly proportioned, she listened as I told her about Bobbi Jo. Her calm intuition was refreshing. She made no judgments about our choices, as she told me about her past. And the more we talked, the less my past mattered to me.

We drank margaritas and Susan got me laughing about her childhood. The time she refused to eat lunch at Camp Lonesome Bull. For five hours. Stubborn runs in her blood she said.

Her memories unfurled like blue bonnets in the Texan sun. She'd had a tough go at times but was in harmony with her mother and father and half-brothers. She had dear friends. She respected herself. She'd created a new life out east. She was proud of who she was and how she'd arrived at this point in her life. Her self-reliance had been gathered around her like handmade quilts by the strong women in her life. People who'd headed west from Arkansas and endured raids, circling wagons at the edge of a bluff, using a natural formation of stone stairs to allow women and children to escape to the river below. At dawn, they rose from where they'd hidden, and found enough men still alive to get them to Fort Worth, Texas.

Meanwhile, I found that my role in the business had radically changed too. I was less of a watch dog and more like a domesticated hound who greeted whoever arrived at the doorstep of the business. Maybe it was the strength of Big Boy Movers' dependable reputation, but I felt less wary of imminent disasters. We were functioning like a well-oiled machine. Without Bobbi Jo around, I wasn't as physically distracted, and was more available to visit job sites and even help on moves, though that always inspired "old man on board" jokes.

I had found a good match with our new manager, Steve Bowes, a fellow musician who had a brilliant creative streak, allowing him to improvise when problems arose. Downstairs, he managed the office with pacifying authority. His manner of delegation calmed workers and kept me out of confrontations, the unnecessary Heavy Hand. He had legible penmanship and respected personal boundaries. He'd return from morning dispatch, looking like a teenager in shorts, and as he re-banded his ponytail, he'd fix me with a veteran's gaze. Then a smile would rip across his face and I'd hear about some unexpected disaster he'd just managed.

I paid bills, handled tax stuff, made sure the DMV cards were in the trucks, and waited for a gargled curse or a muttered prediction. But they never came. Big Boy Movers was thirteen years old. Bobbi Jo and I might not have been able to have a child, yet this thirteen-year-old was borne solely from my efforts. I felt a poignant sense of relief, knowing we had each created "children," but so far, even on the boardwalks of summer, mine was not behaving like a reckless teen.

I wondered how single motherhood was treating my ex-wife, and how her son would be doing when he turned thirteen. I knew I wasn't his father. Letting go of what could have been was becoming an old song I was starting to forget. I felt shadows of what might have been passing over me, but I also caught the flickers of hopeful blue light peering in through my window. I began to sense a loosening of what had always bound me to wonder what lay ahead. If I had a child "out there," perhaps that child had found out that I was divorced from Bobbi Jo and would find the courage to approach me again. It became a new kind of worry. Whoever she was, I'd felt my blood in the body of the letter she'd written me.

My first children napped and were awakened whenever I pulled them out of the notebooks they slept in on top of my piano. They continued to arrive unexpectedly, but I always made time for them to wander where they would, often returning months and sometimes years later, changed, the minute I embraced them on the worn keys of my Knabe spinet. The relief I got from my anxiety about my "other" children was a sonic blanket that soothed me, as if my music was my mother or father, comforting me as they reminded me that I had not fallen from some two-story window.

Somewhere in my salt-rimmed reverie I saw two pale blue

illuminations forming, as lustrous dust outlined their figures in a window. The weathervane rattled on the roof, and thunder ripped by overhead. A neighbor's dog, long dead, barked as it had once, in a yip of wind. In that twist of time, I felt a sense of approval; a nudge from ancestors who watch over me. And Susan's eyes had never left mine.

CHAPTER 43

WHO'S ROCKY? (1993)

*Love's a song
in a woman's heart*

"The River"

I was rattled. After my experience with detectives who seemed unable to give me answers about the break-in, I had gradually accepted that it was a random accident, a fate I must have deserved on some level. Whatever had been stolen was gone forever, and whoever had done it would never haunt my dreams again. I'd had my suspicions about the coincidence of Bobbi Jo not being at home at the time of the burglary, but I had given up trying to make sense of her actual whereabouts. She was believably upset but refused to discuss who she'd been with during that time. To the professionals, it was just another burglary. Unsolved and of less concern with every passing year since 1988.

It had been almost five years that I'd been working on leaving those uncomfortable questions behind me when the police phoned. Maybe they finally had some answers.

But the call which rattled me had come from a homicide detective. My head swam. One of our best drivers, Bob Gordon, who had been dependable from day one, had spent eight years in the penitentiary for manslaughter. And as Susan had said, "He's the nicest murderer I've ever met." I sure hoped Bob hadn't done something stupid. Behind his gentle smile was a spitfire temper.

The way Bob Gordon had explained it, when the guy broke the beer bottle over his head, Bob had gone "just a little kooky." He hadn't meant to kill him. Hell, the guy was a retired clown, trying to be funny about how Bob was short and how maybe his wife wanted something normal sized. As Bob told me this, I tried to measure his grin, all the way through the part about how he'd used the broken leg of a barstool to finish the job, because he needed to make the guy stop laughing. But then all that blood had made Bob feel sick, and he'd slipped in it, and the bouncer had handcuffed him to the pay phone, and it started ringing, and Bob answered it, and sure enough, it was Bob's wife saying she'd been looking for him. "How's that for ironic," he said.

The homicide detective asked to meet Sunday morning. The church bells chimed as he ducked his head through my front door, and his thin lips smiled wanly. I remembered him from the night of the Thanksgiving disaster. He was the one who kept calmly asking if Bobbi Jo and I had been arguing. If she'd been "seeing someone."

We sat outside. I was nervous. I had Bob's file in my hand, and several letters from customers, writing to tell me that Bob was a careful mover, and a real gentleman. But before I could begin bragging about how well Bob had been doing, the raincoat-clad detective slid photographs across the patio table. I felt something stabbing behind my eyes as I recognized the display box of coins I'd found metal detecting, and my 1923 Peace dollar and the Civil War-era gold pieces I'd collected. "What the fuck?" I growled. Cold sweat gathered on my hands as I paged through the pictures. This was not about Bob Gordon.

There was a gun, not mine, and a man's watch. Not mine either. There was also a photo of a bound leather volume, with the word 'Diary' embossed on it. "What the fuck?" I said again as my eyes met his.

He held his blank stare and declared, "All this was found in a location where a fatality occurred. I can't show you any pictures of the body, but we know the deceased had worked for you. He had Big Boy Movers T-shirts in his room and one of your hand trucks in his closet. We don't know who his accomplices were, but they may have had some disagreement that led to his death. He was obviously close with your ex-wife."

Bobbi Jo was super attractive, so sexy that men had literally followed us home at times. And the movers craved her. It had become an inside joke. Who was going to screw the boss's wife? But I had no idea as to who would have become so entangled with her that it would have cost him his life. I didn't like how this was making me feel. I understood why I was involved in this investigation, but I was a victim. I also understood how frustrating it was that I hadn't been able to provide the detectives with any solid help regarding my wife's whereabouts. I made sure that my eyes never left his as I said, "Sir, I have no idea who my wife was consorting with; that's one of the reasons we got divorced."

He opened another envelope and I saw a nude shot of Bobbi Jo, standing under a pier in Oceanside, California, her black leather jacket open. It was one of the pictures that had been stolen from my dresser upstairs. She'd inscribed it to someone with a heart. But whatever she'd written on it was covered with a Fairfax County police evidence sticker. I assumed that it had been a reward, but for what? The conglomeration of mysteries all centered around her absence on the night of the break-in. That spoke volumes to me. I accepted her sexual appetite; I was at peace with her infidelities. But was there a more sinister reason for her to be rewarding some mover with a gift like that?

"We think the male fatality had been hired to break into a house where a young female was staying. We found nothing of value, just the robbery victim's diary; at least, we think it's hers. There's no name or address anywhere in it. Just sporadic entries. She says she believes her father owns a moving company. She was trying to contact you and she wrote that she had a run in with your wife." Thin lips took a long breath. He focused on something beyond the pool. I felt exhausted, imagining what was still unknown.

"What else?" I asked. No answer came, just the peeling of church bells, delighted in how the Divine had given us life. In one ear, I felt a breath, in the other the muted sound of gunshot. The detective had gone silent, but I heard a scratchy voice coughing in my head. "You'll be fine, boy. I came back from France, bayonet stuck me, but I made it. Toughen up."

Blue light danced across the pool for a second. A thought escaped my lips. "Do you think it's my daughter?"

The detective shrugged. His tall shadow had turned colder, the table glass was a mirror now, and I sensed that he saw panic in my face. "We found other documents that may belong to her, a birth certificate; hospital records, adoption papers, that sort of thing, all in the possession of the deceased. We're not sure if it belongs to the same person, and anyway, we can't find her. Did she ever contact you?"

I didn't tell him about the letter.

The mover had a reason to dig through this girl's things. Was someone looking for proof of some financial claim on my estate? I was beginning to see a pattern. My daughter would be entitled to as much as a wife expected to receive in my will.

He saw my dazed expression, but he continued. "It's taken us a few years to put this together, but from what I've read, the young woman traveled from Florida, looking for family." He tapped the envelope. A small color photo slid out. It was me, in a bathing suit, leaning against a palm tree. I was tan and skinny, and wearing an Orioles baseball cap. I held it and tried to remember who'd taken it. On the back someone had carefully printed "Del Ray, Florida, 1977, your Daddy!" I was twenty-six then. My daughter would be about sixteen now, if she'd been born that year. I also couldn't fully accept that I had a daughter. I couldn't believe how much of her life I had missed. It was hard to embrace a loss, if that loss wasn't really mine.

I asked again, and this time he heard me. "Do you know where she is now? Is there any way that you can help me find her?"

He looked back at me, and I knew he was a father. The emptiness in his flat expression told me. They had no idea where she was. She had vanished. But that didn't mean I'd stop looking for her.

So Bobbi Jo was close to a mover who might have been involved in the burglary. Had it cost him his life? Had she hired him to do two robberies? Make quick pawnshop cash and dig up my connections to this daughter; destroy proof, problem solved? It amused me in a sick way, to think that my ex believed I was worth so much that a daughter might limit her from getting her imagined share of all my wealth. I was president of three corporations. She assumed that they were worth a hundred times more than the certificates I kept in my file cabinet.

In the end she'd given up. Maybe the fatality had scared her, and she'd decided that forty thousand dollars was all she could get out of me. I knew Bobbi Jo's history was colored by some unusual risks that she'd taken. I knew her material temptations ran deep. But I'd also seen the Light in her spirit. She'd made some disordered decisions, but she wasn't a bad person. There was so much undeniable good in her. She would never condone what had been done to that mover. She might have simply gotten too close to the edge of disaster and had fallen into it, unable to control where she landed. We've all been known to leap into the Great Beyond. That was one of the reasons I'd fallen in love with her.

And the mother of this possible daughter. Where was she? The detective closed his notebook. He'd told me he couldn't offer any further information, only promising that I'd get my property back as soon as the investigation was over.

I'd kept that unsigned letter in my sock drawer. After the detective left, I opened the envelope. For whatever reason, I had not looked deeply enough into the lowest corner. Two little black-and-white photos were stuck in its depth. I coaxed them out. In one, a bald woman in a narrow bed, her smile still delicately crooked as she stared blankly toward the camera. Melinda. That was her name. I remembered her lying beside me on the sand, telling me she was leaving Florida. To go home to Minnesota. I recall her voice, asking me if I'd write.

We'd walked away from the others. The band had gathered around the bonfire; it was a Primadonna beach party, half naked drunks, and us, upwind from them on a deserted stretch of Del Ray beach. I heard one of the roadies and his shitty guitar screaming Lynyrd Skynyrd songs. Melinda asked me to hold her, offering kiss-me-goodbye lips. Driftwood flames threw shadows around us. The stars and the smell of the ocean spoke to me, reminding me: she's a wild creature, migrating. I knew I couldn't hold on to Melinda. She knew it too.

Blonde Melinda, our fingers wandering under our towels until she said, "Wait," and then we'd broken loose, stumbling into each other for the last time.

The other little photo puzzled me. A shaggy-haired muscular dude and the crooked smiling Melinda leaning against him. He had his hand on her stomach like he was measuring something. The note on the back proclaimed: "Melinda and Rocky, 1977, Augusta, Georgia!!" Who was Rocky? Maybe Rocky got the same 'are you my Daddy' letter I got. Maybe somebody was hoping I'd know where he was. I wanted to do the right thing. But as I stared into the shadows of my sock drawer, I realized that sometimes we have to walk away from mysteries that we cannot solve.

Faith in Divine light never blinds us. It lets us see without our eyes. And I knew that I was being shown truths that might be unsettling, but that they were all my teachers. Something from that envelope rose behind me, its blue hands settling softly on my shoulders. A gentle voice told me I'd done the right thing. Even if I wasn't sure what that was. Faith in my actions were indeed blessings that a gracious God was sharing with me.

Susan found me passed out on our bed, cradling my pillow like it was a child.

Whatever it was, Susan knew. She had the vision to see the goodness in me. And the worry that she knew I'd need help losing. She saw the father in me.

CHAPTER 44

A STAR-KISSED GLOW (1995)

*I had flash and
snakeskin boots*

"Love Was a Lie"

"Turn right at the next light. Up there. See it! Hey just past that three-way intersection," and those words, imbued with the dramatic tenor of his voice, became a heavy metal scream as Garth shouted, "Look out!" and I slammed on the brakes of the E Truck, just a hair away from the rear of a minivan which had rammed into the tractor trailer ahead of it. From his passenger seat, Garth commanded, "Go," thrusting his right arm bravely outward, demanding our entry into one lane and then another, and another, until four lanes later, as horns blared, we received some merciful blessing from highway angels in the form of perfectly timed green lights which parted the traffic ahead of us to allow our ascension onto an exit ramp that would deliver us to our preordained destiny. A barbecue joint called "Fricks," just beyond the last clogged aorta of Breezewood. "They've got great Mennonite cider," Garth had said.

Garth knew all about this joint, as his band, Strangle, always stopped there when they did their mid-west tours. He was their bass player and had been happy to hit the road with me, to make a custom delivery to a young woman in Canton, Ohio. Plus, he'd assured me that he knew a shortcut through

Breezewood, which was a relief, as I always dreaded my treks through that maniacal maze, where the air smells like diesel because Maryland, Ohio, and Pennsylvania all deposit their concrete bowels into the latrine that is America's Largest Truck Stop.

After lunch, the cab got quiet. I had to admit, I still heard the feral call of road life and it tempted me. Susan and I were married now. Domestic life was steady and sweet. But riding along next to a fellow musician gave me a chance to remember the thrill of never knowing what lay ahead for the band. Would the gig be sold out? Would the accommodations include massage service? How would the new songs go over? Would there be some hot fans who'd want to party after the show? Would management from New York surprise us with good news?

It took a couple hours, but the long loping miles began to unspool in less appealing ways. I remembered the hunger of needing to be loved by audiences, venue owners, agents, managers, and record labels who all believed we could be bought and sold like a commodity. As Garth snored, I thought of Strangles' financial entrapment to their record label. My heart took a celebratory leap as I realized I was no longer bound to an industry which really didn't care if I succeeded or failed. Until I succeeded, which then meant I'd be legally enslaved to them. I was free from the bondage of being a costume on stage that I'd grown out of.

And it seemed more than coincidental that Susan had come into my life as I had freed myself from a similar superficial bond. Susan's belief in me, at what we might do together, was compelling. Her invincible confidence had warmed my hand as I held hers. This was not a Bobbi Jo intoxication, but healthy fire catching, its draft coming from how I saw the possibility of family growing around us. There were rose petals in her bathtub, but there was also a discussion about Emily Dickinson as she stimulated me in ways that I'd never imagined. Our talks felt like poetry we'd both been waiting to share with each other. And it fed our minds long after she married me.

There was a solidness in the lives entwining mine. Downstairs, the office hummed with the business of moving. Upstairs Susan glided about, catlike, with graceful strength. She smelled like fresh water which had sprung from its source and found its way into a desperately thirsty field the size of my heart. Six months into our marriage, there had yet to be anonymous flowers delivered, evasive answers, or mystery hickeys. We had one argument about the best way to brush teeth, but that was no measure of unsteadiness.

I might have missed the excitement of the road, but the thrills I'd pondered as I drove seemed cheap compared to the riches of being my own man, on stage as a solo act or as the founder of a moving company. Freedom wasn't something I ever thought I'd lost, but as I looked in the rearview mirror of my life I saw that I'd left behind everything and everyone that had kept me caged.

When Garth woke up, we were just outside Canton. "Thanks man," he said, "for hiring John to manage Big Boy." John was the drummer in Strangle. Steve Bowes had trained him well, and so far, so good.

I said, "Absolutely. A fellow drummer. Always a good fit!"

John Pettit was happy to have a more lucrative job after his band's European tour. Customers overlooked his piercings and dreadlocks and respected his steady demeanor. We played off each other, and he kept the rhythm of the business as if he was still behind his drums, supporting the challenges of the moves like songs in a set. It was as if the Divine had known exactly who I'd needed to keep my creation thriving. John exuded patience, humility, and kindness whenever he spoke to customers, movers, and to me. As with Steve Bowes, chaos turned more quickly to harmony with a musician at the helm. And my respect for both of them ripened into friendships that I value to this day.

A star-kissed glow filled the trucks as band members and even Strangle's road manager became movers. Hair grew longer and new tattoos appeared on the Big Boy Movers ensemble. I experienced Strangle's music from a distance; a riot in a dishwasher between animals choking on silverware. Superbly played, just not my cup of tea. John's office wall displayed glossy posters of their bare chests and black broccoli hair; with a logo of bladed instruments emblazoned with Viking symbols. Homage to an earlier style of touring.

Garth looked past his blown smoke ring and started talking. He was a fine bass player, and fans loved his ability to jog toward a stage wall and propel himself up it, crow hopping until he somersaulted; his dreadlocks sweeping the floor as he landed. It felt natural to have veteran musicians working at Big Boy Movers. We knew the fantasy of stage life, relished the thrills, but we were able to see the value of making a good living that didn't require any pretense or ego. That commonality made for a precious bond.

I told Garth about lighting heads on fire, standing on my drum stool, hurling flaming dolls into a crowd. The fog, strobes and explosions, the fans as cute as kittens, flashing me, watching me pump adrenalin. Those six-minute drum solos, flying from hi-hat to snare, around the toms. Like a jockey on a horse, I rode them, the wooden reins in my hands sprinkling blood everywhere. Garth knew. Better than any orgasm, a tornado of cheering, lifting you from all that keeps you earthbound. I missed the glory of the band circus. He could tell.

"But what I really love, what keeps me going, is the writing. I just can't see myself ever not writing songs." I didn't tell him about my spiritual guides, the blue-lit emanations, or my quest to dig deeper into my own life for song material. But he understood my hunger to perform. And I wanted to. Maybe not in huge arenas in Europe, but a table of six people in some dive bar loving my songs was worth more than ever.

Garth nodded. "Man, Ben," he said, "we should go on the road. Do your tunes; use a drum machine."

I said I'd think about it. The eyeball tattoo on his neck stared past me, unblinking.

When I got home, I played some new songs for Susan. She liked one in particular, about me running down an old road where the playground's closed for good. And how I can see two children like shadows in the woods.

But she couldn't see the performer who still needed audiences to applaud his work. Because he was the same one who craved silence, far from stages littered with broken dreams.

Either way I'll keep writing songs. And appreciating how they bring me divinity and truth.

And give us children, and shadows in the woods.

CHAPTER 45

THE BLUE FIGURES (1955-1995)

You might see our shadows,
standing in the rain

"Peaches and Honey"

The nickel-colored tube seemed harmless. I was in a loose gown, socks on, and all ears. The nurse was explaining why it was important to lie still so that the best MRI images could be obtained. As I was mechanically eased into it, headfirst, I noticed the light inside it seemed a bit off. It was not normal light. It was what I used to call igloo light; a muted icy gray, but warm in the way that being inside a snow tunnel used to make me feel. I remembered being on my back, when I was around seven, in a snowbank tunnel in the Mockingbird Hill winter hush, with just the sound of my own breathing in my ears. But my recollection of silence was interrupted by the clanging burps of something metallic on both sides of me. I imagined the cacophony as some acid jazz drum solo and tried to follow its rhythms. I let the irregular noises become informative and hopeful as I focused on my doctor's experience. He'd be able to make sense of all this. There had to be some scientific logic for why a variety of the blue-lit visions kept appearing in my life.

But the enclosure jerked in ways that were far from musical and that made me wary. What would be discovered? I'd been curious for so long. As I listened to my breath, I tried to accept the idea that some extrasensory ability had been bestowed upon me. I couldn't control it, or understand it, and I was in this tube to see if there was some medical explanation for what I had been experiencing for as long as I could remember. I closed my eyes. The bluish caress of what I saw behind my lids felt like the stroke of a hand, but whose? Did the blue figures originate from the myriad realities that intersect our own? I'd read that quantum mechanics and astrophysics had given birth to a new theory of biocentrism, which teaches that life and consciousness are fundamental to the universe. In other words, our awareness creates our material world, not the other way around. Death of consciousness simply does not exist, based on this theory. Therefore, my guides, my blue smears of matter, could have existed prior to my physical body being born, and in fact, may be beyond the constraints of time and space. Our reality is measured, and we use those measurements to keep our lives in order and in harmony with the world around us. It was a lonely feeling in that tube as I wondered if my doctor could see past what traditional medicine had taught him.

In my freshman year at college, when I began using drugs, hallucinations offered a sense of reality which was compelling. I let my mind travel through mysterious panoramas that gave me vivid glimpses of the "other side," where mystics, medicine men, and sacred prophets had journeyed for centuries. As I followed those inner pathways, I became certain that other realities existed. I saw them. I not only experienced the Buddha and his supplicants, but I met my previous incarnations in mirrors as I tripped. Still, LSD, mescaline, marijuana, peyote, and magic mushrooms never filled my head with blue figures. Other than the spiritual experiences I'd had, what I saw was almost always cartoonish and entertaining, as if the drugs were mental workouts to increase the range and stamina of my own imagination. And looking back on my lyrics, poetry, and drawings, they certainly did what they were meant to do.

All my encounters with my aquamarine entities were when I was stone cold sober. My powder blue figures were with me in times of darkness, when the depths of life were overtaking me. They were there as well, when I needed validation, and could find no human being to give me that. They were me. At least, they felt like they were not additions to my quest for awareness, they were simply with me as I sought it. They could not be bought, sold, or manipulated recreationally.

After I laid off drugs for good, I hoped Truth would come to me unadorned. My faith in how the Divine would guide me toward it became a journey I had to make alone. I had friends, like Shana, who might understand my hunger for a buoyant awakening. But as I meditated on it, I found that being alone, in silence, gave me more opportunities to hear messages I had missed, or been afraid to understand. Much of the work I was meant to do was daunting, because it meant confronting my ego and my mind, which I knew were always riding shotgun with me. But I was the one behind the wheel, and I made sure they knew it.

I didn't feel the need to explain my exercise of awakening to anyone, or to describe the mystery of whatever the blue figures were in my life. But Susan heard me. And in her quiet graceful way she reminded me that no one could make my spiritual journey but me. I kept reading, studying all I could on the sensory experience I couldn't understand.

Still, I knew I had to get an MRI to completely rule out this mysterious anomaly as being connected to anything physically wrong with me. It wasn't schizophrenia—those hallucinations are often more auditory. Mine rarely were, and whatever I heard was usually indecipherable. Visual hallucinations in older age often accompany Parkinson's or Lewy body dementia. If I had any of these health problems, I wasn't aware of it, and neither were my family doctors.

Hallucinations are believed to emerge from different connectivity between brain networks or regions, in the higher order prefrontal areas of the brain that monitor where our sensory information comes from—both internal and external. Brain folding patterns, which develop in utero in the second or third trimester of pregnancy, can scaffold the way we experience the world and whether or not we'll have these unusual sensory experiences.

As I was ushered out of my ride in the nickel-colored tube, I was told to put my clothing back on and find a comfortable seat in the waiting room.

An hour went by. My hands were sweating as I turned the pages of a magazine. Why was he taking so long? Maybe he'd discovered something mysterious in my brain? Curiosity is a quirky companion. It urges you to turn over every stone but forgets to warn you about the spiders and snakes that may lurk beneath the rocks. I tried not to think. Just as I realized that wasn't going to happen, I heard my name being called.

My doctor appeared in the doorway. With a friendly head tilt he said, "Come on back to my office."

I was surprised by his blank face as I described the blue images I had experienced. I explained that they weren't always completely visible, that they were often a smear of bluish light. How they mostly appear when I feel I need them to. Or not.

"They can surprise me," I confessed, knowing how odd that sounded. I didn't tell him about seeing my great grandmother's face in a train window. I imagined him smiling as he'd ask, "And you were how old? Five?" I tried to give him details; describing that there were sounds, whispery, feathery, and that there was a chanting sometimes, but I really began to get the sense that he thought I was just batshit crazy. He'd been my doc for a few years, but I'd never had the courage or confidence to confront him and tell him these things. My truth. And now that I was, I regretted it. I should have written it down. I was struggling to describe something that came and went, and that I never fully saw as having a distinct face. I felt my thoughts unraveling; my voice was faltering. "Just shapes," I told him.

"Always blue?" he asked. "Ever seen any other colors? Polka dots? Two tones?"

He cleared his throat and began reading from a book on a shelf behind him: "Yes, we decipher broken brains. We can even track neural codes, the actual spatial-temporal firing patterns for particular objects in the hippocampus, and we can even install an implant that replaces a faulty circuit in the prefrontal cortex . . . "

My blood pressure was rising. My shirt was sticking to my back. This was the wrong guy to have come to, but he droned on, saying, "Insurance will cover everything today, and I don't see any reason for a follow up, but . . . " I held up my hand.

The white-jacketed doctor paused and squinted. After his glasses had collected enough of the overhead light in his of-fice, he swiveled around toward me.

"Sounds expensive, doesn't it?" He grinned. "I'd tell you if I saw aliens in your film."

I got on the elevator feeling emotionally drained: I'd come to an expert with a riddle, I'd sat and eaten myself up inside, imagining the worst, hoping for the best, drinking bad coffee in an empty waiting room, for what? For him to make me feel like a freak? I didn't see that coming.

As I was putting on my seat belt something slipped in behind me. In the mirror, a serene mist of a face. Water blue. With the most peaceful smile I'd ever seen.

My guides are gifts, and yet I can't thank them, except by being open to whatever they are conveying to me. I made up a prayer to say when I'm wanting to reach them: God give me the strength to find peace, God give me the faith to know peace, and give me the grace to share the peace I've found. It came to me so naturally, that I wonder now if perhaps they spoke it into my ears as I slept.

Our souls are constructed from what the universe is made of, and that very fabric also houses our brains, which are just amplifiers and receivers for the proto-consciousness. All is one. All is connected. If there is no death of consciousness, then whatever I've seen as a blue-lit guide may simply be part of the fabric of the universe, and in fact, "it" may live on long after my body is gone. Einstein said: "Religion is science," but I wasn't going to let science tell me what to believe.

My heart never questions why my Creator keeps sending me visions of beings I have yet to understand. There are no words to question Him with, but I promise I'm never going to turn away from where I'm being guided. I will surrender to uncertainty and do all I can to help others, as my Creator has helped me.

CHAPTER 46

LOVE WAS A LIE (1997)

*We gave each other blood,
we gave each other bone*

"Everything That Matters"

Song ideas are like tadpoles, ripening and wriggling up through me until they're caught in a net of chords on my piano, where they stretch and astonish like sleeping babies do.

I might have talked about it, but I never wanted to become a real father, even when I was married to Bobbi Jo. I believed my destiny was to be a songwriter and performer. That was the life I lived. I stayed on that path of dreams, writing for the radio, recording, hoping; always with one eye on the golden prize that was constantly just out of reach. Then I met Susan. My song "Love Was a Lie" is a reflection of how grateful I am now. I dedicated it to her when I performed, though she was seldom in the audience.

*My first children were my songs
They were happy when you came along
When you left and the house turned cold
They were all I had to hold
I had fire and a brush with fame
Now nobody's clapping
And calling my name
Love was a lie but I made it sound true*

Love was a lie 'til I met you
Shadows run through this old house
In golden light that never goes out
Fingerprints on windowpanes
From little angels who flew away
Precious ghosts who stay with me
That's the blessing of memory
Love was a lie I finally saw through
Love was a lie 'til I met you.

Fatherhood is a song I've just begun writing. Fame was a song I never finished. And family is a song I'll sing with my sons.

Susan and I had been trying to create a child for two years. She'd had more than one miscarriage. I'd felt pretty helpless when those had happened, and I never seemed to find the right words to comfort her. But finally, on the tenth day of February 1997, a miracle was born. His name is Henry Fox Mason.

He was presented to me in the latex-gloved hands of a tough talking nurse, still connected to the lifeline that sustained him for nine months, while his landlady abided by uncertain terms with her tenant. I was given scissors. My first son stared past me, as confident and focused as a man arriving at his own bus stop. Two transparent blue hands surrounded mine as I severed Henry's cord. He smiled at what only he could see.

Each of us is our own universe and every universe is in motion. But Divine motion has yet to charge me for what it has transported into my life: Art, words, rock and roll; which brought the truck I grew into a business, and Susan, who helped create the music of real family which I never thought I'd have in my life.

Love was a lie. Until I experienced the truest love of all. The love of a child.

I'd believed that my choice of profession would always surround me with family. Which I thought of as the guys in whatever band I was in, those freewheeling poly-marriages that were sustained by our constant attempts to give birth to our dreams of fame. Even Big Boy Movers was enough of a pseudo-family that it satisfied my need to shepherd children.

I knew I was a father figure, and sometimes, when Davo had downed one too many six-packs, he'd call me Dad. I was Dad . . . to many movers. For decades I gave them shelter, financial support, and picked them up when they fell in the quagmires that tempted them. All those years of fatherly role play are still a proud song in my heart. But there is no comparison to the pride I feel every day for my real children, and I have only Susan to thank for that.

Divine motion would also deliver our second son, Arlo John Mason, within three years of Henry's arrival. Arlo is tuned to the same key as I am, and from his first breath, I heard his melody reaching toward mine. I'm the audience The Divine allowed me to become. The only charge for my attendance is the heartache that comes with it. But that fades as I imagine my sons in the blue yonder of what never dies. My relatives, long gone, are the lights that shine from their eyes into mine. My sons are the best songs I've ever written.

We are held in the hand of Love
Of all that gives Spirit flesh and bone
Our lives are the dreams God has
As we learn to find our way Home

By the time Henry was eight months old I was working on

a new record. I birthed the songs half asleep and wrote "Me and Cleopatra" with one hand on the piano as I held Henry. I booked a studio, employing pot-smoking hipsters on bass and drums, with Jeff "Cool Shoes" Severson producing. He knew his way around the studio. His band "Four Out of Five Doctors" had been signed to CBS Records, toured with Hall and Oates and opened for The Cars, and The Clash.

This second CD, "Forty Eight States of Love", was playful. The material burst out of me, almost as if I'd written the songs to capture a child's attention. There were bold, kaleidoscopic creatures roaming throughout the album, like "Lizard Queen" (who has a pretty purple tail that falls off in my hand), "Mambo Genesis" (which describes a llama in a bathtub, a rooster who steals a wedding ring, and a song-weaving spider), "It Rolls" (an account of a holy hound dog who screams out Bobbaloo), and "She's a Cat" (about Susan), which Henry would eventually sing from his car seat. As a new dad, I wasn't always sure what I was doing. But I'd been raising my first child since I was thirteen in the Infernos.

I was too overwhelmed to release the record, and too busy being a surrogate father to crews of boy-men who toddled in and out of Big Boy Movers' nursery. Meanwhile, our sleep-starved life was in full production, and John was driving the G truck because one of my boy-men broke his hand in a bar fight. So I held down the desk, half asleep.

"Big Boy Movers: Hello? I'm sorry to hear that." I squeezed my tea bag until it delivered into my mug, reminding me of the diaper I should check upstairs.

An agitated voice continued, "Do you have a crew available? Today?"

I heard despair in the woman's voice, but there was nothing I could do to help this person. The voice became a bluesy

keening, "We're all packed," she said, and I felt it, an exhausted, raw-faced woman, her hands sore from the boxes she'd
wedged into her car, the heat draining her, as someone on the
cool side of Moving Day stared out, useless, chain smoking
for breakfast because his kitchen was empty.

She named the movers who stood her up; "Assholes, fuck-
ers, sorry, pardon my French." She sighed, but I recognized
the names; they used to work for me.

She'd hired the cheapest movers she could find; booked
them weeks before. But someone else who also had to move
today was probably paying those cheap movers double or triple their normal rate. So they told this sobbing woman that
their truck blew its engine or the exhaust fell off. It was summertime and the lying was easy.

Consoling her brightened my azure headlamp. I focused it
on her as she said, "Thank you and goodbye, I'll keep looking."

Seconds later, the phone roared like a monster organ lick.
A bassoon voice wanted to know what the fuck I was trying
to pull.

"You promised three men. Ninety an hour. You sent an
extra guy here!"

I asked bassoon voice to put his wife on the phone. She
was a fourth-grade teacher and we'd had no communication
problems when she booked the move. She chirped pleasant-
ly but didn't understand that four men did her job in three
hours at one twenty per hour, and that three guys would have
taken five hours or longer. So it got done faster, for less than it
would have been. "Mungo didn't explain that before the move
started," she said.

It was a cruel feeling, being an hour away from a conflict
I'm sure I could resolve in person. I told myself to take a deeper breath, as I caught the bluish wisp of a shape sweeping past

the basement office window. I could feel my nerves binding together in my shoulders, in my hands, and I couldn't help the tone that began rising in my voice. This was simple math; why couldn't she understand that? But before I could find a nice way to say that, I heard her crying.

Bassoon grabbed the phone; sputtered I was "a little prick." I said something unprofessional. We both apologized, and I knocked sixty bucks off the bill. Hopefully they'd tell people we treated them right.

Upstairs, Susan was singing to Arlo and Henry—something soothing.

I'd never heard her yell at anyone. Where was her anger? Maybe she'd left it in California or New Orleans or back at her corporate job that ended when she moved in with me. Susan taught yoga until a month before Henry was born. She was the eye in a hurricane of leotards.

Early in our relationship, Susan had noticed my tendency to react heatedly, and she'd given me two books about anger to read. The problem was, I had never seen my fire as a detriment. I'd harnessed it for the physical work it took to build businesses, and in the spiritual work it took to seek mindfulness. I was hurt that Susan felt pain from anything I did. I read the books, but I bore resentment that she wasn't able to appreciate that my fire is what made both sides of my being thrive.

I reminded myself that balance had to be a model for our children, and our family. I told myself that this higher love is what were born to find and share. That it was simply God's will. I promised myself that I would show Susan that higher love; that she was the one who I'd waited a lifetime to share it with. I needed to tamp down my fire. It was time.

CHAPTER 47

A NEW HEART BOX (2000)

Faith is the nail that builds this house

"House of Hope"

Would the child I raised for almost twenty-one years thrive without me tucking it in at night, in the house where it was born? Big Boy knew Daddy was moving. Susan and I wanted to raise Henry and Arlo in the country, in the midst of nature, away from the concrete confinement of the DC area. But it would be challenging on levels I couldn't describe to Susan. She sensed my anxiety, my fear of disrupting a business that had allowed us to make this plan. Manager John insisted, "Go, I got it covered." But he wasn't me.

By now we were already a mobile operation. John and I had cell phones, and the drivers did as well. No more complicated pager codes, hunting for pay phones, or asking to borrow the customer's landline. Electronics kept Big Boy connected, but we'd never been more disconnected physically. The organization I'd had in my head since 1979 was in one central location: my house. It was where the moving company operated and often camped, awaiting orders to advance in campaigns I could always monitor from my basement bunker. That army was now only in the field, its home base permanently deactivated.

We adjusted. The physical location of trucks and moving

supplies, logs of worker info, graphs of profit and loss, journals of booked moves, Strangle posters, the desk, two wobbly chairs, and a gooseneck lamp; all these existed now as transitory geographic points in space. The only constant was my realization that it was all slipping away from me.

Would John avoid operating problems by shrinking the operation? If I was two hours away from household moves and the six-wheeled beasts that died at inopportune times, how could I instantly appear to raise the dead, calm the fury, and charm the livid into writing checks for imperfect moves with damaged furniture? John couldn't perform miracles. That would still be my job.

It wasn't arrogance. It was fact. I was the only one who had that power. It would mean more drive time if I couldn't resolve the problem from a distance. My dreams had taken over twenty years to come to life, and they gave me the hindsighted confidence to take on any threat to their demise. But had I become too deeply rooted in the location I had transformed into the hub of my business to physically leave it? And the creativity I had freely let flow, would it simply remain here, where it would exist without me, forever completed and unmovable? What about all the years that had been spent redesigning the wrought iron entry, the arched front door, the leaded glass side windows, the crown molding, the addition of all the landscaping which surrounded the house and the backyard pool? The decking, which was woven in sections throughout the rear of the house, flowed outward from a covered porch I had personally sanded, stained, and decorated with a vine-covered lattice wall. I'd be leaving behind a portfolio of my artistic abilities. I'd be saying goodbye to every commitment I'd made to reform a plain 1935 brick Cape Cod into a showpiece that was truly a work of art.

But what always came back to me in those moments of curious wondering was one inescapable fact. My beautiful creation was surrounded by endless, discordant noise: speeding cars, sirens, rocketing metro trains, and neighbors so loud that I overheard confidences I was forced to digest. That weave of constant clamor wove itself around me like an ugly Christmas sweater. I wanted to be free of it, and whenever I doubted Susan's compass, which always pointed us toward Rappahannock, I felt the constraint of that garment which was starting to feel more and more like a straitjacket. I imagined my decades of efforts, as artful as they were, as a finite, passionately conceived, three-dimensional structure. Moving away from it would allow it to become forever finished, framed, and hanging in the only place that mattered. My own heart.

To repair myself, I was building a new heart box, for our family. With no stage lights or wet panty contests. There'd be water, maybe a river where I could moderate my fire, where the reminders of my rock and roll lifestyle were just shooting stars in its pitch-black skies. Where I could close my eyes and not hear the sound of my thoughts blaming me for giving away so much of myself to satisfy the hollow hunger I'd shared with Bobbi Jo. Where there was enough space for all my guardians of twilight blue illumination.

Rappahannock County nestles up to the Blue Ridge Mountains, and it's just far enough from the DC area to keep an onslaught of sightseers away. Because who wants to drive two hours to look at low-lying mountains? And hiking? There's plenty of that, but I don't see getting poison ivy as alluring as what the Eastern Shore and Maryland and Virginia beaches offer. There are no geologic anomalies that pull crowds out here, unless they simply want to see unique beauty hidden in plain sight. And drink clean water and breathe fresh air. All concepts easily overlooked.

Rappahannock drew us to it. For five years we explored its bounty of uncrowded secrets and affordable real estate. Coming home to Falls Church had become an odd readjustment. Convenience and familiarity always greeted us, but something began following me. As I fell asleep, its message matured in my head until words rose with every breath. They were "silence . . . songs . . . water."

We kept looking at properties—month after month. We asked questions. I did some front seat pondering about that unsigned letter from the writer wondering if she's my daughter. Thinking out loud, I asked, "I wonder if she decided Rocky was her dad. That would make sense," I muttered, remembering the muscular dude with his right hand on Melinda's stomach. "The whole thing doesn't add up, but I'm having a hard time letting go of it."

Susan said, "If she's your daughter she'll find you. When she's ready. Bobbi Jo might have scared her off, but would that stop your kid? Let it go. If she's really yours she'll prove it."

The pieces of my life might not fit together yet, but the mosaic was still being shaped. I understood that. When we got in bed that night, I imagined a black canvas above me filled with abstract ruminations that I saw as a work in progress.

Part of me wanted to stay rooted where everything grew predictably, and my routines were perfectly sized for who I was. The safety of the past was intoxicating, but it could also be a numbing stupor which would keep me from hearing voices and sounds calling from Rappahannock. I meditated on letting go, and the unsolved equations faded as I drifted off. Something was drawing me toward music I had not yet written, lyrics I had yet to sing. There were other wordless signs that the Divine had sent for me to heed, like the messages I caught as I stood in acres of little blue stem hay and saw the figures I had begun to trust. Always just out of clear sight, moving as if they held a sacrament, a sun-blessed mystery they knew I was bound to follow. With my family. Even when I felt lost in Rappahannock, I saw vision and light. Maybe peace and curiosity too. Maybe what my guides wanted me to see.

God's grace was giving me the opportunity to embrace the missing pieces of my life.

CHAPTER 48

RAPPAHANNOCK (2000)

Old voices keep calling me

"Rappahannock"

It is said that we will walk past a serial killer seven times in our lives. It is said that in a lifetime of swimming, thirteen deadly diseases will pass by us as antibody remnants. It is said that we are always within inches of the treasures that lie buried beneath our feet: Native American artifacts, Colonial-era relics, and even underground fungi, like truffles, all of which can often be worth more than gold per ounce.

We are luckily stupid and stupidly lucky. A man has a bladder infection. He walks to the back of the plane on a flight over Tunisia and an unsecured door blows open. He falls thirty thousand feet, lands on haystacks and crawls into a deserted mosque. He drinks his own infected urine and eats bats and lizards for sixteen days until he's discovered by a herdsman. We are all falling, landing where we are meant to be.

After five years of searching, Susan and I found a place in Rappahannock like none of the other forty-four properties we'd been shown. Even though it had to be torn down and re-built so we could live there. Even though when we first pulled into its circular driveway I didn't want to get out of the car. One day earlier our realtor had called to tell me that this was the place we'd be buying. She knew me that well. As I stared at the beaten-looking, mansard-roofed wreck, I thought she had to be kidding.

But it's never what real estate looks like. It's what you look like when you imagine it. It might be a battleship gray dumpster, but if it sits on heavenly acreage with river frontage, then start packing: you're moving. As we walked the property and took in the views from it, I became overwhelmed with the promises it offered.

Sonically, I was intrigued by sounds I'd caught as we'd driven the mile-long lane that led us to the house. They were not chattering echoes of life led by humans on treadways to whatever success they were seeking. No mechanical clatter trailed us from the city. There was only a bittersweet tonelessness that taunted and teased me, challenging me now, to listen carefully to what lay between the breaths of breezes and the sigh of wind sweeping the hay field behind the house. And that desolation guided me, promising me I would make new creations. That I would tell new stories and weave them into art, that there would be encouragement from my blue champions who chanted in time with the current, as I drifted off that afternoon against a warm rock beside the Thornton River. This land would hold me. The water would heal me.

This place on Blossom Lake Lane in Castleton could be recreated into a flourishing structure within and without, where Susan and the boys and I could play and work and live blissfully. Pretension could be left behind; it would survive on its own. It always does.

I also visualized a recreated home for my musical expression. My rock star persona wasn't dead, just in a state of suspended animation. That fire was infinite, crackling in my ears as the hopes that honored it stirred inside me. Kingfishers and a blue heron swept closely past as if I was on stage with them at Club Thornton. Lyrics came to me, as free flowing as the river below me. I didn't need a microphone to express them:

Heavenly dancing fish scales in brown and wind green water
Are perfectly unspoiled like Nature's newborn daughter
They're rushing by like blessings in this Thornton River vein
Reminding me to see that everything is made of rain.
The best way to remember this is to feel the breath of spring
Her perfume falls like feathers from every bluebird's wing
Her blood is clear and warm, it's simply who we are
Made of everything that flows in this river made of stars
And when the pavement doesn't kiss you, and the cement
*   breaks your heart*
When the promise on your screen turns empty, cold, and dark
Walk away, put down the phone . . . come on out where the
*   garden grows*
Leave that life you think you own, leave it all . . .
*   and come on home.*

To deliver the goods in the business of music requires inspiration. I never realized how much I had needed a fresh infusion of it until that moment in the Rappahannock twilight.

I always wanted to live by the ocean, to satisfy my beachcombing hunger, but the river carries more diverse manmade and natural oddities past me here. The Pamunkeys used gummy river clay to make containers that were baked to burnished reds over slow fires to harden. I don't know why they broke them, but they always did when they left this area. I've found pieces of pottery stuck in the riverbank and even a flint arrowhead. I've dug up their tools, quartz spear points and axe heads, and even a fingerprint on one piece of delicately inscribed pottery. They were drawn to this spot, just as I am. They have left behind a plethora of artifacts as proof of their love of its bounty.

The river is a vein that leads to the sea, so my desire for

connection to the ocean has finally been satisfied. And it's so clear, that I can see a chunk of Unakite. It's Virginia's state stone and it's been here over seven hundred million years. There's wildness in her blood. I'll take a piece to Daddy. He'll love all its colors.

My Native American heritage is that of the Wampanoags, a tribe from New England. I am in fact, the tenth grandson of Yellow Feather, who greeted the Mayflower landing party at Plymouth in 1620. My father is named after his son, Metacomet or "King Philip." Perhaps it was this kinship that invited me to a similar place where people like my ancestors had lived; close to water, in the cradles of forest and field. The Pamunkeys depended on water. This river sustained them. It offers me a very different but just as essential sustenance. This is where I need to be to begin to heal myself. It feels like home. I believe my family will see the changes that I have felt aligning with my heart for some time. I used to find my true self in the spotlight. Now, I want to simply be in The Light.

Above me now, a pale green cataract, unutterably beautiful above the horizon, eclipses any stage light ever cast upon me. Fake fog and flash pots seem cartoonish beneath a sky so clear that the Milky Way becomes a luminous shawl.

This is our first night on the property. And our first bonfire in the backyard. I've gotten it going with pine boughs and packing paper from moving boxes, which makes the fire dance giddily. I see Susan and the boys inside, and from here their wide-eyed wonder is contagious. "Come on out," I shout toward the house. Susan carries Arlo, and I hand Henry the hose. The logs I'm leaning into the blaze are creating crazed sparks that are perfect targets for a three-year-old to shoot down. We move the lawn chairs back, the fire has grown fast, and as we retreat, I help Henry use the hose to quench the embers that enflame the dry grass around the bonfire.

"Couldn't do this in Falls Church," I tell my fire crew. Bright orange tongues waggle in agreement, at a wavering height of at least ten feet. With no wind to blow smoke in our faces, it is simply sublime, beyond all my suburban expectations. The pine logs seem to know they have an audience while they writhe and pop, as heat meets sap. Each flaming ghost of wood lifts my sense of what home means, as sparks find Heaven, up where I believe God watches over us.

CHAPTER 49

KENTUCKY GIRL (2002)

You are like the seasons, always perfect always leaving

"I Can't Make You Do Anything"'

I've sold Big Boy Movers Inc., for seventy-nine thousand bucks to Chazco Van Lines. It doesn't matter that it grossed over three million dollars during the twenty-five years I owned it. Or that it was my precious baby, born from nothing but a showman's sense of command. Or that I raised it amid the conformation of two marriages, in a ceaseless storm of work that battered flesh and trucks, and what they carried. Hundreds of people have come in and out of my life because of this morphing creation that started from nothing but a rock and roll dream. It gave me inspiration and the gift of time to travel. It also gave me acidic headaches and blistering breakdowns. I know the fire I harnessed to create it is still alive. But now I feel it in my heart, not in my ego, where it once urged me into confrontations with movers, customers and trucks. My legacy is no longer available to be rejuvenated. Or to blame me for. I won't leave my sons a business that starts fires.

Yet, the dilemmas which appeared on the road before me every day created an ever-growing confidence in myself which I will cherish. I always felt like I did behind the drums or at the piano; listening, reacting, and playing in sync with whatever new music was being birthed around me. Letting go of always being a featured soloist allowed me to find peaceful harmony with uncertain disorder which I could never predict. I composed solutions as I learned about the nature of my movers, our clients, and the six-wheeled beasts which transported countless belongings.

I will miss the victories, large and small, and the elixir of shared beers at the end of arduous days. I'll miss the glow of satisfied signoffs for the moving services we had provided. I'll miss the calls to congratulate me for sending fine young men to help a family become settled in their new home. I'll also miss how I've grown able to resolve problems like damages to furniture and misbehavior by my movers during the work they did so tirelessly. I'll always be grateful that I learned how to comfort unruly movers, to give them words of encouragement, after bad mistakes were made. Even as I fired them or as they quit the following day.

I'm proud of the fact that I could be a man with an expansive heart. Without my movers around me, that empathy will be an instructive reminder that I discovered my inner strength, that I wasn't an angry dictator, that in fact, I loved what I did and all the ruffians who worked for me. Maybe that reminder will reveal itself in more essential ways, as I raise my sons, without the constant distraction of those unpredictable collisions which always appeared on my previous highway of life. A new road is beckoning our family forward, but Big Boy Movers created our entrance to it. Relief feels like the heaviest and most precious load I'd ever transported.

On the way home from giving John the news of the sale of the company, which he took stoically, Daddy called. His voice went in and out as I headed further west on Route 211. "Fairfax Hospital; your mother, she's failing," he said. I made a U-turn at the Rappahannock County line and ran the light; nobody was on the road. The trooper who pulled me over, took my driver's license and handed it back after I told him where I was going. He studied me like he was wondering how he would handle his own mother's death.

In the rear-view mirror, the sky poured lavender gravy over the Blue Ridge. A comforting blue appeared buckled in the seat beside me. Did the trooper see it? His plastic name tag said Corporal Smoot. He had a weary Civil War soldier's face.

I met up with Daddy in the lobby of the hospital. In the elevator I gave him the Unakite. Before he stowed it his winter coat, we both marveled at it in his hand: salmon-colored feldspar, green epidote, blue quartz, and red jasper. "Boy," he said, "That's really something." It felt good to hear a little liveliness in his voice.

My mother was in a white room in the Cardiac Care wing of Fairfax Hospital. She was bunched up on pillows; blipping machines to her left; a tray with a juice box on a metal arm in front of her. Flowers on her windowsill overlooked a helicopter pad four floors down. I told her she's going home tomorrow, just in time to watch the boring Buffalo Bills, and she opened her eyes and asked me who's going to win the Super Bowl. "The Washington Redskins," we both said.

She was always a sports fan, and I remembered how she took me into Annandale Sport and Hobby to buy me my shortstop's glove when I was twelve, in 1963. My father had offered two gloves before that one, both as stiff as shields, deflecting every ball I tried to catch. "Twenty-nine bucks?" I heard him gulp.

And when I was seven, she drove ten miles to buy me five packs of baseball cards. A quarter, it cost her, what I would earn for a week of chores in Hockessin, Delaware. Her dancer's fire forged muscles up and down her body and allowed her to keep palming the floor at seventy-five. Who could do that? She was a diving coach, loved everything about water, and took my sister and me body surfing when we were barely old enough to swim. She built a koi pond and dug it herself, laying rock and breaking ground for dozens of azaleas that were her orange and pink pride. Afterwards, she'd drink her bourbon and say "go man go" as I beat on upside-down metal trash cans and the plastic tops of coffee containers.

And when I sat at the piano in her living room, she'd dry her hands and leave the kitchen to stand beside me. "Play me another song," she'd say before I left. "Just one more."

That day in the hospital her thick white curls made her brown eyes wider as she sailed through the pictures I'd brought. She studied Arlo wearing a Washington Bullets T-shirt, holding his spear aloft. He was in a primal hunter pose, all headband and serious, and she paused on that photo, staring at him, smiling. It's the last picture I ever showed her.

She took it with her into that realm where renegades and little boys are the same, running unbound like she did as a wild little girl in Anchorage, Kentucky, with two pet alligators watching from a bathtub outside. My mother headed toward the Divine an hour after I left. I hope she imagined that Arlo was beside her, as she kidded him about stopping in Buffalo to watch the Redskins win the Super Bowl. Maybe she was threatening to take him to some modern dance performance on Broadway. Maybe Arlo was wearing his Washington Bullets T-shirt, holding his spear, telling her he'd protect her along the way.

Later that evening I stood in the field behind the new house. And I saw my mother sailing above me, her brown hair shining in spotlights of sun. I saw her arms spread like wings, lifting her over stages she never got to dance across, over adoring crowds who never got to watch her fly. I wanted to release her from her frustration, from the denial of her dreams to dance like an angel. I wanted to stop trying to make her happy. I wanted us to release each other—to be just a mother and a son, imperfect, blessed with the gifts of Divine expression. Children and parents always drift apart, sometimes physically, sometimes not. We grow to let each other be who we will be. Are we guided? Are we meant to guide others?

I wanted us to be as perfect as we are now, not as we hoped to become, with our gratitude for each other the only accolade that mattered. And I asked my relatives to help me lighten the darkness that kept us apart.

CHAPTER 50

FOOTPRINTS IN SNOW (2003)

*All is passing and
the current's strong*

"Nothing Ever Stops Us"

Snowstorms in the suburbs always felt professionally managed, as if some overseeing authority was monitoring any accumulations that might threaten our freedom to use our cars. It was entertaining to watch the orange behemoths challenging our streets; the blackness of pavement appearing as cause for celebration. Victory! Over Nature!

All my years of life lived in such a well-guarded environment did not prepare me for the desolation and confinement that a Rappahannock winter delivered. I was now a mile off pavement, and as the ice storm thrashed against the house and froze bushes and small trees into reposes of vivid submission, I saw no rescuing plows headed my way. All I could see were white walls of wind-blown weather. I'd had the TV on, and just as the storm map was showing expected accumulations of eighteen to twenty-two inches, the electricity went out.

I balled up packing paper and loaded the wood stove with kindling and the dry logs I'd brought inside. The fire was warming the room when Susan called. The line crackled as she was telling me that she and the boys were stuck in Falls Church at the home of a young woman who'd been an occasional nanny for our family. It was hard to know when she'd be able to get home; Susan predicted that it might be a couple of days. Then the line went dead.

I needed to get outside.

The sun emitted a feeble glow in the howling snow that danced around me. But my rabbit fur hat, knee-high boots, and heavy coat over my bathrobe kept me warm as I trudged down to the river. It was frozen—but this was where I could become liquid light.

I kicked the snow off a flat rock, undressed, and hung everything on bare branches that offered a hearty welcome to me. At the river's edge I found a lance-like stick. I broke the ice and eased in.

Time stops in cold water; turns transcendental. Arms extended, I became a snow angel, wings barely moving, as I stared up from the Thornton. Whispers skimmed over me. Rising, sweet and still: "Come. Down. Stream."

Male and female. Poetry. "See the dark, don't fear the dark." It felt goofy to hear voices, but I followed the sound. The current twirled me into an eddy, and my head took a good whack. Rocks are soft in water this cold.

I was aware that Susan and I were being pulled by different currents. She'd become exhausted by my anxiety about what we'd taken on. All that she felt I blamed her for. All that I still held onto in Falls Church. But twenty-five years of living in one house made for roots that ran deeper than I could imagine until I tried to pull them out. All that history, all that entrenchment; I could feel it leaving me. I'd been waiting years to find water like this. I'd been the one who'd said "no" to the properties without it, and now that I was in it, it didn't feel painful, it felt like an assuring embrace of the man I'd been longing to discover. And someone I was afraid I might never find again.

I swam without moving, gasping through broken branches. A sycamore had its arms wrapped around shins of granite crouching in the river, and a gnarled hand reached for mine. It pulled me out from between the harp strings that held me. I gathered my towels and clothes and boots and climbed the hill from the river. The pond was an iced mirror reflecting a cat-eyed moon. What did it see? How that answer would come didn't matter.

Back inside, I added more logs to the fire blazing in the Vermont Castings wood stove. How long was I down there? In my coat pocket I found that I had carried up another piece of Unakite; so beautiful.

The blizzard raved on, slam dancing into the trees, assaulting everything. If I was in Falls Church, I'd hear the sound of machinery; comforting, like guards rattling keys, yanking on cell doors. Everybody's locked down in suburbia, doing time together. But we'd also be free, walking down our snowplowed street right now, back in civilization, comparing survival stories with neighbors. As I fell asleep, the storm rampaged, and in slate black darkness I woke several times to feed the fire, my only source of heat.

From my chair I saw dawn approaching. The litter box didn't smell; it was frozen. Coffee brewed with melted snow in a cast iron pot. Boiled eggs were shared with the two cats hunkering down with me as wood smoke greeted the morning light.

Something hooded glided near my car. Petite, fading into an opening between the pines. Snow tumbled from branches. A red cardinal struck an exclamation mark at the end of a question I kept asking.

With work coat and hat over bathrobe, I slogged out. Susan knew my mind on this. If there was a daughter and a paternity test proved it, she'd be family. But she was burglarized, threatened. Maybe she was afraid to get too close. Why were there fresh prints in the snow? Each one was delicately curved, with an arch that looked like a smile. Deep and small they bravely appeared as left, right, left, left, and then they vanished. A strong example of composure. Or panic.

Nothing was under the wipers of my car—no snowy envelope with a letter inside. Blaming me or begging me. If someone found the wrong Daddy, they'd be forgiven. An eight-point buck posed in the field to my left. A tawny doe tilted her rounded ass and faded into the Russian olives. But I wouldn't chase my curiosity into the pines, not this time.

Being seventy-two miles from my established past should have been comforting, but in the tranquility of a new solitude, the joints of my marriage, fatherhood, and my businesses had become loose. My faith had become the cast that steadied my doubts as I held them.

And I knew I hadn't completely left what I once called home. I knocked snow off boots and opened my new front door; and maybe it was my night of fitful sleep, or the aqua-colored light around me, but I clearly pictured how easily I entered the old rehearsal room, back in Falls Church. I could still smell the bar smoke of that noisy blue space, as I remembered the genesis of this person who was seeking me. I saw Primadonna posters on walls, band gear, my airbrushed drum set, and as somebody was tuning his guitar, I recalled how I began stretching a coiled phone cord out into the privacy of the hall, sliding to the floor, knowing I hadn't told anybody about Melinda in Florida, as she calmly informed me she was pregnant and keeping the baby; that I don't have to do anything. Saying she'll "handle everything."

"Who's the father?" I asked her as she hung up. Silence.

I understand I can't move away from what lives inside me. But I've been emotionally pregnant for twenty-six years. It's time to let those boot marks in the Rappahannock snow be deer hooves.

Back inside, sprawled in the cradle of my green leather chair, my fingers gently rake my cats' back, as frozen branches scratch frosted windows. Nature will always have the final word; I can't control it or people. Whatever was out there is unfathomable and will melt into the past like snow. All that matters is the present moment—the steady hum of the woodstove, the purring coming from the blanket beside me, and my acceptance of peace with all that surrounds me.

But in my cradle of contradictions, I am a man who can't always see and a man with sight I never knew I'd find. I wish I understood what doctors can't explain and forgive myself for doubting what it means. I believe it's God's way of guiding me; a sacred gift I'm not meant to unravel. In my solitude it surrounds me, in my silence I hear its call. I didn't arrive here by accident. I feel my cradle rocking. Faith moves forward as doubt pushes it backward. My growing kinship with the blue-lit figures is comforting. They have brought me closer to the Divine than I have ever been. As snow clouds turn from fists to open hands, my mind lets go of all that has bound me. I breathe and believe.

The room is warm. Wet pants and coat are drying, hung in sparkling light from a clear blue sky. Within the hour, I've moved into post-storm mode, broom sweeping snow off bushes that were weighted down, shoveling a walkway out my front door so I can be ready to receive the boys and Susan when the roads are clear. The power has come back on, and tepid shadows have given way to lights I'd left on when it failed.

I'd felt something lifting from me. It wasn't a waking dream. When I saw the snowy white canvas that had fallen around me, I knew the inspiration had come from knowing I could let go of all that had held me down in the city. That I was free to paint a new life. For myself and my family. That I was free to let the Divine direct that fatherless young woman to wherever she was meant to be.

CHAPTER 51

UNAKITE (2003)

*In every lifetime,
I am home*

"Brown Eyes"

One of the first songs I ever wrote, "When I Take the Time," ended up on an album released on Sanctuary Records by a band I was in, the John Wells Delegation. At seventeen, I was too young to appreciate that I was asking myself to be present; to be grateful for every breath, as I shared that song before countless audiences.

I thought I'd live forever, boundless on the waves of God's gift to me. Time to me then was a series of adventures, unfolding so fast that I was engaged mostly by the thrill, and seldom by what they offered me spiritually. I was not ashamed of my fire, or my intensity, as my friends described it. But I believe I knew that it was driving me beyond the speed at which I could absorb the nuances of the life I was passing through. I didn't realize that I was filled with a hunger I could barely control. It gave me the fuel to rise up every morning at 4:30 to deliver papers, to do three drum solos a night, and to make straight As in school. But now I see "When I Take the Time" as me talking to myself. That song was me being my own parent, reminding myself not to take too big of a bite, or chew too quickly; to savor each swallow which the Divine ladled out in the bowl of time before me.

My father tried to teach me this. And though he failed while he was alive, his lessons have come to life in me now, many years after his passing.

Daddy took his time. He stoically faced the horizons before him, just as he had when he was the captain of a sub chaser in WWII. He was patient, but he was present in every moment, even as his health dwindled, and his voyage grew closer to its end. He was always glad to see me, and my brother and I took him out to lunches and walks in his favorite park. But with Ma gone, he seemed more resigned to the weakening of his own physical condition. He lived alone at the house for a while, then gracefully accepted his stay at a nursing home for a month. When the time came for him to go into hospice, I was there, waiting with my brother and sister at its entrance in Arlington.

When the ambulance arrived, I thought of it as a taxi dropping my father off at a quaint hotel. It was lunch time. He'd settle in, stay a few days. Daddy studied the white dental molding over the entryway of the 1910-era house as he was rolled in. He noticed the slate roof and the elderly Virginia pines around the hospice. As he was wheeled to an amber-lit room, Native American flute sounds rose from somewhere. Daddy stared at me. He said, "Everything's going to be okay. Susan, she's doing what she needs to." But no one had told him about our separation and upcoming divorce.

He took on a concentrated expression as if he was measuring the dimensions of something. I brought the boys in. He squeezed their fingers. Henry and Arlo both said Daddy had talked to them. "Without words," Henry said.

I held his hand. He nodded when I reminded him how he'd walk out into the warm saltwater at Silver Beach and fall backward, spreading his arms, pulling himself with cupped fingers, sinking, then floating. How he'd always say, "This, this is why we come here." He took a long breath and closed his eyes. He was in the shallows, surrounded by pillows, pressing his lips together, and I could feel him letting his feet find the undulating sand. He squinted and I saw him measuring the horizon of the Chesapeake beneath an October sky.

I thanked him. For giving me music, for showing me how to be graceful, for sharing the elegant tact that made his life as peaceful as the watercolors he created. I thanked him for teaching me to tie knots, to ride a bike, to drive a VW Microbus stick shift, to write stories, to draw battleships and sing songs, to be direct, to tell people how much you love them, to embrace creativity when no one's there to hold you, to say fuck it when you've done all you can and there's nothing more you can do. For the pragmatism and the poetry, for the strength he was showing me now, for the courage to face death. For having a shepherd's heart.

"All of us get lost sometimes, we need somebody to help us find our way, and I had mine. My father had a shepherd's heart, and when I fell down in the dark he found me. And he brought me home." I knew I'd finish writing that song after he was gone. But I sang it to him anyway. Softly. I'd like to think I heard him harmonizing with me.

I had to leave then. To sing my songs for people who didn't know my father. He would have said "Play it pretty," if he could have. He let go of my hand as I kissed his bristly cheek. My sister and brother said he drifted away about the time I was finishing my last song that night. Peacefully, as if he was floating on his back in the shallows at Silver Beach.

Two weeks later I went by my parents' house. It had sold quickly the day before and I wanted a chance to say goodbye to its long expanses of exposed beams and white carpeted rooms. The house was efficiently empty, except for the dining table with realtor cards on it. I studied the clean white carpet which had been vacuumed by my brother as I followed it down the hall to my old room. I spent several moments there, remembering where I'd become a teenager. As I turned to leave, I stopped. Just ahead of me, in the center of that perfect, white-carpeted hallway, was Daddy's Unakite. It hadn't been there when I'd walked down that hall minutes earlier, toward the room I'd grown up in, the room where my father and I had both marveled at that piece of Unakite in his hand. Daddy taught me to beachcomb. No matter where we were, he was always curious about what might appear at his feet. That piece of Unakite was his way of saying, I wanted to beachcomb with you one more time. It was a playful wink. It was Daddy, reminding me that you never know what you'll find in this life.

Because time, the immeasurable ocean we travel to cross what we call space, twists and turns in ways we cannot fathom. The Thornton River is a microcosm of all of this; it carries the clear blood of all that is past, present, and future life. I've seen translucent blue figures gathering downstream from me, slippery dark hair like bark in suffused sunlight. It's where the quasi-dimensional becomes visible.

How does this come to me? I believe when I lie between the strings of the river's harp, the vibrations of flesh and bone align with the heart's eternal coherence. Energy is a frequency, and my Wampanoag blood resonates with sacred rhythms when I'm in the Thornton water. The Pamunkey Indians once lived here. In the quantum field of the Infinite, they still do.

Tonight, the Thornton is misty, moonlit water. A kingfisher scolds from her home in the bank, and I see velvety shoulders among the ironwood arms that bend toward the river. The moonlight casts them as blue, opaque, but they gather in a group across from where I float.

I exhale my awe underwater. Beetle-browed fish form mounds of tumbled pebbles: leaf green epidote, white and blue quartz, purple red jasper, pink feldspar, and gray basalt. Maybe my amazement will ripen the eggs they lay in those psychedelic piles.

"Bone turns to mud. Blood goes to sand. The river's like a woman's love, rushing through your hands. Love, too deep to understand." New lyrics rise into my mind, inspired by what's concealed in this water. Truth no one can know until they get absorbed by its darkness. Love can drown a man and it can save him. But Truth reveals what he's meant to see.

The song in my mind is a thought painting, and as I hold my breath, I wait for more words to appear. The river sand beneath me is soft, imploring me to imagine a pony, and as I rise, something rushes into my ears. A sound I've never heard before. Coming from where I saw the figures gathering. Upstream now, it's a chant. As clear as the wandering breeze that carries it toward me. Male and female, like before. The rhythm is steady. The tempo of the chanting goes faster as I begin to walk toward it. I want to understand. I don't call out. I say my name. Then I say my sons' names. The chanting stops. All I hear is the sound of the Thornton, undulating downstream, until it fills my ears with a silence that is as full as the moon above me.

I climb the hill to the house. Three blue figures followed me as I'd begun walking. I looked back once, and they appeared elderly, slowing, in perfect synchrony, until they were just shadows. As I near it I hear it. A faint chant rising toward the house from the river. I hold my breath. Walking in silence, blue reflections in puddles of light before me. The chanting is muffled whispers, a frequency I feel, especially in my fifth chakra. I answer, trying to mimic what I'm hearing, phrases that bend and fall. Keening I'm not meant to understand. But I'm learning to listen. To understand that love never dies. It just changes form.

For decades, the glamorous allure of my life on stage was a spot lit wall I'd never been able to see beyond. It was a self-made mirror where I would preen, imagining my image on album covers, or on my next television appearance. I caught heartfelt signals from the other side of that wall, but I dismissed them, unable to fully put my faith in the guidance they offered me.

A child hears what he can't describe. But my fruit of song grew on my vines until it finally ripened and they heard it. And that brought me to Rappahannock, to silence, where they knew I'd hear my song.

On our wheel of incarnation, we spin in circles, eating, drinking, fucking, wanting; our desire constantly turning us away from that which would nurture us: emptiness, stillness, and detachment. That's why I stuck needles in my arm in 1969. I wanted it all to stop. I wanted to slow the spinning, even for thirty minutes.

That was a careless misstep, but I don't regret it.

It let me see the darkness. So I could find the light.

EPILOGUE

"This life is a beautiful thing, and it doesn't end. I can hear the ancient ones in the hills, whispering . . . Rappahannock. Old voices keep calling me. Rappahannock. Life is more than what the living can see. Rappahannock, may your blessings always be." I wrote that the first summer I was here.

They've always been with me. In the woods behind our house in Hockessin, Delaware, as I followed them into hiding places, my wooden spear in hand. In freshly plowed fields, where their sharp arrowheads let me feel their will to survive. In all the ways I've felt them guiding me wherever I've lived.

Maybe I was too young to know them then, but I feel them now, as I walk through these empty bedrooms in Rappahannock. They are beautiful shadows and halos of light, more so than ever, assuring me that even in tumultuous times in my life, it will always be possible to find peace. They'll be with me as I venture backward and forward into the wilderness of what I thought would last forever and what lies ahead of me now.

They promised that the weight of grief and attachment would be lifted, yet I had no proof of that until my family left and I began living alone. My blue figures led me well. Not just because they are my ancestors, or because my Native American lineage connects us. The weight was lifted because they inspired me to embrace the void, to let the inspirations draw closer. To fill the emptiness with art, music, and writing, from places within me that had been chained to a life I learned to let go of.

My blue muses guided me through times which I always imagined would be overwhelming, toward healing processes, like the writing of this book. I have willingly had to relive the story of my adventures, both heartbreaking and joyful, but it has deepened my spiritual journey . . . which continues.

I have no concerns about what I imagine waits beyond a curve in the road ahead. I have been blessed with vision that allows me to see things that I do not need to understand or explain. And whatever those things are, will be perfect. Just like every Universe the Divine has created.

I sit in the leather chair in front of the wood stove, all wrapped up in a lodge of red and black quilts. Meditating. Silence. Detachment. Silence. Eyes closed, returning to the breath. The steaming darkness becomes a Divine weight. The locust wood has pockets, hot enough to whisper and moan, but then, across my folded fingers, I feel cool air. Darkness fades.

They enter, uncountable, people, my blood; ancient and young, dark and light, hair one shade of shadow, bodies weightless and empty. They hold me. Until I let go of fear. Until I know I'm not alone. And when my heart is as full as I can stand, I lift my quilts.

One figure of blue takes my hand. She leads me to my piano.

Sing me one more song, she says. And as I do, she dances.

I believed I was born to be a rock star. I clung to that belief until I was broke and living in an empty house. To find my truer self I had to let go of all which no longer served me in order to receive the guidance of what I've come to call blue lit energy . . . that inexplicable magnetic force that pulls me toward Divine providence.

I believe my metaphysical experiences to be symbolic messages delivered by mysterious visitors from the past and future.

My twisted path through darkness and light was graced with a compass that I learned to trust. I imagine the same is true for others who feel caught in the grip of crushed dreams.

Leaving my coveted identity under the spotlight of the stage allowed me to receive the light of Divine inspiration. For that, I remain forever grateful.

Ben Mason

High praise to Jeff Severson for his encouragement in 2012 that graced the birth of this memoir. Thank you to Leanne Tankel, Leslie Petit, Lessandra MacHamer, Laurice Herberghs, Pamela More, Sue D'Alessio, Karen Jones, Michael Barry, Mike Tramonte, Ron McMillan, Beth Harbison, JJ Gormley, and Dr. Tom Lawson.

Gratitude to Scott Severson for the artwork he did on all four of my albums. Musical thanks to Steuart Smith, Daryl Davis, Steve Van Dam, Nate Brown, Craig Honeycutt, Marco Delmar, Paul Eckert of Lucky Penny Concerts and Cerphe Colwell and Music Planet Radio.

Primadonna encores to Michael Yuhas, Ryan Michael Galloway, Donny Bobick, Robb Inglis and Richard Price.

Deep appreciation to John Wells, my guide when I was sixteen and he was twenty six as JWD weathered ten years in DC, New York, and Nashville. Much love to him, Tom Murtha, Holly Garber (RIP) and to Teddy Garber who carries the tradition of our brotherhood forward, making his father proud as he wears his old man mask up in Heaven.

Grateful salutes to my Big Boy Movers soldiers: Ted Billy Filer, Dave MacLary, Steve Runge, Mike Ganley, Eugene wherever you are, Rob Marquart, Steve Bowes, John Pettit, and Pat Hendren. And thankful blessings to Charlie Lemmer and to Deb, his Godsend.

Neighborly thanks to my Rappahannock friends, Kitty Keyser, Dawn Story, Bart Ciuba, Paul Reisler, Miranda Hope, Kiaya Abernathy, John Halberg, Mo Day, Cheryl Crews, Elizabeth Lee, Annie Williams, Bob Lucking, Charlie Butler, Cathy Kiley Martin, Betsy and Roger Hille, Amy, Gary, Evan and Dylan Hitt, Teresa and Dez Boardwine, Terry Waggoner, genius winemaker Bill Gadino and best neighbor ever, Bobby Carroll.

Applause to my Nashville friends: Billy Weisband, Richard Leigh, Vince and Barbara Santoro, Jonathan Kupersmith, Judy Paster and Erica at the Bluebird.

Starlit thanks to Joan Michelson who found me the perfect home for my memoir in the brilliant embrace of JuLee Brand, of W. Brand Publishing and infinite thanks to her developmental editor, Christina Frey of Page Two editing.

Much love to my family: Brother Jim, his wife Cindy and their daughters Kara and Jaimie, sister Bitsy, her husband Dave and their son Taeo.

Extra treats for my new dogs, Victor and Betty White, courtesy of my ex-wife, and the best mother in the world, Susan Hatley. May she forever know that this book would never have been written if she hadn't guided me out to Rappahannock. Rest in peace, Susan, you'll live forever in my heart.

And in heavenly conclusion, I thank my parents, Phil and Libby Mason, who walked beside me in darkness and in light, as I made my journey toward this paradise I call home.

Ben lives in the foothills of the Blue Ridge Mountains, on the site of a 3,000-year-old Indian village. He creates his songs, art, and stories on sacred land, and feels the passage of those who came before him in the stone tools, jasper arrowheads, and clay pottery rising from the Thornton River that runs through his property.

Ben released his fourth CD, *Flesh and Bone*, in February 2018. The album features Steuart Smith from The Eagles, as well as Steve Van Dam and Nate Brown of the band Everything. *Flesh and Bone* displays Ben's artwork and lyrics in a sixteen-page booklet which comes with the CD. "Sunshine," the first single from *Flesh and Bone*, is enjoying airplay in the US and Canada as well as Great Britain. Ben has enjoyed promotion of the record with multiple interviews on iHeart Radio and various FM stations.

Ben has been a performing musician in the DC area since the '70s. He's played the Birchmere, Jiffy Lube Live, the Cellar Door, Blues Alley, the Bayou, The Kennedy Center, Baltimore Civic Center, and many venues now long gone.He opened for Billy Ray Cyrus in Washington, DC before 110,000 people for Rolling Thunder and he returned to their stage again from 2015 through 2019, where crowds of 40,000 people gathered at the Lincoln Memorial. Ben was on Lifesong Records (Jim Croce), RCA Sunberry/Dunbar, was signed to Nashville's Cedarwood Publishing as a writer, has appeared as a musical guest on *The Today Show*, written two nationally-aired film scores for NBC television documentaries, was the Grand Prize winner in the 10th Annual Mid-Atlantic Songwriting Contest, has appeared on over one hundred albums and appeared as the opening act or recorded with Foreigner, Styx, Don Felder,

Steve Laurie of The Hollies, The Dillards, Poco, Rick Derrin-ger, Steuart Smith of The Eagles, Bo Diddley, Gary US Bonds, Dave Mason, Chuck Woolery, Mary Chapin Carpenter, and John Cougar Mellencamp. His first solo album, "River Deep In Me," was produced by John Jennings, who also produced Mary Chapin Carpenter.

Ben released two other solo albums, *48 States of Love* and *Loveland*, which include songs that are featured in the film *Recludere* and on MSNBC's show *Juvies*. *The Young And The Restless* has used two of his songs, "I Can't Make You" and "The Only One" in recent episodes, and Disney licensed "Every One of Us" for a yet-to-be-released movie. Ben is signed to a publisher in LA who works exclusively in television and film and was the force behind CBS Music for twelve years. Ben sings the closing song on *Maybe By Next Year*, a Kid Pan Alley CD released in 2022, which also features musicians who play in the Robert Plant Band, Kenny Loggings Band, Bruce Hornsby Band, Dave Matthews Band, Bella Fleck and The Flecktones, as well as with Quincy Jones and Miles Davis. In January 2023 *American Songwriter* magazine awarded him third place in its lyric contest, out of several thousand entries, for his song "Love Was A Lie."

He continues to record, playing piano and singing songs he's written about his life and the world around him. Ben is also a mixed media constructionist, creating and selling works of art that can be seen on his website.

His websites are www.benmasonexperience.com and www.benmasonsongs.com

He can be found on Facebook at: Ben Mason, Ben Mason Experience, and on Instagram at @benmasonwriter

The Infernos
Live in Annandale: 1965

John Wells Delegation
Nashville, The Cedarwood Sessions: 1968
One of These Days: Sanctuary Records 1975
Rodell Studios—Overdub vocals/instruments on 33 various albums, private and government: 1971-1975
JRB Studios—Overdub vocals/instruments on 22 albums, various artists: 1972-1976
3 live albums, never released: 1969-1974
Life Song Records,
2 albums, never released: 1973-1975
The Speed of Love: 1977

Primadonna
RCA/Sunberry Dunbar, *A New Shade of Blue*—never released: 1979
3 live albums, never released: 1977-1979

***Friends of Dave Allen*: 1992**
***Friends of Dave Allen, Live at the Birchmere*: 1992**

Ancient Steams Still Present, with JJ Gormley: 1994

The Oxymorons
Forlorn Hope: 1996

Lunar Grove
From the Coast of Mars: 1996

Jimmy Jenkins
The Post: 1998

The Curb Feelers
Back to the Cul-de-sac: 1999

Karin Ringheim
Welcome to the Hard Luck Café: 2007

Pat Chapman
If I'd Only Known: 2007

John Wells
Alive and Well in Key West–
Ben's song "Haven't Met You" included: 2008

Dick Wright
Obsessed: 2008

Craig Stroud
House of Gold: 2008

Tom Kara
Native Birth: 2008

Unknown Artists
Monkey Boy Studios–
Ben's background vocals on 3 albums: 1996-2011

Ben Mason solo albums:

River Deep In Me: 1991

48 States of Love: 1997

Henry's Song: 1999

Rappahannock Festival: 2002

Wassail Weekend, December: 2004

Hearthstone Festival Live: 2004

10,000 Dreams: 2007

Dojo Recordings: 2008

Ben Live in Sperryville: 2008

Ben Live at the Abbey: 2009

Loveland : 2009

Ben and Bill Abernathy Live at Oasis: 2010

Jesus in a Chevy, with Jon Carroll: 2012

Live at Gypsy Sally's, with Jim Mason and Andy Hamburger: 2015

Holy Rain: 2016

Flesh and Bone: 2018

Maybe by Next Year, Kid Pan Alley: 2022